DISCARDED

ECONOMIC INTEGRATION IN CENTRAL AMERICA

empirical investigations

To those who have taught me, including my parents
and my friends in Central America

ECONOMIC INTEGRATION IN CENTRAL AMERICA

empirical investigations
by JEFFREY B. NUGENT

the johns hopkins university press
baltimore and london

Copyright © 1974 by The Johns Hopkins University Press
All rights reserved. No part of this book may be reproduced or
transmitted in any form or by any means, electronic or mechanical,
including photocopying, recording, xerography, or any information
storage or retrieval system without permission in writing from
the publishers.
Manufactured in the United States of America

The Johns Hopkins University Press, Baltimore, Maryland 21218
The Johns Hopkins University Press Ltd., London

Library of Congress Catalog Card Number 74–6832
ISBN 0–8018–1451–0

Library of Congress Cataloging in Publication data
will be found on the last printed page of this book.

contents

tables

figures

preface

Progress in science, in general, and economics, in particular, is the result of the repeated interplay between theoretical reasoning and empirical investigation. It is empirical investigation which makes possible the comparison and evaluation of alternative explanations for the behavioral phenomena under consideration. Without systematic empirical investigation there would be no means of distinguishing (in the course of time) better explanations from poorer ones or of separating socially beneficial policies and institutions from detrimental ones. Empirical tests call attention to conventional reasoning that needs to be rejected or modified, thereby highlighting the need for new theorizing and/or the need for better methods of measurement and more data. In addition, empirical investigations can provide the basis for the quantitative assessments of the benefits and costs of alternative policies, upon which policy decisions should be based.

Successful empirical investigation requires the coordination of theory and statistics in such a way as to assure that the variables included in the theoretical analysis can be defined operationally, that these variables are relevant to the assessment of the theories, policies, or institutions under consideration, and that the statistics which are collected and utilized actually measure the relevant variables or concepts.

Because the theoretical models in the field have revealed that economic integration may bring about many different kinds of outcomes which are both sufficiently different in character to make generalization risky and sufficiently uncertain to render the assignment of probabilities to the various alternatives difficult if not impossible, there would seem to be few fields in which empirical investigations are as potentially important. The present study is undertaken in the belief that there are indeed issues in this field for which the nexus between and among theory, operationally defined variables, measurement, and institutional social cost-benefit analysis needs to be strengthened.

This study attempts to utilize the Central American experience to accomplish the following tasks: (1) to assess the impact of the Central American Common Market (CACM) on each of the economies of the region; (2) to develop a series of small short-run econometric models for each of the countries of the region and for Central America as a whole for use in prescribing and evaluating alternative monetary and fiscal policies; and (3) to obtain a rough estimate of the potential improvement (in terms of income) that each country could obtain if each of the member countries would agree to coordinate its monetary and fiscal policies at the regional level.

Since satisfactory achievement of any one of these tasks would require a sizable research effort, the scope must necessarily be rather severely limited. We have chosen to limit it by excluding considerations that are primarily "political" or "social" in nature and by confining it to the macroeconomic level, thereby leaving to future researchers the tasks of explaining the effects of economic integration on economic structure and on the distribution of income and wealth among individuals and groups, etc.

The presentation proceeds as follows: chapter 1 considers the usefulness of the Central American experience in studying the potential effects of various forms of economic integration among developing countries and provides a descriptive background on the economies of Central America and on their efforts toward economic integration. Alternative theoretical approaches to and methods of quantitatively assessing the various different effects of customs unions are presented and criticized in chapter 2. Several of these approaches (as well as some new ones) are applied to the Central American case in chapter 3.

The three small econometric models are described and estimated in chapter 4. These models are then utilized in chapter 5 as the behavioral and accounting constraints for estimating the potential gain in welfare attributable to policy coordination within the region.

Conclusions, qualifications, suggestions for further research and some policy proposals are presented in chapter 6. The monograph is completed by a selective reference list and two appendices. Appendix A contains the data utilized in the study; appendix B presents some calculations supplementary to those accompanying the text in chapter 4.

acknowledgments

The author gratefully acknowledges the encouragement of Brian Bosworth and Oliver Sause in undertaking this project. He also expresses his appreciation to Eddie Betanco, Lic. José Guillen Villalobos, Roberto Mayorga, Gabriel Siri, Gerald Wein, Alan Cohen, Ford Cooper, John Eddy, Richard Rueda, Jr., and Wendell Belew for assistance in obtaining the data which is utilized. Bill MacReynolds, Glen Gotz, Anna Gee, Yvonne Hastie, Paul Lande, Nick Patapoff, and especially Charles Williams provided the computational and programming assistance without which this study could not have been completed. The cooperation of the University Computing Center at the University of Southern California is also gratefully acknowledged. The author has benefitted greatly from discussing with and/or receiving comments from Bela Balassa, Jean Waelbroeck, Joel Soffin, Michael DePrano, Constantine Glezakos, Glen Gotz, Paul Montavon, Dick Cooper, Dirck Stryker, Peter Gordon, Ross Eckert, Samia DeClercq, Selwa Baasiri, Charles Williams, and Meredith Burke. None of these helpful people are responsible for the errors that may remain.

Although initial research for this study was financed by the Agency for International Development/ROCAP, the final results and the views expressed are those of the author alone and do not necessarily represent those of AID.

abbreviations

AID	U.S. Agency for International Development
BCIE	Central American Bank for Economic Integration
CACM	Central American Common Market
CAFMS	Central American Fund for Monetary Stabilization
C.A. Peso	A Nonexistent Monetary Accounting Unit = 1 U.S. Dollar
CR	Costa Rica
CU	Customs Union
DW	Durbin-Watson Statistic
EACM	East African Common Market
ECAFE	United Nations, Economic Commission for Asia and the Far East
ECLA	United Nations, Economic Commission for Latin America
EEC	European Economic Community
EFTA	European Free Trade Association
ES	El Salvador
GATT	General Agreement on Tariffs and Trade
GDP	Gross Domestic Product
GNP	Gross National Product
GU	Guatemala
HO	Honduras
IMF	International Monetary Fund
LAFTA	Latin American Free Trade Association
LDCs	Less Developed Countries
NI	Nicaragua
$\bar{R}^2$	Coefficient of Determination (standardized for degrees of freedom)
ROCAP	Regional Office for Central America and Panama (of AID)
SIECA	Permanent Secretariat of the General Treaty of Central American Economic Integration
UNCTAD	United Nations Conference on Trade and Development

For definitions of abbreviations of specific variables used in the export performance model of chapter 3, see section A2 of chapter 3. Similarly, for definitions of the symbols used in the econometric and programming models of chapters 4 and 5, see table 4-1.

1 | introduction

A. THE USEFULNESS OF THE CENTRAL AMERICAN CASE

As the world heads into the last quarter of the twentieth century it seeks new and more effective ways of helping the "less developed" or "developing" countries (LDCs) to gain a more favorable share in the economic development that has been achieved by the world as a whole in recent decades. In pledging their support to various forms of economic cooperation and integration among the LDCs, various developed countries and the United Nations, itself, have apparently become convinced that economic integration will be a most important, if not essential, vehicle for achieving higher levels and rates of economic development in the less developed regions of the world. In its blueprint for development of the 1970s, the General Assembly of the United Nations unanimously approved the following resolution which commits almost every country in the world to do its part in assisting the process of economic integration among LDCs.

> The developing countries will continue their efforts to negotiate and put into effect further commitments for instituting the schemes for regional and subregional integration or measures of trade expansion among themselves. They will, in particular, elaborate mutually beneficial and preferential trade arrangements which foster the rational and outward-looking expansion of production and trade, and avoid undue injury to the trading interests of third parties, including third world developing countries.

The developed market economies will, through the extension of financial and technical assistance or through action in the field of commercial policy, support initiatives in regional and subregional cooperation of developing countries. In this connection, they will specifically consider what help can be given to any concrete proposals that may be put forward by developing countries. In the efforts of developing countries to carry out trade expansion, economic cooperation and regional integration among themselves, the socialist countries of Eastern Europe will extend their full support within the framework of their socioeconomic system. United Nations (1970, p. 11).

Any form of economic cooperation or integration, of course, will require some sacrifice in terms of national objectives and sovereignty which the LDCs, many of which have only recently won their independence, may understandably be reluctant to make. Likewise, in granting assistance to economic integration among LDCs, the developed countries will impose upon themselves real costs consisting of the foregone alternative uses of the resources involved.

While the United Nations, various national governments, and the public at large have apparently been confident that economic integration provides a perhaps indispensable means of achieving development, the studies of professional economists have virtually never demonstrated that economic integration has provided or could provide substantial benefits. Remarkably, the professional literature on economic integration has devoted almost exclusive attention to the trade aspect, i.e., the effect of free-trade associations or customs unions. Very little attention has thus far been given to measurement of the potential benefits of other forms of economic integration, such as policy coordination, monetary union, movements of capital and labor, etc.[1]

One might say that there is a credibility gap on the issue of the benefits of economic integration between the scientific community, on the one hand, and the pronouncements of our national and international leaders on the other. The main problem the scientific community has faced is that the number of historical examples of economic integration is extremely small. Although the European Economic Community has been strong enough and remained in existence long enough to offer economists a fairly adequate opportunity to evaluate its impact, the several schemes of economic integration among LDCs have not generally offered the same opportunities.

The Latin American Free Trade Association (LAFTA), involving Argentina, Bolivia, Brazil, Chile, Colombia, Ecuador, Mexico, Paraguay,

---

[1]Thanks to the work of Kemp (1969) and Corden (1972b), some progress has recently been made in the theoretical analysis of these problems.

Peru, Uruguay, and Venezuela, is the largest scheme among LDCs, but its impact does not appear to have been very significant. Its coverage has been limited and, according to the 1969 Protocol of Caracas, any decision as to whether or not to adopt a common external tariff has been delayed until at least 1974. Although intraregional trade among LAFTA countries has risen somewhat to a little over 10 percent of their total trade, considering the large number of countries involved and the fact that some of these countries are landlocked and thus heavily dependent on trade with neighboring countries, this percentage remains surprisingly small. A smaller subregional group known as the Andean Group (Acuerdo de Cartagena), including Bolivia, Colombia, Chile, Ecuador, and Peru, is scheduled to adopt a common external tariff and to encompass more commodities than LAFTA. But, since it came into existence only in 1969 and since many of its provisions are to come into effect only gradually, it is much too early to afford evaluation of its effects. The partial free-trade association among the smaller countries in the Caribbean area (CARIFTA) is also of very recent vintage; moreover, its effects have been mitigated by the incorporation of various measures to offset inequities.

The Central African Customs and Economic Union (UDEAC), consisting of four countries (The Central African Republic, Cameroon, Gabon, and the Peoples' Republic of Congo), has apparently not yet fully implemented its ambitious plans for a customs union and for harmonization with respect to local taxes on manufacturing. The lack of full-fledged implementation is attested to by the fact that intraregional trade is still only about 2 percent of total trade in that region.

The experience of the East African Common Market (EACM) offers a much better opportunity for studying the effects of a customs union among developing countries. Indeed the EACM has been in effect in one form or another for more than fifty years. It incorporates features of a true common market in that there has been a considerable degree of capital mobility and a number of common services. There was even a monetary union until 1966. These factors are reflected in the fact that intraregional trade has been accounting for 15–20 percent of the total trade of the region in recent years.[2] However, the EACM case may be somewhat special in that (1) Uganda is a landlocked country which is dependent on imports from Tanzanian and Kenyan ports (some of which are processed before being forwarded to Uganda) and (2) income levels

[2]Actually the intraregional trade share had risen to almost 20 percent in 1966–68, but declined to about 15–17 percent in 1970–71, and in view of the military and political tensions in the area has probably declined further in 1972–73.

are so low—barely $100 per capita—that the possibility of local manu-
facture even for a regional market with a moderate amount of protection
is extremely limited. The unfavorable geographical position of Uganda,
together with the economic backwardness of Tanzania, have seemingly
combined to bring about a considerable amount of polarization of economic activity in favor of Kenya. The political pressures for offsetting
or compensating for these apparently accumulating inequities resulted
in substantial revisions in EACM arrangements in 1967. Among the
new arrangements are some degree of decentralization of the common
services and the temporary and partial taxation of imports from intraregional trade surplus countries (Kenya) by deficit countries (Tanzania
and Uganda). While the EACM provides an ideal case for studying the
distributional effects of customs unions among LDCs, and in this respect
has received much attention,[3] assessment of the net benefits to the region
as a whole is impeded by the difficulty of estimating how the East African countries would have performed in the absence of the EACM. Thus,
while there has been virtually unanimous agreement that the distribution
of benefits has favored Kenya at the expense of Uganda and Tanzania,
estimates of the net effect on the region as a whole have varied widely.
Recently, trade has further been impeded by border conflicts between
Uganda and Tanzania.

The effectiveness of the free-trade association among Egypt, Syria,
Iraq, and Jordan (known as the Arab Common Market) has been limited
by an apparent lack of enforcement of its provisions and also by the
relative importance of quantitative restrictions and other administra-
tive controls on trade which apparently persist and thereby continue to
restrict trade even though tariffs on most items produced in the region
have been eliminated or reduced. Intraregional trade in the case of the
Arab Common Market accounts for a somewhat more significant proportion of total trade (over 5 percent) than in some of the other trade
arrangements, but that proportion represents only a modest increase
over that of the preunion period.

Aside from the Central American Common Market and the various
other existing arrangements mentioned in the above paragraphs, several
other trade arrangements have been considered, experimented with,
or adopted among LDCs—the RDC among Pakistan, Iran, and Turkey,
ASEAN in Southeast Asia, the Maghreb grouping in North Africa, and
the UDEAO grouping in West Africa—but none have achieved a status
comparable to those we have mentioned above.

[3]See Brown (1961), Ghai (1965), Newlyn (1965), Hazlewood (1966), Green and Krishna
(1967), and Robson (1964), etc.

A few serious studies of hypothetical customs unions among LDCs have been undertaken,[4] but in no case has a demonstration been made that economic integration would offer significant benefits to its participants. In any case, hypothetical cases can hardly provide concrete evidence.

The Central American Common Market, which came into effect in 1961 among Guatemala, El Salvador, and Nicaragua, and was joined by Honduras and Costa Rica within the following year and a half, offers considerably greater potential for useful examination. Not only has it been operative for a fairly substantial period of time but also its coverage is rather general both in terms of free trade within the region and the application of a common external tariff. Finally, thanks to an international effort in the early 1960s, a fairly satisfactory base in terms of national-accounts data and trade statistics are available on a comparable basis both for the precustoms union period of the 1950s and for the postunion period of the middle 1960s. With the unfortunate and important exception of the border war between Honduras and El Salvador in 1969[5] and the resulting bitterness which, among other things, has led Honduras to reestablish preunion tariffs, the Central American Common Market (CACM) has survived relatively well.

Since intraregional trade has jumped from something less than 5 percent of total trade in the region in the 1950s to some 25 percent in recent years, that the CACM has had a substantial impact cannot be questioned. The importance of intraregional trade implies that the Central American economies are now quite interdependent. Furthermore, the prospects for, and the pace of, achieving higher levels of integration are generally considered to be greater in Central America than elsewhere. The similarity of historical experience, social, and economic institutions and the absence of extreme differences in the stage of development in the five Central American countries (at least relative to other groupings), undoubtedly have facilitated the degree of integration achieved thus far and will continue to smooth those additional steps that may be undertaken toward more complete economic integration.

[4]See, for example, Cohen's (1969) evaluation of the potential benefits of integration between India and Pakistan and Keesing's (1965) discussion of a common market in Southeast Asia, and other United Nations studies for Africa and Southeast Asia.

[5]This war sprang up ostensibly over a soccer game but, in fact, it is traceable to the decision of the Honduran government, in the face of growing domestic social problems between its poor landless agricultural workers and large landowners, to expand a cautious program of land reform by appropriating land from illegal Salvadorean squatters. In retaliation for this action, the Salvadorean government then authorized a military incursion into Honduras in order to protect what it considered to be the property rights of its nationals.

It is for these reasons that the CACM offers a particularly favorable case study both for evaluating the benefits and/or costs attributable to the creation of a customs union and for simulating the benefits and costs which other forms of economic integration would entail.

Except for some recent studies by Willmore (1972a, b, c) Wilford (1970), McClelland (1968), and Schiavo-Campo (1971), all of which are limited to very specific aspects of integration, the Central American experience remains relatively unexplored.[6]

B. AN OVERVIEW OF CENTRAL AMERICAN GROWTH AND INTEGRATION SINCE 1950

In order to familiarize the reader with the nature of the Central American economies, in this section we present a brief description of some of the salient characteristics of these economies, of their recent growth, and of the integration movement itself. In the early 1950s, few places in the world may have appeared less promising from the point of view of the potential for successful economic integration than Central America. Per capita income was a meager $200; total population was under eight million of which a large portion remained outside the monetized economy; although the Central American countries were not strictly "banana republics," their economic structures were certainly similar: 70 percent of the population was engaged in agriculture, 35–50 percent of total national income was contributed by the agricultural sector, an additional 9–12 percent by industry, and the rest by the services sector; each country possessed roughly the same geological, geographical, and climatic conditions—tropical underpopulated coastal plains surrounding an overpopulated central highland. Given these similarities, it was not surprising that each of their economies was heavily concentrated on the same agricultural commodities: coffee and bananas[7] as far as cash crops were concerned and corn, beans, chick peas, and peppers as far as subsistence crops were concerned. Complementarity, as measured by intraregional trade, was negligible.[8] Two-thirds of both imports and exports originated in or were destined for a single country, i.e., the United States; significant amounts of the land, financial, and other forms

[6]There is, of course, the usual plethora of descriptive or institutional studies: Wiónczek (1968, 1973), Castillo (1966), Hansen (1967), Segal (1967), Schmitter (1970), Cable (1969), Villagràn-Kramer (1967), Kahnert et al. (1969), Pincus (1962), and Moscarella (1964).

[7]These commodities accounted for 80–90 percent of total exports in the early 1950s in all countries of Central America except Nicaragua, where coffee and bananas accounted for only about 60 percent, the rest being accounted for by cotton, wood, and sesame.

[8]Intraregional trade was about 2 percent of total trade in 1950.

of wealth were owned or controlled by a small number of individuals or firms (in some cases foreign enterprises such as the United Fruit Company); similarly, political power was often concentrated in the hands of a landed oligarchy. Feudalistic institutions, including indentured service to creditor landlords, even if officially illegal, played a significant role in most countries of the region; the social services and infrastructure so important for trade, exchange, and development were grossly deficient in all countries except Costa Rica.

Nevertheless, there were some important historical, cultural, and political influences fostering the movement toward integration. Most important among these influences were the common language (Spanish), the common colonial heritage (Spanish) which had been superimposed on an earlier and very significant Indian civilization in part of the area (Mayan), and a common interest in diminishing what had alternatively been regarded as excessive dependence on, domination by, or interference from the United States and other foreign powers. Indeed, for over two hundred years under colonial rule, and again during almost twenty years after achieving their independence in 1821, the five Central American countries had been united in an economic and political union. Moreover, subsequent to its breakup there were numerous attempts to reconstitute the union in one form or another.[9]

Although these political and cultural influences were probably most important, economic considerations also played some role in the movement toward economic integration. On the one hand, after the collapse of the coffee boom in the mid-1950s, prices of traditional exports were generally declining. Moreover, the possibility for increasing the quantities of traditional exports was limited by (1) the lack of idle land in the case of El Salvador; (2) the high cost of settlement of the vast tropical rainforests and wilderness areas of the other countries; and (3) the fact that the export markets of two of the most important exports (coffee and sugar) were determined by bilateral international agreement on a quota basis. On the other hand, the difficulties of fostering and sustaining industrial growth via autarkic development were becoming increasingly obvious from the experiences of other countries. Thus, from the long-run development point of view, the alternatives to economic integration were not very attractive.

External influences were also largely favorable to integration. The Economic Commission for Latin America played a very active role both in the early movement toward integration and later in the establishment of the secretariat for the CACM. Despite some early vacillation on the matter, the United States government, having taken a position favorable

---

[9]For a detailed account of this experience, see Karnes (1961).

to the establishment of a common market in Europe, could hardly oppose integration in Central America. Moreover, as the CACM was in the process of being formed, the United States went a step further by committing itself to providing financial assistance to developing countries in their efforts toward economic integration, making Central America an outstanding candidate for such assistance.

Although some trade liberalization within Central America preceded the formation of the CACM (in the form of a series of bilateral trade agreements between El Salvador and each of the other Central American countries), most of the trade liberalization is the immediate result of the CACM itself. Under the Multilateral Treaty on Free Trade and Central American Integration (signed in 1958 in Tegucigalpa, Honduras), the Central American countries committed themselves to gradually reducing the tariffs on intraregional trade and to reaching the goal of a common market. In 1960 this treaty was expanded and to some extent superseded by the General Treaty of Central American Integration (signed in Managua, Nicaragua) which effectively freed intraregional trade of many commodities immediately and set a specific timetable for the elimination of tariffs on the remaining items of intraregional trade and for the unification of tariff rates among member countries.

For all practical purposes, the free-trade provisions became effective between El Salvador, Guatemala, and Nicaragua in 1961, for Honduras in 1962, and for Costa Rica in 1963. By 1966 more than 95 percent, and by 1969 more than 98 percent, of trade items in the CACM standardized trade classification (NAUCA) were subject to free trade for those products originating from within the region and to a common external tariff for those originating outside the region.[10] Aside from the treaty itself, the integration movement has sprouted a whole complex of regional institutions: the Permanent Secretariat of the General Treaty of Central American Economic Integration (SIECA), the Central American Bank for Economic Integration (BCIE), the Central American Institution for Research and Industrial Technology (ICAITI), the Central American Defence Council (CONDECA), the Central American Clearing House, regional commissions, institutes or councils on civil air navigation (COCESNA), telecommunications (COMTELCA), nutrition (INCAP), sanitation (OIRSA), chambers of commerce, higher edu-

---

[10]Among the commodities not yet subject to free trade or a common external tariff are those export commodities subject to country quotas in international agreement (coffee and sugar), certain subsistence crops which are subject to quantitative restrictions (rice and corn), and items subject to governmental monopolies (alcoholic beverages and petroleum refining).

cation, tourism, exporters, agricultural sciences, and others too numerous to name.

Various attempts have been made to extend economic integration into the areas of policy coordination, the ultimate goal being complete monetary union. Among the most important of these efforts to date have been an agreement in 1969 on industrial incentives legislation—the purpose of which is to avoid competitive proliferation of indirect subsidies to industrial investment—and more recently the agreement to establish the Central American Fund for Monetary Stabilization, which is supposed to provide assistance to individual members in balance-of-payments crises.

Two fairly important and probably quite unfortunate modifications have also taken place since 1966. The first was the imposition in 1967 of a common surcharge on the common external tariffs for a period of five years. This action, approved in what became known as the San José Protocol, was prompted by the balance-of-payments and fiscal pressures which had become intense throughout the region by 1967, due to the slowdown of the growth of extraregional exports and reductions in government revenue collections resulting both from the trade-diverting effects of the CACM itself and from the accumulating tax rebates, tax holidays, etc. offered by the individual countries in their increasingly generous packages of industrial investment incentives. Naturally, the surcharge had the effect of increasing the rate of discrimination in favor of Central American goods.

The second modification came in 1970 in the form of a unilateral reimposition of tariffs on intraregional trade by Honduras, implying its effective withdrawal from the customs union.[11]

By comparing the changes in the relative as well as absolute intra-regional trade flows between 1968 and 1971 in table 1-1, the reader

---

[11]This drastic action was partially based on growing concern in Honduras that it was not receiving its fair share of the benefits of the CACM. (In table 1-1 below, it can be seen that by 1968, both Honduras and Nicaragua had become major deficit countries in respect to their intraregional trade. The deterioration of the position of Honduras was probably most striking because Honduras seems to have had a positive position relative to the rest of the region before the establishment of the CACM). At the time, Honduras seemed prepared to accept financial compensation from its partners in return for its agreement to remain in the CACM and to keep its roads open to transit trade between its neighbors to the north and to the south. Still seething over the 1969 conflict with Honduras, however, El Salvador refused to sign the accord which was to finalize this agreement. Thus, it was in reality the continuing bitterness arising from the border war that triggered Honduras to withdraw from the CACM. Although subsequent attempts to repair relations between the two countries and to reconstitute the complete CACM have thus far met with failure, the Honduran withdrawal has not yet come to be regarded as permanent; many observers are optimistic that greater political stability, which would enable both combatants to make the required compromises, will be forthcoming.

Table 1-1. Direction of Central American External Trade in 1953, 1961, 1968 and 1970/71

| | Imports | | Exports | | Intraregional trade | |
| | Share from C.A. | Share from U.S.A. | Share to C.A. | Share to U.S.A. | Imports (c.i.f.) | Exports (f.o.b.) |
					(in million U.S. dollars)	
1953						
Costa Rica	.004	.601	.006	.657	0.3	0.5
El Salvador	.090	.599	.033	.821	6.5	2.9
Guatemala	.010	.645	.017	.766	0.8	1.5
Honduras	.037	.716	.062	.778	2.0	4.2
Nicaragua	.025	.651	.020	.455	1.1	1.1
Central America	.033	.637	.027	.713	10.7	10.2
1961						
Costa Rica	.047	.466	.026	.563	5.4	2.2
El Salvador	.136	.394	.126	.338	14.7	15.0
Guatemala	.067	.477	.078	.534	8.9	8.6
Honduras	.089	.517	.127	.590	6.5	9.3
Nicaragua	.039	.491	.026	.472	2.9	1.8
Central America	.078	.465	.081	.488	38.4	36.9
1968						
Costa Rica	.172	.382	.212	.226	49.3	36.5
El Salvador	.314	.294	.405	.196	66.1	85.6
Guatemala	.167	.413	.323	.281	41.2	70.9
Honduras	.263	.459	.169	.439	48.6	30.3
Nicaragua	.252	.383	.153	.289	46.2	24.6
Central America	.242	.385	.263	.329	251.4	247.9
1971						
Costa Rica	.219	.326	.203	.407	76.6	47.1
El Salvador[a]	.252	.284	.334	.234	60.4	78.1
Guatemala[a]	.219	.337	.287	.327	62.9	88.9
Honduras[b]	.239	.452	.076	.520	52.0	15.0
Nicaragua	.256	.331	.246	.352	54.0	46.0
Central America	.234	.343	.237	.361	305.9	275.1

[a] Expanded to full year on basis of figures for first three-quarters of year.
[b] Data refer to the year 1970.

Sources: [a] United Nations, *Direction of International Trade*, Annual Issue 1938, 1948, and 1953–1956.
[b] IMF, *Direction of Trade*, Annual 1960–1964, 1966–1970, and various monthly issues of 1972.

can see that they have continued to grow at impressive rates, despite the Honduran withdrawal. As of 1971, the share of intraregional trade in total trade has fallen only slightly from its impressive peak of 25 percent in 1968, and, when the complete 1971 statistics are available for El Salvador, Guatemala, and Honduras, they could show a slight increase in relative terms over 1968. Subsequent to the Honduran withdrawal and to the interruption of trade between Honduras and El Salvador, it is not surprising that the regional trade shares of Honduras and El Salvador have declined fairly sharply. On the other hand, the regional trade of Costa Rica, Guatemala, and especially Nicaragua has increased almost rapidly enough to compensate for the relative decline of El Salvador and Honduras in the CACM trade. Indeed, Nicaragua may have benefitted somewhat in Salvadorean and Costa Rican markets from the withdrawal of Honduras.

As of 1971, Costa Rica's intraregional trade deficit was the largest in the region, but its intraregional trade position was not significantly worse than its extraregional trade position. Guatemala has replaced El Salvador as the major surplus country as far as intraregional trade is concerned.

As noted above, an important aim, if not the primary purpose, of the Central American integration movement was to facilitate the achievement of a change in economic structure and to decrease dependence on the United States. The remarkable extent to which these goals were achieved is illustrated in tables 1–1, 1–2, and 1–3.

Table 1–1 shows that simultaneous with the increase in the share of CACM regional trade in total trade from 3 percent in 1953 to 23–25 percent in 1968–71, the trade dependence on the United States has declined from about two-thirds of total trade to about one-third.

Table 1–2 shows that the dependence on coffee and bananas, which alone had accounted for more than 80 percent of Central American exports in 1953, also declined sharply—to a little over 40 percent—in 1968–69. During the same period, the share of manufactures in Central American exports increased from less than one percent to more than 20 percent. Various other nontraditional exports such as meat, shrimp, mining products, and miscellaneous items also burgeoned rapidly.

In table 1–3 we show the sectoral composition of Gross Domestic Product in 1953, 1961, and again in 1968. The share of agriculture declined from 37.9 percent in 1953 to 28.7 percent in 1968. Conversely, the share of manufacturing increased from 11 percent in 1953 to 16.5 percent in 1968 and undoubtedly is considerably higher at the present time.

However, while the formation of the CACM has undoubtedly had a lot to do with these structural changes, its influence in this respect

Table 1-2. Commodity Composition of Central American Exports 1953, 1961, 1968, and 1969
(in millions of U.S. $ at current prices)

	Coffee	Bananas	Cotton etc.	Sugar	Cocoa	Wood	Meat	Cattle	Shrimp	Sesame	Maize	Rice	Mining	Manufactures	Other	Total
1953																
Costa Rica	33.6	35.8	—	0.6	4.0	0.2	0.3	—	0.1	—	1.0	0.3	—	0.2	4.1	80.2
El Salvador	76.6	—	7.5	—	—	—	—	0.8	—	—	—	—	—	3.0	0.9	88.8
Guatemala	68.2	12.6	—	—	—	—	—	—	—	—	—	—	—	—	8.1	88.9
Honduras	11.9	41.2	0.2	1.0	—	3.5	0.1	1.8	—	2.5	0.2	0.2	5.0	0.1	3.4	67.6
Nicaragua	21.3	0.3	9.3	—	—	4.2	—	1.6	—	—	0.5	3.5	—	—	1.5	45.7
Central America	211.6	89.9	17.0	1.6	4.0	7.9	0.4	4.2	0.1	2.5	1.7	4.0	5.0	3.3	18.0	371.2
1961																
Costa Rica	44.9	22.0	0.4	3.3	4.8	0.3	2.8	1.9	1.3	—	—	—	—	1.7	0.8	84.2
El Salvador	70.0	—	21.4	2.0	—	—	0.7	—	—	—	—	—	—	21.5	3.5	119.1
Guatemala	69.1	13.9	10.1	1.0	0.2	0.9	0.8	—	—	—	0.1	—	1.5	6.4	8.4	112.4
Honduras	9.1	39.5	0.5	—	—	7.5	1.6	3.1	0.1	—	0.5	—	4.5	3.3	7.6	77.3
Nicaragua	19.7	0.1	20.9	2.8	—	2.9	4.0	1.6	0.4	2.4	—	0.1	3.1	0.7	1.9	60.6
Central America	212.8	75.5	53.3	9.1	5.0	11.6	9.9	6.6	1.8	2.4	0.6	0.1	9.1	33.6	22.2	453.6
1968																
Costa Rica	55.3	43.7	2.2	9.3	3.3	0.2	12.0	0.5	1.5	—	—	—	—	32.7	10.1	170.8
El Salvador	92.2	—	16.1	9.7	—	—	—	0.4	4.2	—	—	4.0	—	70.1	15.0	211.7
Guatemala	73.4	14.1	45.1	8.0	—	1.2	8.6	4.0	0.9	—	0.1	—	—	55.5	22.0	232.9
Honduras	21.0	84.1	4.9	1.6	—	13.5	4.7	2.8	0.4	—	2.9	—	10.1	16.5	16.0	178.5
Nicaragua	23.0	3.2	67.5	5.5	—	1.7	15.9	0.1	5.1	2.9	1.3	0.2	5.6	18.9	6.4	157.3
Central America	264.9	145.1	153.8	34.1	3.3	16.6	41.2	7.8	12.1	2.9	4.3	4.2	15.7	193.7	69.5	951.2
1969																
Costa Rica	55.8	52.6	1.4	9.5	7.6	0.3	15.2	0.1	1.1	—	—	—	—	34.3	11.8	189.7
El Salvador	87.2	—	22.4	6.4	—	—	—	0.8	5.0	—	—	1.8	—	66.6	11.9	202.1
Guatemala	81.5	17.0	45.3	6.6	—	1.1	12.0	1.2	1.7	—	—	—	—	62.0	27.0	255.4
Honduras	18.5	75.8	4.0	0.6	—	14.3	9.0	1.9	0.5	—	1.9	—	15.6	15.6	8.1	165.8
Nicaragua	21.4	2.2	51.3	8.3	—	2.0	21.0	0.2	6.8	2.5	1.2	0.6	5.1	23.4	8.6	154.6
Central America	264.4	147.6	124.4	31.4	7.6	17.7	57.2	4.2	15.1	2.5	3.1	2.4	20.7	201.9	67.4	967.6

Source: United Nations, *Yearbook of International Trade Statistics,* 1955, 1964, and 1969.

Table 1-3. Structure of Productive Activity in Central America 1953, 1961, and 1968
(sector value added divided by GDP at factor cost)

	Share of agriculture	Share of manufacturing
1953		
Costa Rica	.406	.117[a]
El Salvador	.355	.111
Guatemala[b]	.324	.120
Honduras	.498	.088
Nicaragua	.411	.102
Central America	.379	.110
1961		
Costa Rica	.286	.147[a]
El Salvador	.323	.159
Guatemala[b]	.296	.131
Honduras	.464	.131
Nicaragua	.330	.097
Central America	.329	.135
1968		
Costa Rica	.238	.194[a]
El Salvador	.271	.182
Guatemala[b]	.274	.157
Honduras	.384	.153
Nicaragua	.302	.129
Central America	.287	.165

[a]Includes mining and quarrying.
[b]Based on data in constant prices of 1958.

Sources: United Nations *Yearbook of National Accounts Statistics*, 1953, 1969. Central Bank of El Salvador.

cannot be said to have been exclusive. As can be seen from these tables, these structural changes were partially felt prior to the formation of the CACM in 1961,[12] and thus post-CACM changes may have merely continued changes that had already been initiated by, and were more closely related to, other factors. Some of these factors were probably noneconomic and connected with the gradual erosion of traditional non-market values and institutions, on the one hand, and the increasing penetration of modern values and institutions from the mass media, commerce, increasingly active religious and social organizations, migration, education, touristic exchanges, etc., on the other hand.

Private foreign investment may also have played a role. As shown in the balance-of-payments accounts of the region in table 1-4, inflows of this sort were much greater from 1962 to the present than from 1957-61. While some of these inflows may be attributed to the formation

[12]Some of the structural changes that took place prior to 1961 are attributable to the bilateral trade agreements initiated by El Salvador. Since these arrangements were really all part of the integration, it may well be justifiable to attribute some of the pre-1961 changes to the CACM.

Table 1–4. Balance-of-Payments Summary for Central America 1957–70
(in millions of U.S. dollars at current prices)

	1957	1958	1959	1960	1961	1962	1963	1964	1965	1966	1967	1968	1969	1970
A. Goods and services	-81.7	-80.0	-62.6	-81.7	-53.1	-62.5	-96.4	-148.6	-192.8	-206.9	-267.0	-209.1	-200.4	-239.8
1. Merchandise (f.o.b.)	n.a.	-7.5	3.2	-34.4	9.5	20.9	-7.5	-15.2	-33.2	-14.4	-71.0	1.4	1.2	-39.4
2. Services[a]	n.a.	-72.5	-65.8	-48.3	-62.6	-83.4	-88.9	-133.4	-159.6	-192.5	-196.0	-210.5	-201.6	-200.4
B. Net current transfers	32.8	26.9	24.0	25.3	33.9	22.6	24.2	34.3	35.5	39.1	40.6	40.9	49.7	51.9
1. Private	1.1	0.4	1.2	0.7	4.0	3.1	9.3	19.7	21.0	20.8	23.1	24.8	32.5	39.0
2. Public	31.7	26.5	22.9	24.5	29.9	19.5	14.9	14.5	14.5	18.3	17.5	16.1	17.2	12.9
C. Balance on current account (A + B)	-48.9	-53.1	-38.5	-56.4	-19.2	-40.0	-72.2	-114.3	-157.3	-167.8	-226.4	-168.2	-150.7	-187.9
D. Capital account	37.9	57.4	44.5	67.5	45.2	74.2	95.1	148.7	209.3	100.0	172.6	111.4	139.6	166.5
Private	34.0	21.4	24.4	31.4	26.1	68.9	88.1	91.6	107.8	92.2	159.2	125.9	138.4	130.3
Public	14.4	8.8	5.3	3.3	-10.6	0.9	27.8	42.9	85.3	13.8	21.8	25.1	17.0	56.9
Commercial banks	-1.2	-3.0	-0.7	10.3	-0.5	8.2	11.5	-3.0	-9.8	-28.2	-13.0	-31.9	-10.8	-3.3
Monetary authorities	-9.3	30.2	15.5	22.5	30.2	-3.8	-32.3	17.2	26.0	22.2	4.6	-7.7	-5.0	-17.4

[a]Including transport, insurance, travel, return on capital, wages, films, correspondence courses, etc.

Sources: International Monetary Fund, *Balance of Payments Yearbook*, various years. SIECA, *Tercer Compendio Estadistico Centroamericano*, 12 Oct. 1963. SIECA, unpublished worksheets.

of the CACM, some of them may alternatively be more closely related to increased political stability and other factors. It can also be seen from table 1-4 that public foreign investment, while much more volatile than private foreign investment, has been greater in the postunion period (1962–70) than in the immediate preunion period (1957–61). Once again, some of these investments may have been induced by the CACM, while others may be explained by many other factors. A good portion of these public foreign investments were used in highway construction in the region. The investment in highways was channeled in part through the Central American Bank for Economic Integration (BCIE) and was strongly and deliberately biased toward the integration of the road systems of the five countries. This undoubtedly had the effect of complementing the formation of the customs union and other institutional arrangements in rendering regional trade more profitable than it had previously been. (Indeed in chapter 3, we shall give special attention to this factor and try to separate its influence from that of the CACM itself in explaining overall income growth in the region.)

As a result of fairly rapid growth of traditional exports, especially of bananas, sugar, and cotton in the 1960s, along with the remarkably rapid growth in nontraditional exports induced in large part by the CACM, Central American export growth since 1950 has been excellent— ranging from about 4 percent per annum in Honduras to more than 9 percent per annum in Nicaragua. The generally fine export performance has been reflected in a growth rate of national income in the region as a whole of about 5 percent per annum between 1950 and 1967.

This is not to say that everything has been perfect. Indeed, population has been growing in the region at a rate that is perhaps as high as 3.5 percent per annum, and thus the rate of growth of per capita income has probably not reached 2 percent per annum. Moreover, most observers feel that the degree to which income and wealth have become more equally distributed is not significant. Moreover, many Central Americans are already becoming aware of the high cost in terms of profits outflow and future debt repayments that must be paid for the foreign borrowing that has taken place in recent years.

In certain respects, even the customs union itself has not been without its more unfavorable trade-inhibiting aspects. On the basis of the Central American tariff structure before and after union and input-output coefficients for other countries, Nugent (1968) and Lawrence (1966) have shown that as a result of the CACM itself and also the increasingly generous fiscal incentives offered unilaterally to industrial investors by the individual countries,[13] there is evidence that the effective rate of

[13]These incentives have almost always involved tariff exemptions on capital and raw material imports for new industrial activities.

protection on consumer goods manufactures (sections 6 and 8 of the Standard International Trade classification) has increased somewhat over the period and is now generally as high as, if not higher than, that on similar products in other highly protective Latin American countries. The San Josè Protocol of 1967 further increased the overall rate of protection, at least until 1973. However, the outlook for additional overall tariff increases does not seem bright and the protocol on industrial incentives should have the effect of stopping, if not actually reversing, the trend toward increasingly favorable investment incentives. In other respects (which will be discussed later) the CACM, in particular, and the integration movement, in general, have had the effect of rationalizing and homogenizing the Central American tariff structure to some extent.

2 theoretical and empirical analysis of customs unions

The purpose of the present chapter is to provide a brief review of the theoretical and empirical analysis of customs unions (CUs). We emphasize the way in which the analytical apparatus has been applied at the empirical level in order to arrive at quantitative estimates of the social benefits relative to costs of CU participation.

Our presentation is divided into two parts: the analytical apparatus itself in section A and the empirical methods of applying that apparatus in section B. Each of these sections is in turn divided into two parts: one which treats the effects of CUs directly on trade and indirectly on efficiency and income, and a second which deals with other more direct effects on efficiency and income. Since the analysis of CUs has thus far been limited primarily to the trade effects, we start with the analysis of these effects and then take up the other effects on a more ad hoc basis.

A. THEORETICAL ANALYSIS OF CUSTOMS UNIONS

1. The Trade Effects

The classical treatment of the trade effects of CUs is that of Viner (1950). Although it is only a partial equilibrium analysis, it provides the building blocks and the terminology upon which general equilibrium analysis has subsequently been developed.

Figure 2–1 shows how Viner analyzed the welfare effects of a CU in terms of the now familiar concepts of "trade creation" and "trade diversion" with respect to an individual commodity. In this diagram, the domestic supply and demand curves of the commodity in question are given by Sh and Dh, respectively. If one assumes that the individual country portrayed in the diagram is a small country, foreign supply in the absence of a tariff is given by the horizontal line Sf. With the help of this model, one can consider three alternative institutional possibilities: free trade, a nondiscriminatory tariff, and a tariff which discriminates between members and nonmembers, i.e., a CU.

In the first case, i.e., the free-trade case, the foreign price Sf would also be the domestic price. Domestic supply and demand would be determined by the points of intersection of Sh and Dh with the price line Sf. Thus domestic consumption would be Ch_1, domestic supply would be Sh_1, and the difference $(Ch_1 - Sh_1)$ would be imported.

In the second case, i.e., that of the nondiscriminatory tariff, the effective foreign supply curve is the former foreign supply curve (Sf) plus a fixed tariff (t) which is shown by the line $(Sf + t)$. The equilibrium consumption position is now at B, implying domestic consumption of Ch_2. The equilibrium production position is at A, implying that domestic supply is Sh_2. The excess demand $(Ch_2 - Sh_2)$ is therefore imported.

In the third case (i.e., the CU case) the tariff applies only to nonmembers of the CU, the members of the CU being exempt from the tariff. Suppose, for example, that there is one partner whose supply curve Sp, as shown in the diagram, is higher than Sf but lower than $(Sf + t)$. In this case, equilibrium in consumption is at C, implying domestic consumption of Ch_3; equilibrium in supply is at D, implying domestic supply of Sh_3; the excess consumption $(Ch_3 - Sh_3)$ is imported from the CU partner instead of from the more efficient extraregional supplier.

Since the CU case is only one of three possibilities, it can, in principle, be compared either with the free-trade case or with the tariff case. However, it is generally assumed that the free-trade position is ruled out on grounds of political acceptability; if this is so, the relevant choice is, of course, that between the alternatives of a nondiscriminatory tariff regime and a CU.

Vis-à-vis the nondiscriminatory tariff case, the creation of a CU has both trade-creating and trade-diverting effects, because trade is increased by $(DE + FC)$ but, at the same time, the original level of trade EF is diverted from the more efficient foreign suppliers to the higher-cost suppliers in the partner country.

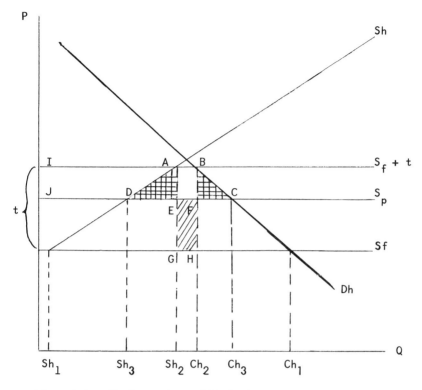

Figure 2-1. *Trade-creation and Trade-diversion According to Viner.*

Using traditional consumer surplus analysis, total consumer surplus in the preunion nondiscriminatory tariff case is measured by *PIB*, whereas, after union it is the larger area *PJC*. The difference or the change in consumers' surplus is measured by *IBCJ*. One part of the difference, namely, *IADJ*, represents a transfer from producers to consumers and another part, *ABFE*, represents a transfer from government (tariff revenue) to consumers. (This latter redistribution is usually assumed to take the form of neutral consumption subsidies as otherwise additional study would have to go into the distortions introduced by the nonneutrality of the subsidies.) The remaining areas (i.e., triangles *DAE* and *BCF*) represent net welfare gains (as opposed to simple changes in distribution in favor of consumers), but these gains are offset by additional losses in government tariff revenue of *EFGH*. Trade creation, therefore, brings gains of *DAE* plus *BCF*, while trade diversion brings a loss of *EFGH*.

The above analysis is subject, of course, to numerous limitations. Some of these limitations—particularly those dealing exclusively with the trade effects—can be overcome relatively easily by slight amendments or additions to the analysis. These will be discussed in the present section. Others require much more substantial revisions and often are not capable of being incorporated into the formal analysis. The discussion of these latter limitations will therefore be postponed until the next section.

An example of a limitation that can easily be overcome is the assumption that the tariff rate is unaffected by the formation of the CU.[1] If the (external) tariff for a particular country is changed as a result of its participation in the CU, there can be additional trade-creating or trade-suppressing effects, depending on whether or not the postunion tariff is lower or higher than the preunion tariff. Such effects are usually distinguished from the ordinary "trade-creation" and "trade-diversion" effects of a constant tariff by calling these "external trade-creation" in the case of a tariff reduction or "external trade suppression" in the case of an increase in the tariff rate. Naturally, since preunion tariff rates are likely to vary among countries, CU participation can bring about external trade creation in some CU members and trade suppression in others. Trade diversion may take place in countries of either type or in countries in which trade is neither created nor suppressed.

Another limitation that can be overcome relatively easily is the partial equilibrium character of the model. Indeed, this shortcoming is serious when estimates of the impact of CU participation on the economy as a whole are desired. Since CU participation is likely to affect the whole structure of relative prices, a partial equilibrium framework is generally unable to consider all the adjustments which lead to the new equilibrium. Fortunately, the same analysis can be incorporated rather easily into a general equilibrium framework through the use of the familiar single-country, two-commodity international trade model shown in figure 2–2.

In this diagram, the curve TT represents the domestic transformation function and the nonintersecting curves $U_1, U_2, \ldots U_5$ represent the set of community indifference curves. All of these curves are given in terms of the same two commodities: an exportable commodity (X) and an importable one (Y).

If free trade prevails and there are neither transport costs nor domestic taxes, the relative prices in world markets given by f_1f_1, f_2f_2, $\ldots f_5f_5$ are also the prices facing domestic producers and consumers.

[1]Rules of the General Agreement on Tariffs and Trade (GATT) prohibit increases in the average tariff rate in CUs. But many countries which may consider the possibility of CU participation are not signatories to GATT, and even those that are may not be forced to adhere to this provision very strictly.

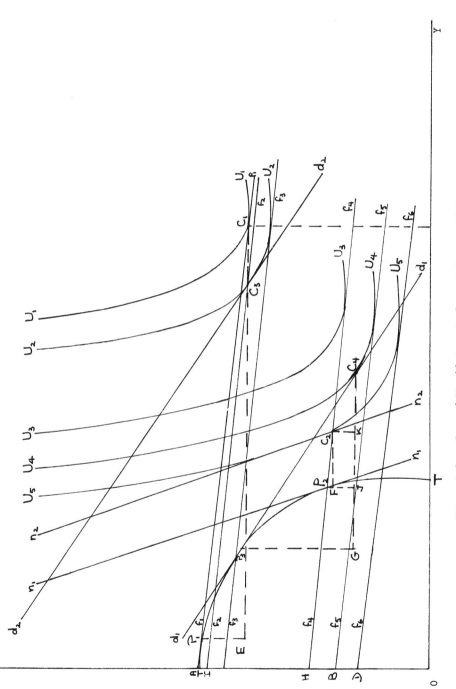

Figure 2-2. *General Equilibrium Analysis of Customs Unions.*

P_1 on TT is thus the equilibrium production point; from this point the country trades P_1E of X for EC_1 of Y in the world market in order to arrive at the optimum consumption point C_1 on U_1.

If a nondiscriminatory tariff is imposed on Y, the relative price of Y in terms of X could be raised, yielding a new set of domestic prices, e.g., n_1n_1, n_2n_2, ... At this new set of relative prices, optimum production is at P_2, from which (assuming both that the country's international terms of trade are unaffected by the imposition of the tariff and that tariff revenues are redistributed to consumers in the form of neutral consumption subsidies) the country trades P_2F of X for FC_2 of Y along f_4f_4 in the world market in order to arrive at the optimal consumption point C_2 (where the distorted price line n_2n_2 is tangent to the indifference curve U_5 on which C_2 rests). C_2 on U_5 reflects a distinctly lower welfare position than C_1 on U_1.

Assuming (1) that the individual country joins a CU in which it is small in size relative to other members (or at least relative to the union as a whole) and (2) that there is at least one member of the CU which can supply Y at a lower price in terms of X than that indicated by n_1n_1, n_2n_2, etc., it is reasonable to expect that domestic relative prices in the CU case would be given by the slope of d_1d_1, d_2d_2 (i.e., intermediate between those under free trade and those under the nondiscriminatory tariff). In this case, optimal production is at P_3 from which the country trades, P_3G of X for GC_3 of Y from its partner at the terms of trade available in the partner country (given by the slope of d_1d_1) so as to arrive at C_3 on U_4. Income or welfare can be measured in terms of either X or Y by converting one to the other at (undistorted) world prices. Thus, while in the free-trade case welfare is measured in terms of X by OA, in the nondiscriminatory tariff case it is measured by OD, and in the CU case it is measured by OB. As has previously been mentioned, since most evaluations of CUs have proceeded from the assumption that the free-trade case is ruled out for political reasons, the relevant comparison is usually that between CU and the nondiscriminatory tariff. In the particular case shown in figure 2–2, CU participation would raise welfare measured in terms of X by BD. As in Viner's partial equilibrium analysis, the improvement in welfare is attributable to the fact that trade creation of $GJ + KC_3$ exceeds trade diversion of JK. However, it is perfectly possible to construct examples in which the reverse would be true and in which CU participation would bring about a welfare reduction vis-à-vis the nondiscriminatory tariff case.

A vital assumption in the above evaluation is that the country under consideration (country A) is small both with respect to the rest of the world (country C) and with respect to its CU partner(s) (country B). Only when this assumption holds will the postunion relative price of X

in terms of Y in country A be the preunion relative price in country B. If only the first part of the assumption holds, the postunion relative price will not differ from what it was before union; without a change in domestic relative price there can be no welfare gain in country A, although there would presumably be a terms-of-trade gain in country B. In general, it is likely that the postunion terms of trade will lie somewhere in between the preunion relative price in country A and that in country B. The exact position (i.e., the slope of d_1d_1, d_2d_2 . . . .) cannot, of course, be determined in a single-country analysis. In order to overcome this shortcoming of the single-country analysis, Vanek (1965) extended this general equilibrium analysis so as to include two or even three countries on a graphical basis. To do this, he used an "Edgeworth box" analysis involving the indifference curves of both CU partners as well as the trade offer curves of both countries and the rest of world, thereby showing exactly how the terms of trade are determined. Although this analysis is very rich indeed, like its earlier partial equilibrium counterparts (Viner 1950 and Meade 1955), it yields a large number of alternative outcomes depending on a myriad of circumstances—size of tariffs, structure of tariffs, differences in preunion tariff rates among countries, size of countries, demand and supply elasticities in the different countries, complementarity of resource endowments, size of the preunion trade deficit, etc., from which it is difficult to generalize. Vanek's treatment of two countries was further extended to include three and/or four countries by Arndt (1968, 1969) and was further generalized algebraically by Kemp (1969). These extensions have demonstrated that, once the small-country assumption mentioned above is dropped, welfare of country A, of the union and of the world will no longer generally coincide. Distributional effects between and among union partners and between and among nonunion countries and between union members as a whole and nonunion members as a whole become possible and, in fact, probable. The analysis of the welfare effects of a CU thus comes to depend upon the particular CU and upon the particular country or countries inside or outside of the CU, i.e., the individual partners A or B, or individual nonunion countries C or D, or A and B, or C and D, or A, B, C, and D, together.[2] Krauss (1972) has suggested that the distributional effects could justifiably be considered in even greater detail, such as at the level of producers of Y in country A, or even at the level of the owners of factor K in industry X in country A, etc.

[2]Vanek, however, has argued that the analysis can be facilitated through the assumption that the CU adopts a "compensating common tariff," i.e., a set of tariffs on different commodities which leaves the volume of trade and the terms of trade of the rest of the world unchanged. The analysis of the net, as well as distributional, effects can thereby be confined to the effects on the union partners alone, i.e., the effects on countries A and B.

If the membership of the CU is sufficiently large that collectively the members of the CU can exercise some degree of monopsony power as far as their imports are concerned or of monopoly power with respect to their exports, CU participation can bring its members some terms-of-trade benefits (at the expense of the rest of the world) above and beyond those benefits considered in figures 2–1 or 2–2. Although in such situations CU participation may not offer the only means of capitalizing on these benefits, Arndt (1968) has pointed out that it may constitute one of the *most durable* and *effective* means of doing so.

While these extensions of the general equilibrium version of the traditional analysis to include three (or four) *countries* are important in understanding how the terms of trade are determined and what effect such changes in the terms of trade may have on welfare, they are not sufficient for analyzing the effects of CU participation on the *structure* of *relative prices* and thereby on welfare in member countries. For this purpose, an extension to three *commodities* is required.

Since, except for the inclusion of a third commodity, such a model does not differ in any substantive way from the graphic model presented in figure 2–2 above or from the algebraic counterpart of that model presented by Johnson (1965a), we shall confine our presentation to a brief outline of the procedures followed. (The details can be obtained from the author on request.) The procedures lead to algebraic formulae for the welfare cost of tariffs that will be utilized in chapter 3 in order to quantitatively assess the importance of one particular effect of CU participation: the tariff-homogenization effect.

The approach follows Johnson (1965a) in assuming (1) that each of the commodities is a final good (i.e., there are no intermediate goods) and (2) particular mathematical forms for the transformation and utility functions given by TT and the curves U_1, U_2, . . . , respectively in figure 2–2. The transformation function in two commodities (X and Y) assumed by Johnson was of the form:

$$(2.1) \qquad X^2 + Y^2 + MXY = K^2$$

If $M = 2$, equation (2.1) implies that $X + Y = K$; thus the transformation curve TT would in this case be the straight line drawn between the point $X = K$ on the X axis and the point $Y = K$ on the Y axis. If $M = 0$, equation (2.1) is the formula for a circle of radius K, and thus TT would be the northeast quarter segment of such a circle drawn around the point of origin 0.

The three-commodity counterpart to equation (2.1) is given by:

$$(2.2) \qquad X^2 + Y^2 + Z^2 + MXY + LZY + NXZ = K^2$$

Although this transformation function (like its two-commodity counterpart) has not been derived from an underlying production function, when the curvative coefficients L, M, and N are confined to values between zero and two (as they will be in subsequent use of the model), it possesses the shape and other properties that are usually assumed or desired.[3]

The marginal rates of transformation of Y for X, Z for X, and Z for Y can easily be derived. They are:

(2.3)
$$\frac{dY}{dX} = \frac{2X + MY + NZ}{2Y + MX + LZ}$$

$$\frac{dZ}{dX} = \frac{2X + MY + NZ}{2Z + LY + NX}$$

$$\frac{dZ}{dY} = \frac{2Y + MX + LZ}{2Z + LY + NX}$$

Corresponding to each alternative institutional assumption—free trade, nondiscriminatory tariff, or CU—there is a particular set of price ratios. Assuming (1) that the exportable commodity X is exempt from a tariff; (2) that the importable commodities Y and Z may be subject to tariff rates of t_1 and t_2, respectively; (3) that there are no transport costs; (4) that each of the three commodities can be measured in units such that these units exchange in the world market at a price of unity; (5) that tariff proceeds are returned to consumers in the form of neutral consumption subsidies; and (6) that domestic prices are determined by world prices plus the distortion (if any) introduced by the tariff (broadly defined to include any type of distortion), the respective price ratios would be:

(2.4)
$$\frac{Py}{Px} = 1 + t_1$$

$$\frac{Pz}{Px} = 1 + t_2$$

$$\frac{Pz}{Py} = \frac{1 + t_2}{1 + t_1}$$

---

[3]This formulation is a special case of the extremely general transformation function advocated by Christensen, Jorgenson, and Lau (1973). The specification that L, M, and $N < 2$ rules out the possibility of multiple equilibra considered by Foster and Sonnenschein (1970), but unless the imperfections in factor markets are extreme, this restriction seems realistic. See Johnson (1966).

Naturally the price ratios will vary according to the institutional case. For example, in the free-trade case $t_1 = t_2 = 0$. By setting the marginal rates of transformation (from equation [2.3]) equal to the domestic price ratios given by equation (2.4), one can find the optimal production point P (with optimal production of X, Y, and Z) corresponding to each alternative institutional assumption in the following way:

> Solve for X and Y separately in terms of Z yielding (quadratic) expressions in terms of the curvative coefficients L, M, and N and the tariff rates t_1 and t_2.

> Substitute these partial solutions for X and Y in equation (2.2) to obtain a solution for Z and subsequently for X and Y in terms of K (which subsequently cancels out) and the parameters L, M, N, t_1, and t_2.

Recalling the convention about units, gross national product at world prices (GNP) is given by:

(2.5) $GNP = X + Y + Z$

Thus, by substituting the solution values for X, Y, and Z corresponding to the CU case into (2.5), one can obtain an expression for the optimum value of GNP at world prices in the CU case (GNP_{cu}) in terms of the parameters L, M, N, t_1, and t_2. This process can be repeated for the nondiscriminatory tariff case yielding the optimal GNP (GNP_t) or alternatively for the free-trade case yielding the unconstrained or "first-best" optimal GNP solution (GNP_f). Since all of these expressions for the optimal GNP are of identical form and involve the same five parameters, they can easily be compared. The relevant comparison here is that between the nondiscriminatory tariff case and the CU case. The percentage change in GNP attributable to the change in production points from P_2 to P_3 is thus $(1 - \dfrac{GNP_t}{GNP_{cu}})$. This, too, is a quadratic expression in L, M, N, t_1 and t_2.[4] Assuming that L, M, and

[4]Specifically, the expression becomes: $1 - \dfrac{1 + D + E}{1 + D' + E'} \cdot \dfrac{S'}{S}$

where $D = \dfrac{(N - 2 - 2t_2)(2 - M - Mt_1) - (N - L - Lt_1)(2 - N - Nt_2)}{(M - 2 - 2t_1)(2 - N - Nt_2) - (M - L - Lt_2)(2 - M - Mt_1)}$

$E = \dfrac{(2 + 2t_2 - L - Lt_1)(M - L - Lt_2) - (N - 2 - 2t_2)(L + Lt_2 - 2 - 2t_1)}{(2 - N - Nt_2)(L + Lt_2 - 2' - 2t_1) - (N + Nt_2 - M - Mt_1)(M - L - Lt_2)}$

$S = \sqrt{D^2 + E^2 + MDE + LD + NE + 1}$

and D', E', and S' are the same as D, E, and S, except that in the former, t_1 and t_2 pertain to the preunion tariffs, while in the latter they pertain to the postunion common external tariffs.

N are technical parameters that would not be affected by institutional changes, differences between GNP_t and GNP_{cu} can arise only if the tariff rates (t_1, t_2) differ between the CU case and the nondiscriminatory tariff case.

Now let us turn to the choice of the optimal consumption point C. In this case, Johnson assumed social utility functions of CES form. In the three-commodity case, the CES utility function can be expressed as:

$$(2.6) \qquad U = (AX^{-\rho} + BY^{-\rho} + CZ^{-\rho})^{-\frac{v}{\rho}}$$

where A, B, and C are the distributional parameters ($A + B + C = 1$), v is the homogeneity parameter, and ρ is the substitution parameter which is related to the elasticity of substitution (σ) by $\sigma = \dfrac{1}{\rho + 1}$. The assumptions that A, B, and C and ρ are constant and that $v = 1$ (the constant returns to scale assumption) imply that the income elasticities of demand for X, Y, and Z are unity and that the marginal utility of income does not vary with the level of income. Utility can thus be expressed in terms of aggregate GNP defined in (2.5) above.

The marginal utilities of the three goods are:

$$(2.7) \qquad \begin{aligned} \frac{\delta U}{\delta X} &= A\left(\frac{U}{X}\right)^{\rho+1} \\[2mm] \frac{\delta U}{\delta Y} &= B\left(\frac{U}{Y}\right)^{\rho+1} \\[2mm] \frac{\delta U}{\delta Z} &= C\left(\frac{U}{Z}\right)^{\rho+1} \end{aligned}$$

Efficiency in consumption requires that the ratio of any two of these marginal utilities should be equal to the corresponding ratio of their prices.

Thus, the set of ratios $\dfrac{\delta U/\delta Y}{\delta U/\delta X}, \dfrac{\delta U/\delta Z}{\delta U/\delta X}$ and $\dfrac{\delta U/\delta Z}{\delta U/\delta Y}$ obtained from (2.7) should be set equal to the set of relative prices given by equation (2.4). As in the case of solving for the optimal production point, one can proceed to separate solutions of X, Y, Z and (from equation [2.5]), therefore, of GNP at world prices for each institutional alternative. Then, one can compare alternative solutions for the GNP corresponding to the alternative optimal consumption points. Again confining our attention to the comparison of the nondiscriminatory tariff case with that of CU, the percentage change in GNP attributable to the improved efficiency in consumption resulting from CU participation is again $(1 - \dfrac{GNP_t}{GNP_{cu}})$. In this case, the expression turns out to be a complicated one involving the relative shares of each commodity in total consumption under free-trade conditions (r_x, r_y, and r_z), the elasticity of substitution in consumption (σ) (assumed to be the same for all commodities), and again the tariff rates (t_1 and t_2).[5]

Since σ is a technical parameter that would probably not be affected by the type of tariff regime, and because r_x, r_y, and r_z pertain to the free-trade position, once again differences between GNP_{cu} and GNP_t can arise only if CU participation affects the tariff rates. This would seem to imply that this model could apply only to situations of external trade-creation or trade-suppression where the external tariff rates are affected by CU participation. However, since one can define the tariff rates used in this analysis broadly enough so as to include the effects of any distortion whose influence is increased or diminished as a result of the CU, this limitation need not be confining.

Finally, the total effect of CU participation on efficiency can be obtained by summing the effect on productive efficiency (given by footnote 4 above) and the effect on consumptive efficiency (given by footnote 5). Since both of these component effects are traceable to changes in tariff rates, the total effect on efficiency is also attributable solely to differences between preunion and postunion tariff rates (broadly defined).

2. Other Effects

However, when other assumptions of the above analysis, such as the assumption of constant or decreasing returns to scale, or that countries automatically operate on their production frontiers, are dropped, more serious modifications in the analysis are required, generally involving considerably greater complications and/or ad hoc departures from the analytical model. For this reason, in the present section we shall be content to call attention to these assumptions. In section B, we shall attempt to give some reference as to how these assumptions may be relaxed and as to how their importance may be assessed. For example, if economies of scale are introduced, it becomes virtually impossible to obtain solutions via general equilibrium analysis except in special cir-

---

[5]Specifically, this expression for the percentage change in welfare attributable to adjustment of consumption to the change in relative prices resulting from CU participation is $1 - \dfrac{F}{F'}$, where

$$F = \left[\frac{r_x}{r_y}(1 + t_1)^{\sigma-1} + \frac{r_z}{r_y}\left[\frac{(1+t_1)}{(1+t_2)}\right]^{\sigma-1} + 1 \right]^{\frac{\sigma}{\sigma-1}} \left[\frac{r_x}{r_y} + \frac{r_z}{r_y} + 1\right]^{\frac{1}{1-\sigma}}$$

and F' is the same as F, except that the tariff rates t_1 and t_2 included in F are the preunion tariffs, whereas, those in F' are those which would yield the postunion set of relative prices.

cumstances. In a partial equilibrium setting economies of scale can be handled by imparting a downward slope to Sh and/or Sp in figure 2-1. The net result is, however, simply to require consideration of a number of additional factors, such as the relative position of the average cost curve of union members, the elasticity of cost with respect to scale, differences in average cost among CU members, etc., making generalizations even more difficult. Economies of scale can be of the internal variety that would accrue to the firm or industry itself, or they can be of the external variety that accrue to other firms in the form of lower prices or higher quality. Except in cases where no union member is able to compete with imports from the rest of the world at the preunion tariff rate, it is likely that the benefits of CU participation would be greater in the presence of economies of scale than without them.[6]

Closely related to economies of scale are the learning-by-doing benefits. If (1) the attraction of a larger market, or a larger pool of resources made possible by CU participation makes it possible to start local production in a certain industry before the date at which it would have been possible to without the CU, and (2) efficiency increases with experience in production or investment, then additional economies derived from the learning can and should be attributed to CU participation.

No matter how narrowly commodities or industries are defined, the level of aggregation is bound to be excessive, thereby causing some potential advantages of CU participation to be ignored. This is because, aside from economies of scale, learning-by-doing, and inter-industry specialization, competition between different firms in the same industry may induce the individual firms to take advantage of economies derived from longer production runs and from reducing machine "down-time" for conversion of equipment to different product lines and specifications, thereby achieving greater specialization and efficiency within the industry.[7]

Also overlooked in the traditional model of CUs is the possible effect of increased competition on "X-efficiency." Whereas, in the conventional analysis (e.g., of figure 2-2 above) it is usually assumed that all firms, industries, or economies are operating in such a way that the production points P_1, P_2, P_3, etc. are always on the production frontier TT, the advocates of X-efficiency argue that, in fact, they tend to operate at points such as P_4 inside of TT. Through the greater competition that intraregional trade would be likely to engender, managerial personnel may be forced to face up to the competition by becoming

---

[6]See Corden (1972a) for a discussion of several alternative possibilities of CU benefits in the presence of economies of scale.

[7]These economies have received much attention in the work of Balassa (1965b, 1971b). See also the questions raised about the likelihood of such effects by Grubel (1970).

technically more efficient in the sense of moving closer to their production frontiers, thereby raising the level of income and welfare.[8]

The traditional analysis also assumes that the quantity and quality of factors of production are given, as implied by the fact that the transformation curve TT in figure 2–2 is given. However, increasing recognition has been given to the fact that factors of production are mobile internationally. Scarce factors, such as capital and skills, are particularly likely to move to areas where exports are increasing and the composition of trade is changing, thereby bringing about changes in relative factor prices which, in turn, help induce additional factor flows. Thus, the supply of productive factors may be affected by CU participation through its effect on the level and composition of trade. There may be not only a net inflow of productive factors to the CU but also, and particularly in the case of a common market, a redistribution in the supply of productive factors within the region so as to achieve greater efficiency in allocation.

Alternatively (but what may amount to the same thing), as Caves (1965), Fei and Ranis (1961), and Lewis (1954) have pointed out, there may be surplus resources which can be used for producing the products that can be exported to other members of the CU. If in a foreign-exchange-constrained world trade balances are improved as a result of CU participation (as has been suggested by Resnick and Truman [1972] and various others), the relaxation of the foreign exchange constraint can lead to increases in income and welfare. In each of these circumstances, even trade-diverting CUs can be beneficial, especially if the CU involves some sort of payments arrangement which conserves on foreign exchange.

Transport costs are also ignored in the traditional analysis. In some cases where internal exchanges are encumbered by large distances or physical obstacles, CU participation may encourage the exchange of commodities between contiguous portions of different countries, thereby economizing on transport costs.[9]

[8]Leibenstein (1966) made a strong case for this view. However, the implication that in the absence of perfect competition firms do not maximize profits raises questions as to why not and, if they don't, what it is that they maximize. Using one particular definition of X-efficiency in which X-efficiency is a function of managerial effort and the utility of managers is a function of income and leisure, Corden (1970) has shown that an increase in X-efficiency could take place only in rather special circumstances. However, these special circumstances involving some asymmetry in behavior between exporters and import competitors may be quite realistic (Williamson 1971).

[9]For example, before the effective partition of Pakistan into Pakistan and Bangladesh, Cohen (1969) argued that a customs union between India and Pakistan would be beneficial in enabling both East and West Pakistan to take advantage of transport savings in trade with contiguous parts of India rather than with each other. On the other hand, where customs unions are formed between noncontiguous countries, transport costs might be increased rather than lowered as a result of CU participation.

Being entirely static in its outlook, the traditional analysis ignores both the possibility of dynamic externalities associated with CU-induced changes in income distribution, or in industrial structure. It also ignores the possibility that technological change might be induced by the increased trade.[10] Moreover, it overlooks the possibility that advantages could be derived from harmonization and coordination of policies among member countries resulting from CU participation. Since the external tariff rates of CUs are settled by negotiation at the regional level, usually on the basis of some rather general formulae for harmonizing preunion differences in tariff rates among countries, CU participation has the effect of freeing (or at least relieving to some extent) public officials from the constant harassment of local interest groups pressing for higher rates of effective protection. As Tullock (1967) has argued, this permits entrepreneurs to go back to what they should be doing: running their businesses rather than courting government officials.

While most of these shortcomings in the traditional analysis have at least been admitted in the literature, there are undoubtedly others which have been completely overlooked. One such limitation derives from the assumption that the *structure* of tariffs would not be affected by CU participation. As shall be pointed out below, however, CUs may definitely have the effect of reducing the relative variation in tariff rates among commodities.

B. EMPIRICAL ANALYSIS OF INDIVIDUAL EFFECTS

As the above analysis has revealed, there are many possible effects of CU participation and in most cases neither the magnitude nor even the direction of these effects is entirely predictable; so much depends on particular circumstances.

For example, whether the union will be trade-creating or trade-diverting depends rather definitely on the size of the preunion tariff rates. This is illustrated in table 2-1 below. Given the cost differentials in the example cited, it can be easily seen that in the presence of a 50 percent tariff CU participation would have the effect of diverting imports of *B* from efficient producers in the rest of the world to less efficient producers in country *B*. If, alternatively, the tariff rate were 100 percent, union participation would create trade, as imports from *B* would

[10]See Cooper and Massell (1965), Johnson (1965*b*), Bhambri (1962), Balassa (1965*b*, 1971*b*), Mikesell (1965), and Kreinin (1964) for advocacy of some of these more dynamic effects.

Table 2-1. Illustration That Customs Union Participation Is More Likely to Be Trade-creating the Higher the Preunion Tariff Rates

Country of origin	100 Percent tariff: trade creation			50 Percent tariff: trade diversion		
	Production cost per unit	Pre-union price after tariff	Post-union price after tariff	Production cost per unit	Pre-union price after tariff	Post-union price after tariff
Country A	20	20	20	20	20	20
Country B	16	32	16	16	24	16
Rest of world	12	24	24	12	18	18

replace supplies from domestic producers whose costs are even higher than those of the CU partner.

It could also be shown that the cost-benefit of CU participation may depend on country size, the degree of complementarity or competitiveness among participating countries, the future direction of their policies, etc. However, while in any such case it may be possible to make qualitative statements, such as that CUs among countries with high preunion tariff rates are more likely to be trade-creating than those among countries with low ones, there is no way that quantitative assessments can be made on *a priori* grounds. Moreover, since the overall effects of CU participation depend on a whole host of factors, some of which may be complementary, but some of which may be offsetting, overall assessments of the benefits relative to costs of CUs require detailed empirical investigations.

1. Measurement of Trade Effects

Use of the Vinerian Model. Given the imprecision with which some of the more "dynamic" or unconventional effects (discussed in section A2 above) have been formulated and explained, and the difficulty of getting at them empirically, most empirical assessments of the net benefits of CU participation have been confined to the trade-creation and trade-diversion effects and have relied rather heavily on the traditional Vinerian model which gave rise to these concepts in the first place. Each such attempt at quantification is thus based on measurement of the areas pointed out in figure 2-1—namely, the size of the two shaded triangles *ADE* and *BCF* (indicating trade creation) relative to the cross-hatched rectangle EFGH (representing trade diversion).

Assuming that demand and supply curves can be adequately represented by straight lines, the welfare gains (or losses) of CU participation can be estimated if, and only if, it is possible to estimate the length of certain of the relevant sides *and* the slopes of the supply and demand curves. It is obvious from reference to figure 2-1 that the areas of *ADE* and BCF can be estimated if, and only if, estimates of (1) $(Sf + t) - Sp$ and (2) either (a) the slopes of the demand and supply curves or (b) $(Sh_0 - Sh_1)$ and $(Ch_1 - Ch_0)$ can be obtained. Likewise, the area of EFGH can be estimated if, and only if, it is possible to estimate both $(Sp - Sf)$ and $(Ch_0 - Sh_0)$.

Most studies have relied heavily on country differences in the pre-union tariff rates to estimate the relevant changes in prices on the vertical axes.[11] A few studies have alternatively tried to estimate cost differentials by comparing different countries with respect to performance in the recent past in different industries.[12] Liesner (1958) suggested a third alternative of obtaining cost estimates from interviews, trade journals, engineering data, etc., but in practice rejected it on the basis of his (undoubtedly correct) belief that this approach would require a research effort of enormous size.

In order to estimate the changes in quantity on the horizontal axis, most studies have combined one of the above methods for estimating the changes in prices with "plausible assumptions" about the demand-and-supply elasticities.[13] Verdoorn and Mayer zu Schlochtern (1964) and others,[14] have attempted to estimate some of the changes in quantity by changes in shares of members' imports or exports in world markets. However, an increased trade share could be due either to trade creation or trade diversion, or both, and hence is not immediately translatable into welfare gains or losses. This defect was removed by further disaggregation in the "trade matrix" approach of Williamson and Bottrill (1971). Truman's study (1967), which was later updated by Major and Hays (1970), would appear to be unique in estimating all the changes in production and apparent consumption directly, i.e., by comparing extra-regional imports, intraregional imports, domestic production, exports and apparent consumption for each industrial category. Industrial use of commodities, however, can usually only be estimated indirectly through the use of input-output coefficients and assumptions about the

[11]See, for example, Bentick (1963) and Verdoorn (1954).

[12]Liesner (1958) has followed this procedure. However, it is difficult to see how this approach can provide anything but qualitative estimates of potential gains unless certain highly restrictive assumptions are made.

[13]See, for example, Verdoorn (1954), Janssen (1961), and Scitovsky (1958).

[14]Among the other studies using this rather incomplete approach are those of Lamfalussy (1961), Waelbroek (1964), and Duquesne de la Vinelle (1965). The Verdoorn and Mayer zu Schlochtern (1964) and Duquesne de la Vinelle (1965) studies make some attempt to distinguish the "common market effect" from changes in competitive position, and other demand and supply changes. Johnson (1958a) has approached the issue somewhat differently by calculating the cost to a prospective member (UK) of a hypothetical free-trade area in Europe, in terms of the loss the prospective member would have to suffer in order to achieve the same level of exports without trade preferences as with trade preferences. Nevertheless, the areas whose magnitudes need to be estimated, turn out to be the same.

constancy of such coefficients over time. Also it is necessary to assume that the preunion shares in apparent consumption of domestic production, partner supply, and external supply would have remained constant in the postunion period if it were not for the formation of the CU. Only then can all observed changes be attributed to CU participation.

Balassa's Method. Although still requiring the assumption that all changes in trading relationships must be attributed to the formation of the CU, Balassa (1967) suggested a much simpler and more operational method for estimating trade-creation, trade-diversion, and the welfare gain of CU participation than the more cumbersome methods employed by Truman, Major, and Hays, etc. His method consisted of two simple steps: (1) to compute income elasticities of demand for intraunion, extraunion, and total imports between the preunion and postunion periods;[15] and (2) to convert the increase in the income elasticity of demand for total imports (thereby representing net trade-creation) into national income terms by multiplying by the assumed efficiency gain implied by a one percent increase in imports relative to national income.

Aside from being simple to apply, Balassa's income-elasticity approach has the advantage of being somewhat more general than the previous approaches. This is so because there is nothing in its application requiring an assumption of constant returns to scale or specifically excluding economies from intraindustry specialization. To the extent that these factors influence trade without also affecting income, such effects would tend to show up as an increase in the income elasticity of demand for imports. Since Balassa has deliberately tried to eliminate from his estimates the effects of income growth on imports, and since most effects of CUs on imports would also affect income directly or indirectly, the extent to which such effects would be picked up in the Balassa method would seem to be limited. However, in his choice of an efficiency conversion factor, Balassa chose a relatively broad concept of efficiency, so as to include the efficiency gains derived from economies of scale, etc., in addition to the ordinary static gain of increased trade.

Applying his method to the members of the EEC, Balassa found that the income elasticity of demand for total imports increased by approximately 0.3. Borrowing Walters's (1963) estimate of the efficiency conversion factor of 3/10 (which was based on the experience of the United States in the early twentieth century!), Balassa computed the increase in the income growth rate of EEC countries attributable to participation

---

[15]This approach is not without possible modifications. For example, Walter (1967) used average propensities to import as the basis for these comparisons, instead of income elasticities.

in the EEC to be about 0.1 percent per annum. Although admitting that his estimate was biased downward by the omission of the growth effects in estimating trade-creation via step (1), Balassa pointed to the small size of the estimated increase in the income growth rates as evidence that this bias was small. This argument involves a certain amount of circular reasoning. If the original estimate of trade-creation (step 1) had not been biased by the omission of the growth effect of CU partici-pation, then the contribution to the growth rate computed from step 2 might have been considerably larger.

Therefore, Balassa's approach would seem valid and unbiased only as a measure of what it was specifically designed to measure: trade-creation in the fairly narrow Vinerian sense. Its main advantages in this respect are that it is much simpler to apply and to interpret the results of than the other alternatives and that it avoids the need to make assumptions that differences in tariff rates reflect differences in costs, or that the elasticities of supply and demand take on certain specific values, etc. It would seem, however, to represent neither a satisfactory method of measuring total trade-creation (including the growth-induced effects on imports) nor a method of capturing the total effects of CU participation, as some practitioners would seem to like it to be. Since any new industry that becomes located within the region after the forma-tion of the CU would be identified as an example of trade-diversion, both the Balassa and Viner methods would have the effect of under-estimating net trade-creation in the broader sense.

General Equilibrium Simulations. The approaches outlined in the previous sections both rely exclusively on the partial equilibrium Vinerian analysis. The use of general equilibrium approaches, such as that for a single country outlined above, or for several countries as advocated by Vanek, Arndt, and Kemp and referred to in section A1 above, is rendered difficult by the facts that the variables included in the analysis are not easily measured, and that the number of factors which could affect the outcome is quite large.

The closest that it seems possible to come to empirical application of such models is to make certain general assumptions about the mathematical form of the building blocks of these models, i.e., the transformation and utility functions, and then certain additional assump-tions (on the basis of empirical plausibility) about the specific values which the parameters in these functions may be expected to take. These parameters could then be substituted into the appropriate formula for the maximum potential GNP under different alternative institutional assumptions, such as that of nondiscriminatory tariff protection and CU. Indeed, the basis for this approach has already been developed in section A above. If the assumptions about the general mathematical form of the transformation and utility functions are thought to be valid, and the simulated calculations are found to be rather insensitive to the choice of parameter values (within what are considered to be their realistic ranges), then the need for detailed empirical investigation may be alleviated.

Alternatively, one might adopt more restrictive assumptions about the mathematical forms of the transformation and utility functions, such as that they are simple linear functions of the type that could be included in a linear programming model. This might lead to detailed empirical investigation of the members of a certain CU before and after union, through the use of data obtained from multicountry input-output tables, consumer surveys, etc. The shortcoming of such studies is, of course, that it is difficult to derive tests to determine whether or not the linearity and other assumptions of any such model are sufficiently realistic that the results can be trusted.

Both sorts of general equilibrium approaches to quantitative assessment of trade policies have been undertaken. Parameter simulation studies have been carried out in different circumstances by Johnson (1965a), McKinnon (1966), and Nugent and Akbar (1971). Empirical linear programming studies of tariff protection have been undertaken by Cabezon (1969), Lage (1966, 1970), and Evans (1970, 1971, 1972). However, as yet neither type of approach has been applied to assessment of the effects of CU participation. The explanation for this probably lies in the fact that, unless one goes into a two- or three-country analysis, thereby increasing the complexity of the model and multiplying the number of parameters which have to be assumed or estimated, the prices of tradeable goods upon which efficiency in production and consumption depends are simply given exogenously. As we have seen, these prices are usually assumed (the "small-country assumption") to be the prices on the world market plus the tariff rate. In such circumstances, welfare gains or losses of CU participation can arise only if and to the extent that the tariff rates change as a result of the union. This is, however, the case only when there is external trade-creation or trade-suppression. In principal, however, it should be possible to define the tariff rates sufficiently broadly as to represent any and all sources of domestic price changes associated with CU participation. In chapter 3 we shall apply the simulation approach to assessment of the benefits of tariff homogenization in the Central American Common Market.

The Export Performance Approach. As we have noted, a major limitation on the use of any of the above approaches to empirical assessment of the trade effects of CU participation is the lack of realism in the assumption (implicit or explicit in such studies) that all differences in imports, import shares, or import elasticities between the preunion and postunion periods can be attributed to CU participation itself. In reality, many other influential variables are likely to change and thereby exert some influence over the trade variables.

One approach that attempts to account for these other influences is the "export performance" approach. This approach attempts to compare the performance of different countries (including both members and nonmembers of CUs) with respect to exports (E) over a period of time. The period of time should be sufficiently long as to mitigate the influences of transitory factors, such as droughts, floods, strikes, political crises, etc., which can dominate in the short run. The differences in export performance among countries can then be explained in terms of both demand factors, such as the world or regional demand pattern for the commodity bundle exported by the individual country in the base period, and supply factors, such as the price of exportable goods relative to home goods, tax policies with respect to exports and export earnings, income,[16] and finally the particular CU (if any) with which the country may have become affiliated during the period.[17]

The shortcoming of this approach is that through the use of international cross-section data, certain differences between countries that are not accounted for by the other variables may inadvertently be attributed to the country's affiliation (or lack of affiliation) with a particular CU, or, conversely, certain effects of CUs may be attributed to certain other variables included in the model that happen to have occurred simultaneously with participation in the CU. Nevertheless, if an effort is made to include most of the more important systematic influences, and if the mutual correlation among variables is not too high, these dangers should not be great.

2. Measurement of Other Effects

Each of the above approaches to assessment of CUs has been limited to their impact on trade directly. As has already been mentioned, the effects of CUs on efficiency, income, growth, etc. which affect trade only more indirectly have been treated less frequently not because of

---

[16]The use of income as an explanatory variable in export performance is not entirely appropriate, since income growth may be the result of export growth. However, some influence in the other direction is also probable, i.e., if income rises rapidly, the capacity for exports is also likely to rise rapidly.

[17]The use of a single dummy variable for any particular CU rules out the very distinct possibility that a given CU can be trade-creating for some members of the union and trade-diverting for others, but does consider the fact that some CUs will, on balance, be more trade-creating than others.

any general consensus that they are unimportant, but because of the difficulty in obtaining empirical estimates. For most of these effects, progress in measuring them has been very limited. About all that has been done is to show that they play some role and thus should be recognized, but seldom has it been possible to indicate how much influence they have exerted.

For example, in regard to economies of scale, several alternative attempts have been made to estimate their magnitude,[18] but no one has yet put a precise magnitude on the extent to which CU participation contributes to taking advantage of economies of scale.[19] Similarly, Balassa (1965b, 1967) and Willmore (1972) have shown that intra-industry trade and specialization have played a large role relative to interindustry trade and specialization in postunion changes in trading patterns of CU members.[20] They have also cited examples wherein the longer production runs and other economies facilitated by this effect have led, or could lead, to substantial cost reductions. Yet no method for making an overall estimate of this gain has been established. As to transport costs, quantitative estimates have been

[18]Naturally, most studies of economies of scale have been confined to particular industries or even processes; even within industries estimates of the magnitude of these economies have varied widely. Another limitation is that almost all such studies have considered only capital costs as opposed to total costs. Even if labor, materials, utilities, and other costs could be included in such estimates, it is extremely difficult to evaluate the trade-off between economies of scale in production and increasing distribution costs. Nevertheless, virtually all works on economies of scale (e.g., Bain 1954, 1966; Haldi and Whitcomb 1967; Stigler 1958; etc.) are agreed that these economies can be very substantial in certain industries.

[19]Two attempts at quantification of these benefits via mixed integer programming models deserve mention: Carnoy (1970) for six industries in a Latin American Common Market and Frank, Meeraus, and Stoutjesdijk (1973) for fertilizers in East Africa. However, the former of these shows optimal solutions which include very small plant sizes, making it difficult to believe that economies of scale were sufficiently considered, and the latter is not really relevant to evaluation of a customs union, since free trade is practiced with respect to fertilizers in East Africa. Both models explicitly indicate the magnitude of an optimal plan involving full regional coordination relative to a suboptimal or uncoordinated one. In the urban studies literature some attempts have been made to measure external economies of scale or agglomeration effects by including city size or some other such variable in industry production functions. See Alonso (1971) for such a survey. For a more general discussion of the role of economies of scale in economic integration see Scitovsky (1963).

[20]Two measures of the change in the relative importance of intraindustry specialization have been employed: (1) the change in rank correlation between pairs of union members of individual industries ranked by the value of intraregional trade, and (2) the change in average "representative ratio" of a particular country, the representative ratio defined by $\frac{|E_i - M_i|}{E_i - M_i}$, where E_i is exports of commodity i, and M_i is imports of commodity i. Balassa and Willmore have drawn their conclusions of increasing intraindustry specialization in the EEC and the CACM, respectively, on the basis of observed *increases* in the rank correlations and *decreases* in the average representative ratios.

of an entirely hypothetical nature.[21] Learning-by-doing effects of experience in production and/or investment have been measured in a number of specific industries and processes and have been shown to be quite significant,[22] but the degree to which such effects derive from, and therefore should be attributed to, CU participation has never been estimated.

In other cases, attempts at quantification have been made but the methods employed are still quite imperfect. For example, Bergsman (1971) attempted quantification of the gains in X-efficiency. Although he specifically dealt only with the X-efficiency gains resulting from free trade, his approach could easily be modified so as to assess the X-efficiency gains resulting from participation in a CU. As such, the approach would be as follows: (1) to identify the n commodities which would be produced domestically both under the nondiscriminatory tariff regime and under customs union; (2) to estimate the preunion levels of domestic production and consumption x_i, $i = 1, 2, \ldots n$; (3) to estimate the change in tariff rates—on the commodities identified in (1)—resulting from adoption of the common external tariff regime; and (4) to calculate the gain in X-efficiency as $\sum_{i=1}^{n} X_i t_i$ where t_i is the *reduction* in the effective degree of distortion due to tariff changes resulting from the union. Since the proportion of home-produced goods to traded ones is usually quite high (even at an equilibrium exchange rate), it is obvious that, if there is any tendency to reduce nonessential tariff rates as a result of CU participation, the estimate of the X-efficiency gain could be quite large. However, this method is subject to severe limitations. First, as Bergsman himself admitted, the measure includes the reduction in monopoly profits and wages which do not represent a real efficiency gain, but only a redistribution from monopolists to consumers. Second, it is probably unrealistic to assume that prices of what are essentially home goods are dictated entirely by changes in tariff rates.[23] Indeed, this will not be the case unless the domestic industry is monopolistic.

With the exception of this attempt to measure the gain in X-efficiency, all of the attempts discussed above, by narrowly limiting their attention to the direct effects on trade, have intentionally avoided the effects of CU participation on income and growth. However, several attempts,

[21]See Mennes, Tinbergen, and Waardenburg (1969), Waters (1970), and Erlenkotter (1972).

[22]The industries that have been studied from this point of view include aircraft, shipbuilding, certain metal working industries, etc. See Hirsch (1965), Rapping (1966), Sheshinsky (1967), and Dudley (1972).

[23]See Anderson (1970) who explains that prices of home goods will, in fact, generally act as the equilibrating mechanism in a general equilibrium system with fixed exchange rates.

usually following along somewhat Keynesian lines, have been made to measure the impact of CUs on income more directly. For example, in his earliest attempt to estimate the effect of the institution of the CACM, McClelland (1968) assumed or calculated: (1) the "normal" growth rate of GNP over the preunion and postunion periods; (2) the value of the export multiplier; (3) the share of exports in GNP. By multiplying the export multiplier by the share of extraregional exports in GNP by the growth rate of extraregional exports, he obtained the contribution of extraregional exports to the overall growth of GNP. On the hypothesis that Central American growth was "export-led," he estimated the contribution of the CACM to the growth rate by subtracting the growth rate attributable to extraregional export growth from the "normal" growth rate. This method is subject to several rather serious shortcomings. First, the concept of a "normal" growth rate is essentially nonoperational. (In practice, the "normal" growth rate was assumed arbitrarily.) Second, the concept of an export multiplier assumes that there are not just in the short run but also in the long run unutilized domestic resources which can be exploited by stimulating demand. Even if one were to concede the validity of the concept of an export multiplier, there are formidable problems of estimation which McClelland ignored by arbitrarily assuming a value of this multiplier. (Naturally, the calculations are very sensitive to the size of the multiplier.) Finally, no justification is given for the assumption that income growth is entirely attributable to the growth of exports.

Another method for calculating directly the income gain attributable to CU participation consists of calculating the increased value added in the manufacturing sector derived from the union. This approach is derived from the thesis of Cooper and Massell (1965) and Johnson (1965b) which states that CU participation is motivated primarily by a desire to secure more industrialization at a minimum of cost in terms of overall efficiency. McClelland (1972) for the CACM and Newlyn (1965) and Hazlewood (1966) for the EACM have attempted to apply this method by computing the value added corresponding to that portion of the increase in intraregional trade in manufactured goods that is attributable to the existence of the union. The major difficulty with this approach is the difficulty of determining what portion of the increased intraregional trade is attributable to CU participation. In practice, estimates of different researchers have differed widely in this respect.

As far as factor movements are concerned, several attempts have been made to measure the effect of the formation of the EEC and EFTA on foreign investment, but with distinctly mixed results (Scaperlanda 1967; Scaperlanda and Mauer 1969; D'Arge 1969; and Schmitz 1970). The importance of these effects of CU participation could only be arrived at after estimating the contribution of the additional capital formation (attributable to the CU) to the growth rate of CU members.

3. Overall Orders of Magnitude

Given the large number of different kinds of effects of CU participation to be measured and the variety of possible ways of assessing them, not to mention alternative sets of data, different countries, etc., one might expect to find an extremely wide range of empirical estimates of the benefits and/or costs of CU participation.

But as Leibenstein (1966) and Heller (1968) have already noted, the range of existing estimates of the contribution of CU participation to national income has actually been extremely narrow, roughly between zero and one percent of national income.[24]

Admittedly, most of these estimates refer to the EEC or to other hypothetical arrangements in Europe, the number of comparable studies for LDCs being limited (for reasons given in our introductory chapter). However, the few such studies that have been undertaken for LDCs have yielded results similar to those obtained for Europe. Lawrence (1968a), for example, concluded that the trade preferences extended by the EEC to the former French and Belgian territories in Africa had been of negligible significance. Similarly, Leibenstein (1966, p. 393) reported a study for LAFTA demonstrating welfare gains amounting to only a fraction of one percent of LAFTA's income. Moreover, in the absence of empirical findings for CUs among LDCs, Allen (1961) and Bhambri (1962) pointed out several plausible reasons why the net benefits of CU participation should be even smaller in the case of unions among LDCs than in the case of those among more developed countries.

Nevertheless, in our critical survey of the theoretical and empirical analysis of CUs, we have revealed several limitations pertaining to the analysis upon which these estimates have been based which could provide a partial explanation for the surprising consistency of these findings. First, some of the potentially more important effects of CU par-

---

[24]Johnson's (1958) estimate of the benefits Britain would enjoy as a participant in a free-trade association in Europe was "a maximum of 1%" of GNP. With the exception of an estimate by Duquesne de la Vinelle (1966) in which Balassa (1967) detected a serious bias toward overestimation, Johnson's estimate would seem to be among the largest. Among the others are those for the EEC by Balassa of some 0.5 percent of GNP, by Verdoorn (1954) and by Scitovsky (1958) of about 0.05 percent of GNP, and by Truman (1967) of 0.2 percent, for Italy by Janssen (1961) of 0.1 percent, and for Germany by Wemelsfelder (1960) of 0.16 percent. Recently, however, with the use of quite original but unorthodox methods, Wonnacott and Wonnacott (1967), Krauss (1968), and Williamson (1971) have obtained considerably higher estimates of the potential benefits of CU participation. However, all of these estimates attribute to CU participation gains which would probably better be attributed to many other factors.

ticipation have not yet been incorporated into the theoretical analysis, let alone into the empirical estimates. Second, most empirical estimates have, in fact, been based on a single effect: the trade-creation/trade-diversion effect. Third, the theoretical model upon which this effect is analyzed is of dubious validity, particularly as far as small, closed LDCs are concerned. Finally, that model has been made operational by additional assumptions of questionable validity.

We do not wish to imply that the empirical work to date has been worthless. To the contrary, if one should allow the above-mentioned (exceedingly small) estimates of the benefits of CU participation to be disregarded simply because the methods of estimation and underlying theoretical models were not completely realistic, the same could be said about every other estimate with regard to every type of behavior. Without such imperfect models and estimation procedures we would certainly be less knowledgeable. The only implication we wish to draw from the above critical remarks is that the apparently consistent finding of insignificant effects of CU participation should not be regarded as a powerful body of evidence, giving one sufficiently strong *a priori* expectations so that one would (in the Bayesian sense) have to reject the outcome of any other empirical investigations that might provide somewhat different findings. Indeed, since almost all the existing estimates have been based on the same model with the same empirical assumptions, the consistency of the findings should hardly be surprising.

3 measurement of the effects of the CACM

In this chapter several of the approaches to empirical estimation of the costs and benefits of CU participation that were reviewed in the previous chapter are applied to the case of the CACM. Estimates of various individual effects, such as those of trade-creation, tariff-homogenization, and industrialization will be presented and critically assessed in section A. This is followed in section B by an attempt to estimate the total effects of CACM participation through estimation of an aggregate production function.

A. MEASUREMENT OF INDIVIDUAL EFFECTS

As pointed out in the previous chapter, because of the ease with which it can be applied and its avoidance of restrictive assumptions, Balassa's income-elasticity approach seems to have gained acceptance as the most satisfactory means of measuring trade-creation.[1] Since the method has already been applied with some success to the EEC by Balassa, and also to the CACM by Wilford (1970) and Willmore (1972a), it should serve as a convenient point of departure for our own empirical investigations of the CACM.

---

[1]For example, Heller (1968, p. 169) has referred to Balassa's method as "the most comprehensive attempt to measure the trade-creating and trade-diverting effects."

1. Application of the Balassa Approach to Trade-Creation

In his study of the CACM, Wilford used aggregate data on imports and income for the years 1953–61 and 1961–67 to compute for the preunion and postunion periods, respectively, the average elasticity of imports with respect to income. The resulting differences in the elasticities were somewhat larger than those Balassa had obtained for the EEC, thereby seemingly indicating the CACM to be somewhat more trade-creating than the EEC. Moreover, application of the same technique to disaggregated (single-digit SITC) import data for the periods 1956–61 and 1961–67 revealed trade-creation in all except two (SITC 3: fuels and lubricants and SITC 4: fats and oils) of the ten commodity categories.

Subsequently, Willmore improved upon Wilford's rather mechanical application of the Balassa approach by incorporating the following modifications: (1) a slightly longer time series (1953–68), (2) slightly more precise breaking points between the preunion and postunion periods (1961 in the cases of El Salvador, Guatemala, and Nicaragua, and 1962 and 1963 for Honduras and Costa Rica, respectively), (3) a different method of computing the elasticities (i.e., by regressing the logarithms of imports on the logarithms of income), and (4) the use of disaggregated data classified by end-use rather than by sector of origin.

At the aggregate level the result of these modifications was a somewhat smaller estimate (0.31) of the increase in elasticity of imports with respect to income attributable to participation in the CACM.[2] This finding indicated that the CACM was on balance no more trade-creating than the EEC; in two of the countries (El Salvador and Guatemala) the results revealed negative trade-creation ("trade-suppression").

At the disaggregated level, Willmore found general evidence of trade-creation, but this was found to be accompanied by trade-diversion (the substitution of intraregional for extraregional sources of imports) in some sectors. At the individual country level, diverging patterns emerged.

While Willmore's results underscored the importance of detailed study of individual countries and sectors, as both Willmore and Schiavo-Campo (1971) have remarked, the degree of disaggregation that would be necessary in order to provide meaningful comparisons[3] by this type

---

[2]Moreover, this difference was not statistically significant.

[3]Truly meaningful comparisons would require (1) that the commodities be homogeneous (and therefore not mix items which have become "traditional" products in the region with new "nontraditional" ones), (2) that quality and price data be available so as to distinguish price increases from quantity increases, and (3) that the data pertain to individual commodities for which preunion and postunion tariff rates are known, and hence one could distinguish between the effects of changes in tariff rates and those of tariff exemptions resulting from CU participation, or the industrial incentives, and the effects of various other trade agreements made in the preunion period.

of analysis is much greater than that permitted by the available data. In fact, import data classified by end-use and country of origin are available for all postunion years, but, for only one year (1958) in the preunion period. Preunion elasticities for such categories can thus only be computed by making assumptions of questionable validity concerning the time path of imports during the period.

Since comparability of the elasticities between the two periods is a prerequisite for satisfactory application of the Balassa approach, it does not seem possible to apply it at a disaggregated level unless the much less meaningful SITC data are utilized. For this reason in the computations which follow we shall confine our attention to the use of aggregate data.

Two further modifications in the mechanical applications of Balassa's method to the estimation of the trade-creating benefits of the CACM seem desirable. In the first place, the comparison of the post-union period with the immediate preunion period (1953–60 or 1956–61) could be biased in one direction or another by the influence of the bilateral trade agreements which proliferated in the region in the late 1950s. Second, to the extent the relationship between the growth rate of imports and that of income is nonproportional, the observed differences in elasticities could be biased if the growth rates of income differed from one period to the other.

In the case of the EEC (as Balassa pointed out) the income growth rates of the immediate preunion and postunion periods were indeed similar. Even if they had differed, no estimation bias would have been likely because in large developed countries, like France, Germany, and certainly the EEC as a whole, proportionality between the growth rate of imports and that of income would seem very plausible.

However, proportionality seems much less realistic in small LDCs, like the five Central American countries or even the CACM as a whole. Because of the scarcity and immobility of several of the productive resources in such countries, rapid shifts in demand (income)—which are typically generated externally through exports and investments in the primary sector—are less likely than small gradual shifts to be matched by increased supplies from domestic sources. Accordingly, a larger proportion of the increases in demand and income is likely to be satisfied by imports in the case of large increases in demand than that of smaller increases in demand. In short, the growth rate of imports is likely to vary more than in proportion to the growth rate of income.

The reader can see that this nonproportionality hypothesis is corroborated in the Central American case by reference to figure 3–1, where the annual growth rate of imports is plotted against the annual growth rate of income for Central America as a whole. It can easily be seen from this diagram that when the growth rate of income is low (but *positive*),

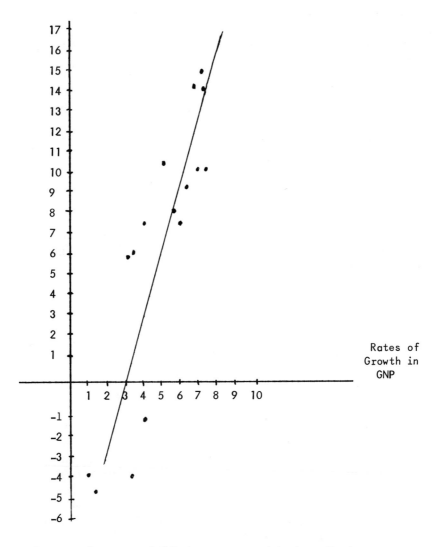

Source: Imports and GNP data presented in Appendix A.

Figure 3-1. *The Graphical Relationship between GNP and Imports in Central America.*

the growth rate of imports is likely to be *negative*. Alternatively, when the growth rate of income is as high as 7 percent per annum, imports grow at 10–15 percent per annum. This nonproportionality between the two growth rates, of course, implies that the elasticity of imports with respect to income increases with the rate of growth of income. Therefore, in the case of CUs among LDCs, in general, and the CACM, in particular, the Balassa method yields unbiased estimates only if the income growth rates of the preunion and postunion periods are similar.

Table 3–1 presents the average annual growth rates of income for each of the Central American countries and for Central America as a whole in each of three periods: the early preunion period (1950–56), the immediate preunion period (1956–61), and the postunion period (1961–67). Income growth rates of the postunion period were in all cases noticeably higher than the income growth rates of the immediate preunion period, which were relied on so heavily by Willmore and especially by Wilford in their computations. Therefore, their estimates of trade-creation and the benefits thereof are biased upward.

Fortunately, the growth rates for the earlier portion of the preunion period (1950–56) are generally rather similar to those of the postunion period, although even in this case they differ significantly in some of the countries (especially Costa Rica and Nicaragua). Since this earlier period is also largely free of the influence of the bilateral trade agreements mentioned above as another source of possible bias, in Table 3–2 we present estimates of the relevant elasticities for this period, as well as those for the 1956–61 and 1962–67 periods.[4] These calculations show that (as expected) the elasticities are quite sensitive to the income growth rate and that differences in the income elasticities between the preunion and postunion periods are (with the minor exception of El Salvador) much smaller when the earlier preunion period (with higher income growth rates) is used in the comparisons than when the later preunion period (with lower income growth rates) is used.

Table 3-1. Average Annual Growth Rates of GNP

	Costa Rica	El Salvador	Guatemala	Honduras	Nicaragua	Central America
1951–56	7.93	5.60	3.80	5.03	8.30	5.22
1956–61	4.30	1.90	3.12	3.95	5.25	3.19
1961–67	6.02	5.20	4.50	5.10	6.30	5.16

Source: Data on GNP and imports presented in appendix A.

[4]Another modification introduced in these computations is the use of constant-price data. This modification seemed desirable on the grounds that without it differences in the rates of inflation or differences between the rate of increase in domestic prices and that of the prices of imports might affect the estimates of the change in elasticities attributable to CU participation in a manner similar to changes in income growth rates between periods.

Table 3-2. Average Elasticities of Imports with Respect to Income

	Costa Rica	El Salvador	Guatemala	Honduras	Nicaragua	Central America
Elasticities						
1951–56	2.94	1.06	0.38	1.63	2.64	1.77
1957–61	0.61	1.24	-0.28	0.30	0.77	-0.84
1962–67	1.90	2.33	1.85	2.64	2.43	2.04
Changes in elasticities						
1951–56 to 1962–67	(-1.04)	1.27	(1.47)	1.01	(-0.21)	0.27
Welfare gain due to trade creation	negative	0.38%	0.44%	0.30%	negative	0.09%

Notes: Figures in parentheses indicate unreliable estimates based on income growth rates that are not similar.
The welfare gain due to trade-creation is defined in terms of the annual contribution to the growth rate and is estimated by multiplying the estimated change in income elasticity by the assumed efficiency conversion factor of additional trade of 0.3.

Source: Data presented in appendix A.

Because of the remarkable similarity in the income growth rates for Central America as a whole between the earlier preunion period and the postunion period, this particular computation is probably the most reliable. It indicates, of course, that CACM participation has raised the elasticity of imports with respect to income by about 0.3. The corresponding changes at the national level, when adjusted very crudely to account for the biases introduced by the use of dissimilar income growth rates,[5] would seem to vary from about nil in Costa Rica and Nicaragua to about 1.0 for El Salvador, Guatemala, and Honduras. These results were not affected substantially when, alternatively, we computed the elasticities by regressing the logarithms of imports on the logarithms of GNP, as had been advocated by Willmore (1972a). Because of the limited number of observations and the rather substantial year-to-year fluctuations, the differences in elasticities are statistically insignificant no matter which method is used in their calculation.

Using the same efficiency conversion factor used by Balassa, i.e., 0.3,[6] these estimates of the change in elasticities of imports with respect to income imply increases in the income growth rates attributable to CACM participation, varying between zero in Costa Rica and Nicaragua to 0.3 percent per annum in the other countries and approaching 0.1 percent per annum for Central America, as a whole. In contrast to the earlier conclusion derived by Wilford, our estimates show that there is little reason to believe that the Balassa method would reveal greater trade-creation when applied to the CACM than it did when applied to the EEC.

In our opinion, its more serious shortcomings are attributable to the facts (1) that, by abstracting from the effect of the CU on income growth (thereby ignoring indirect effects on trade) it fails to capture the most essential reason for CU participation in the case of small LDCs, and (2) that it may attribute to CU participation the influence of various other

---

[5]Since the income growth rates were higher in the 1950–56 period than in the 1962–67 period for Costa Rica and Nicaragua, but smaller in the former period than in the latter for Guatemala, the changes in elasticities have to be adjusted upward for Costa Rica and Nicaragua but downward for Guatemala.

[6]In an alternative attempt to estimate the efficiency conversion factor we have estimated the elasticity of income (GDP) with respect to exports (E) by regressing income (GDP) on exports (E) and investment (I), all variables being measured in terms of the logarithms of one plus the annual growth rate obtained from the same international cross section of time-series data 1949–67 for 38 LDCs that is utilized in the following section. The following result was obtained:

$$\text{GDP} = 2.90 + .216\,E + .122\,I \qquad \bar{R}^2 = .720$$
$$\phantom{\text{GDP} = 2.90 + }(.041)\quad(.049)$$

This implies that a one percent increase in the growth rate of exports (or presumably of imports) would raise the growth rate of GDP by 0.276 percent. Thus 0.276 may be considered an alternative estimate of the efficiency conversion factor.

factors which may differ between periods (only one of which may be the income growth rate which, as we have shown, may be accounted for rather easily).

2. Application of the Export Performance Approach

Since the export performance approach attempts to mitigate these two shortcomings of the Balassa approach and yet aims at capturing the same effects, i.e., the trade effects,[7] it would seem logical that we consider it next.

In the long run, a country's export performance (i.e., the growth rate of its exports) would presumably depend on a multitude of factors, some of which influence primarily the demand for exports (E_d) and some of which affect the supply of exports (E_s). In equilibrium, of course, the supply and demand for exports must balance.

For any particular country we might suppose that the supply of its exports is affected by (1) the relative price of its exportables, (2) its productive capacity, (3) the incidence of policies discriminating in favor of or against exports. On the other hand, the demand for exports might well be affected by (4) its prices relative to those of the rest of the world, (5) the world demand for the commodity bundle it exports, (6) the demand of the geographic region to which it exports, and (7) its participation (or lack of participation) in a particular regional trading arrangement.

In order to give operational content to the model, we define the seven variables mentioned above as follows:

1) The relative price of exportables is the U.S. dollar price of exportables (Px) converted into domestic currency terms by multiplying by the (current) price of foreign exchange (in units of domestic currency per U.S. dollar) (Pfe) relative to domestic prices (Pd), i.e., $\dfrac{Px \cdot Pfe}{Pd}$.

2) Productive capacity is defined in terms of a convenient proxy: gross domestic product (GDP).

3) The discriminatory policies vis-à-vis exports that are considered are the ad valorem tax rate on exports (Tx), licensing requirements on exports (Lx), and the requirement to surrender foreign exchange earnings at fixed rates (Sx).

4) The relative price of country i's exports in world markets is the rest of the world price in U.S. dollars (Pw), converted to its domestic

---

[7]To the extent the export performance approach has a longer time perspective, it should be more capable of picking up the more dynamic and indirect effects of CU participation on trade.

currency equivalent by multiplying by *Pfe*, relative to *Pd*, i.e., $\dfrac{Pw \cdot Pfe}{Pd}$.

5) World demand for the commodities country *i* exports is the commodity-weighted quantum index of world imports of country *i*'s export bundle (COMM).

6) The geographic demand index is the country-weighted index of aggregate imports of the geographic region to which country *i* exports (GEO).

7) The CU variables are dummy variables representing the individual institutional arrangement (if any) with which country *i* becomes affiliated during the period considered, i.e., EEC, EFTA, LAFTA, and CACM.

All variables are defined in terms of the annual growth rates over a period of years, except for the following: *Tx*, which, because it changed infrequently and information for it was limited, is defined in terms of the absolute change in the export tax rate between the beginning of the period and the end of the period; *Lx* and *Sx*, which are defined in terms of a crude index (ranging from 0 to 100) of changes favorable to (+) or detrimental to (−) exports; and the CU dummy variables with values of 100 for participation and 0 for nonparticipation.

Postulating, for simplicity, linear relationships, the model can be formally expressed as follows:

$$(3.1) \qquad E_s = a_{10} + a_{11} \frac{Pfe\ Px}{Pd} + a_{12}\,GDP + a_{13}Tx + a_{14}Lx$$
$$+ a_{15}Sx$$

$$(3.2) \qquad E_d = a_{20} + a_{21} \frac{Pfe\ Pw}{Pd} + a_{22}COMM + a_{23}GEO$$
$$+ a_{24}EEC + a_{25}EFTA + a_{26}LAFTA + a_{27}CACM$$

$$(3.3) \qquad E_s = E_d$$

Several features of this model should be mentioned. First, because it is designed for applications to countries over a period as long as two decades, much more attention in this model is given to supply considerations than in other studies of this type.[8] Second, it includes several important policy variables, such as the exchange rate (*Pfe*) and the tax variables. Third, by including both determinants on the supply and demand sides, it allows one to test the relative importance of each set of influences on export performance over a period of years.

[8] See De Vries (1967), Naya (1968), Ooms (1966).

Finally, the specification of a separate dummy variable for each different regional trading arrangement of consequence recognizes that (for reasons given above) the extent of (positive) or, alternatively, of negative trade-creation (trade-suppression) may vary from one such arrangement to another. However, since the specification in no way distinguishes between countries, it does not allow the effects of a particular CU to be trade-creating for some countries and trade-suppressing for others, as admittedly may be the case.

In order to obtain results in terms of elasticities, all the growth rate variables are specified in terms of logarithms of $(l + g)$, where g is the country-specific growth rate fitted to time-series data for the years 1949–67. Assuming for simplicity that the exchange rate variable (Pfe), domestic prices (Pd), and the proxy for productive capacity (GDP) are all exogenous, a "reduced form" to this overdetermined system can conveniently be derived by summing equations (3.1) and (3.2),[9] yielding:

$$(3.4) \quad \log E = (a_{10} + a_{20}) + (a_{11} + a_{21})(\log Pfe - \log Pd)$$
$$+ a_{11}\log Px + a_{21}\log Pw + a_{12}\log GDP + a_{13}Tx$$
$$+ a_{14}Lx + a_{15}Sx + a_{22}\log COMM + a_{23}\log GEO$$
$$+ a_{24}EEC + a_{25}EFTA + a_{26}LAFTA + a_{27}CACM$$

This equation has been estimated by ordinary least squares with empirical data pertaining to a sample of 38 nonpetroleum-exporting LDCs for which time-series data on most of the variables included in the model were available for the entire period 1949–67. The growth rates and absolute differences employed in the regressions, as well as the data sources, are given in table 3–3.

Several comments on the most important shortcomings of the data are in order: (1) since export quantum indexes were available for only a few countries of this sample, we have had to rely on export figures in dollars and then deflated them by export unit value or price indexes (in dollar terms), as available. (2) Due to the absence of adequate national income or product deflators or other more suitable price data for quite a number of the countries included in the sample, the growth rate of domestic prices of each country has been measured by the cost of living index. (3) Although figures for real GDP were generally more readily available than those for real GNP, where a series of GDP data was not available, data on GNP were utilized; similarly, although we would

[9]In actual fact, these assumptions of exogeneity and the method of deriving the reduced form cannot be valid. Unless at least one of these variables is exogenous, the system would consist of three equations in only two endogenous variables. However, the admission that any one of these other variables is endogenous would almost inevitably lead to the introduction of additional variables and thus greater complexity.

Table 3-3. Data for Export Performance Model 1949-67

		1 E	2 Pfe-Pd	3 Px	4 GDP	5 Tx	6 Lx	7 Sx	8 GEO	9 COMM	10 EEC	11 EFTA	12 CACM	13 LAFTA	14 WAR
1.	Argentina	3.91	2.60	-2.11	3.09	13.5	0	0	5.76	4.70	0	0	0	100	0
2.	Bolivia	-1.01	-6.27	1.36	1.84	4.4	100	40	5.18	-0.21	0	0	0	0	0
3.	Brazil	1.79	0.32	-0.59	5.24	-0.4	0	20	5.82	3.97	0	0	0	100	0
4.	Ceylon	1.76	-0.49	-0.84	3.53	1.8	-50	-20	5.21	1.88	0	0	0	0	0
5.	Chile	3.54	-1.12	1.36	3.93	0	0	0	5.97	5.60	0	0	0	100	0
6.	Colombia	2.22	1.84	-0.56	4.41	-0.1	0	-10	6.26	4.16	0	0	0	100	0
7.	Costa Rica	5.73	-0.80	-0.56	5.48	1.5	50	0	6.61	3.94	0	0	100	0	0
8.	Cyprus	2.76	-3.36	1.44	3.97	0	0	20	7.71	6.18	0	0	0	0	100
9.	Dominican Rep.	2.89	-1.18	0.17	4.22	-13.0	0	0	5.29	3.60	0	0	0	0	0
10.	Ecuador	7.32	-0.73	-0.40	4.47	2.0	-20	-20	5.99	4.06	0	0	0	100	0
11.	El Salvador	7.40	-1.60	0.27	5.05	-8.0	0	-100	6.74	3.43	0	0	100	0	0
12.	Greece	7.69	0.22	0.27	6.11	0	0	10	7.58	3.60	100	0	0	0	100
13.	Guatemala	6.31	-0.62	-0.21	4.93	-5.0	-20	-100	6.38	3.90	0	0	100	0	0
14.	Haiti	0.79	-1.13	-1.30	1.24	5.2	-10	0	7.12	3.51	0	0	0	0	0
15.	Honduras	3.91	-1.81	1.23	3.96	1.0	0	100	6.30	5.66	0	0	100	0	0
16.	Iceland	5.66	2.26	1.87	4.87	0	0	0	7.01	5.21	0	0	0	0	0
17.	India	1.71	-2.05	-0.34	3.66	-5.2	0	0	5.46	3.83	0	0	0	0	0
18.	Israel	15.46	4.65	0.85	9.20	0	70	30	4.92	8.22	0	0	0	0	100
19.	Jamaica	7.85	-2.58	2.18	6.79	0	0	0	4.66	4.67	0	0	0	0	0

Table 3-3. Data for Export Performance Model 1949-67 (cont'd.)

		1 E	2 Pfe-Pd	3 Px	4 GDP	5 Tx	6 Lx	7 Sx	8 GEO	9 COMM	10 EEC	11 EFTA	12 CACM	13 LAFTA	14 WAR
20.	Korea	16.46	5.95	0.27	5.98	0	10	30	11.46	3.62	0	0	0	0	100
21.	Malaysia	3.80	-0.07	-0.31	5.20	0.7	50	0	5.86	2.28	0	0	0	0	0
22.	Mexico	5.14	-2.73	-0.41	5.96	-8.8	0	0	6.31	4.63	0	0	0	100	0
23.	Morocco	3.66	-1.26	0.28	1.96	1.2	0	0	7.23	3.94	0	0	0	0	0
24.	Nicaragua	9.31	-1.57	0.58	5.30	-2.2	0	50	7.52	4.87	0	0	100	0	0
25.	Pakistan	1.78	0.05	-2.04	3.87	-9.0	0	-20	6.61	1.11	0	0	0	0	0
26.	Panama	7.58	-0.39	0.16	6.33	-0.5	-20	0	5.95	5.47	0	0	0	0	0
27.	Paraguay	2.93	2.94	-0.23	3.04	2.9	-20	0	1.85	5.78	0	0	0	100	0
28.	Peru	8.53	-3.50	0.94	5.34	-14.0	70	100	6.35	6.96	0	0	0	100	0
29.	Philippines	5.79	2.23	-0.60	4.55	0	0	0	7.11	1.73	0	0	0	0	0
30.	Portugal	6.55	-1.64	0.75	4.80	-1.1	0	10	6.66	5.04	0	100	0	0	0
31.	Spain	7.14	1.00	-1.37	6.15	0	0	20	6.04	5.05	0	0	0	0	0
32.	Sudan	3.92	-2.87	-0.75	4.83	-1.0	-50	0	4.88	3.30	0	0	0	0	0
33.	Taiwan	13.37	1.53	-1.50	7.88	0	0	20	10.28	3.63	0	0	0	0	100
34.	Thailand	4.93	-0.85	-0.36	5.86	-0.6	50	0	6.11	2.27	0	0	0	0	0
35.	Tunisia	1.02	-0.03	-1.98	3.89	0.2	0	-10	6.83	5.30	0	0	0	0	0
36.	Turkey	1.93	1.01	0.96	4.60	0	40	0	7.97	3.44	100	0	0	0	0
37.	U.A.R. (Egypt)	1.20	0.73	0.03	3.63	3.0	-10	0	6.98	2.67	0	0	0	0	0
38.	Uruguay	-0.72	1.04	-1.44	1.11	13.5	0	-30	5.93	3.04	0	0	0	100	0

Note: All variables have been multiplied by 100.

Sources:

Column 1: *International Financial Statistics*, various issues; *Yearbook of International Trade Statistics*, various years.

Column 2: *Exchange Rates:* In so far as possible exchange rates for export transactions were computed from exports of goods and services in both local currency and U.S. dollars, from the same sources as for column 1. For countries for which this data was lacking or incomplete, official or free exchange rates were used, depending on which seemed most relevant to the average exporter according to the International Monetary Fund's *Annual Report on Exchange Restrictions*, various years. In the few such cases in which multiple rates for exports were in effect, the rates used were weighted averages of the relevant rates, the weights being chosen from the same source. *Domestic Prices: International Financial Statistics* and *United Nations Statistical Yearbook*, various years.

Column 3: Same source as column 1.

Column 4: Development Center, Organization for Economic Co-operation and Development, *National Accounts of Less Developed Countries*, July 1968 and subsequent supplements. Agency for International Development, *Gross National Product: Growth Rates and Trend Data*, July 25, 1968. United Nations Statistical Office, unpublished data.

Column 5: Richard Goode, George E. Lent, and P.D. Ojha, "Role of Export Taxes in Developing Countries," *IMF Staff Papers* 13, no. 3 (Nov. 1966): 453–503. International Monetary Fund, *Annual Report on Exchange Restrictions*, various issues; United Nations, *Yearbook on International Trade Statistics*, United Nations, *Statistical Yearbook*; Marcus Flemming, Rudolf Rhomberg, and Lorette Boissonneault, "Export Norms and their Role in Compensatory Financing," *IMF Staff Papers* 10, no. 1 (March 1963): table 13, p. 144; Colombia: Direccion del Presupuesto, *Boletin Trimestral* (June 1967): 135–40; Haiti: *Rapport Annuel*, Banque Nationale de la Rep. d'Haiti, Département Fiscal, various years; Mexico: Clark W. Reynolds, *Mexican Economy: Twentieth Century Structure and Growth* (New Haven: Yale University Press, 1970). Pakistan: *Budget of Pakistan*, various years, also Stephen R. Lewis, Jr., unpublished data; Paraguay: *Memoria del Banco Central*, various years; Uruguay: Dir. Gen. de Estadística y Censos, *Annuario Estadístico*.

Columns
6 & 7:   *IMF Annual Report on Exchange Restrictions*, various years.

Column 8: International Monetary Fund, *Direction of Trade* and *International Financial Statistics*, various years. United Nations, *Yearbook of International Trade Statistics*, various years.

Column 9: Commodity weights computed from United Nations, *Yearbook of International Trade Statistics*, primarily 1955–59; volume indexes by commodity were obtained for each of the following 96 commodities: abaca, animals-live, animal oils and fats, antimony, apples, bananas, barley, bauxite, beef-chilled, beverages-alcoholic, castor beans, cattle-live, cement, cereals, chemicals, chrome, coal, cocoa, coconut, coconut oil, coffee, copper, copra, cork, cotton, cottonseed, dairy products, diamonds, eggs (in shell), embroidery, fish-dried, fish-fresh, fish-canned, fish-crustacea-molluscs, fish oil, fruit-citrus, fruit-dried, fruit-fresh, fruit-preserved, gold, grapefruit, grapes, graphite, ground nuts, gums-resins-balsam, hides and skins—goats and sheep, iron, jute, jute manufactures, lead, lemon-limes, linseed oil, maize, manganese manufactures, meat-mutton-lamb, meat-canned, mica, olive oil, onions, oranges and tangerines, pepper, petroleum, phosphate, pigs-live, potash, quebracho extract, raisins, rice, rubber, rye, salt, seed cake, sesame, silk, silver, sisal and agave, steel scrap, sugar, sunflower oil, tea, textiles-yarn and thread, tin, tobacco, tungsten, vegetable oil, wheat, wine, wood (in logs coniferous), wood (in logs broadleaved), wool, world exports, yerba mate, zinc. The sources of this data were as follows: for agricultural products, FAO, *Yearbook of Food and Agricultural Statistics*, various years; for forest products, FAO, *World Forest Products Statistics*, various years; for mineral products, *Statistical Summary of the Mineral Industry* 1949–54, 1954–59, 1960–65, 1962–67; for fish products, FAO *Yearbook of Fishery Statistics*, various years; for jute products, Commonwealth Economic Committee, *Industrial Fibres*, various issues; for hides and skins, Commonwealth Economic Committee, *Raw Hides and Skins*; for other products, import statistics (quanta) from UN *Yearbook of International Trade Statistics*, OECD, *Statistical Bulletin, Foreign Trade*.

have preferred to use national product data at factor cost for all countries, in a few cases we have had to use data at market prices. (4) In several countries we have had to use unit-value indexes instead of proper-export price indexes in measuring Px, thereby introducing the possibility of systematic measurement error in the variable, because of the fact that unit-value indexes reflect changes in commodity composition and quality, in addition to changes in price per se. (5) The values of Tx, Lx, and Sx have been based to a large extent on rather subjective interpretations of the essentially qualitative information contained in the IMF's *Annual Report on Exchange Restrictions*—but supplemented by quantitative data from national sources whenever possible. (6) In a few cases (Israel, Korea, Malaysia, and Taiwan) the various growth rates were computed from somewhat shorter time series. (7) Since it was impossible to obtain a different index of world prices appropriate for that subset of the world with which each specific country is most closely competing, the Pw variable has been dropped from the estimating equations. (8) While we have tried to base the weights used in computing COMM and GEO on the mid-years of the period (1956–59), in some cases we have had to use somewhat different years for this purpose. (9) Since both exports and unit values have been based exclusively on data reported by the exporting country, the possibility of some differences between countries with respect to overinvoicing or under-invoicing of exports cannot be denied. (10) The geographical coverage of the sample is quite uneven, being generally heavy on Latin American countries and light on sub-Sahara African ones.

However, since most of the limitations pertain only to a few countries and apply only when there are systematic differences in their incidence between countries and over time, the limitations are hardly overwhelming. The data employed pertain to a larger sample of countries, each with a longer and more complete time series, and a larger number of variables than is usually employed in studies of this sort. Moreover, to the extent these limitations would be expected to affect the results, there is little reason to believe they would seriously bias the regression coefficient of the single variable which is of concern here: the CACM dummy variable.

At the beginning of the period under investigation, several of the countries in the sample were still operating under the abnormal conditions of war—either civil or foreign—from which they would eventually be expected to recover and thus demonstrate above-normal export performance. We have attempted to account for this by including an additional dummy variable (WAR) with values of 100 in countries disrupted by wars in 1948 or 1949 and values of 0 in other countries. Naturally, a positive coefficient of this variable would be expected.

The reader can now proceed immediately to table 3–4 which presents the results obtained by fitting equation (3.4) (modified only for reasons given above by the exclusion of Pw and the inclusion of WAR) to the international cross-section of data presented in table 3–3. The expected directions of the effects (positive or negative) are indicated by the signs given at the heads of the columns.

Regression (1) shows that the estimated regression coefficients generally have the expected signs but are not always statistically significant. Since the Lx, and Sx variables had been estimated only very crudely and were found to have insignificant regression coefficients, they were omitted from regression (2) and all subsequent regressions with no significant change in the results with respect to the remaining variables. Since from the results of regressions (1) and (2), it was apparent that the COMM, EFTA, and LAFTA variables were also of negligible importance in explaining export performance, these variables have been omitted in regression (3), again with little effect on the results. Even with the restricted number of variables the model is able to explain more than 80 percent of the total variance in export growth rates among countries.

In contrast to the pessimistic and fatalistic attitudes expressed in the 1950s and early 1960s to the effect that an individual country is not able to determine its own destiny as far as exports are concerned, these results indicate that factors partially, if not largely, under a country's control have apparently exerted a very considerable influence on the growth rate of exports.[10] Probably because of the fairly long-term perspective of the model, factors related more closely to supply considerations seem to have been more important in determining export performance than factors pertaining to demand.

Of primary interest in the present context is, of course, the regression coefficient of the CACM dummy variable. As the reader can see from regressions (1) to (3), the coefficient is positive and remarkably insensitive to the aforementioned changes in specification. The estimated impact of CACM on the export growth rate can be obtained by taking the antilog of the observed regression coefficient. Thus the observed coefficient of $0.016 - 0.017$ implies that CACM participation has on the whole raised the export growth rate of the Central American countries by about 1.4 percent per annum.

In view of the various shortcomings of data, country coverage, and specification, these conclusions must be regarded as tentative. Of the various possible sources of bias, the two most important are those of excluded variables and simultaneous equation bias. The latter problem

---

[10]This conclusion is consistent with the results of some other recent works, i.e., Kravis (1970).

Table 3-4. Determinants of Export Performance: Regression Results

Equation no.		Constant	Pfe-Pd (+)	Px (+)	GDP (+)	Tx (-)	Lx (+)	Sx (+)	GEO (+)	COMM (+)	EEC (?)	EFTA (?)	CACM (?)	LAFTA (?)	WAR (+)	R^2
1.	E =	-5.089	.375 (.160)	.480 (.322)	1.362 (.233)	-.018 (.063)	-.006 (.011)	.006 (.009)	.499 (.236)	.047 (.240)	-.032 (.013)	.017 (.018)	.017 (.009)	.006 (.008)	.026 (.012)	.824
2.	E =	-5.220	.353 (.170)	.470 (.361)	1.386 (.244)				.537 (.272)	.109 (.268)	-.032 (.015)	.017 (.021)	.016 (.008)	.005 (.009)	.024 (.014)	.822
3.	E =	-4.806	.378 (.160)	.544 (.328)	1.407 (.227)				.493 (.250)		-.035 (.014)		.019 (.008)		.024 (.013)	.812
4.	E =	2.048	.590 (.232)	.919 (.479)					.373 (.371)		-.037 (.022)		.025 (.012)		.054 (.018)	.571
5.	E =	.922	.678 (.256)	.501 (.546)		-.192 (.090)	-.001 (.018)	.007 (.015)	.334 (.398)	.316 (.400)	-.030 (.022)	.023 (.029)	.024 (.012)	-.002 (.013)	.047 (.018)	.666
6.	E =	.113	.633 (.233)	.589 (.474)		-.185 (.086)			.425 (.362)	.397 (.323)	-.032 (.020)		.022 (.010)		.048 (.017)	.655
7.	E =	-.133	.606 (.237)	.439 (.474)		-.187 (.088)			.385 (.369)	.484 (.325)			.022 (.010)			.627

Notes: (1) The following variables are defined in terms of logarithms of $1 + g$ where g is the growth rate computed from 1949–67 annual observations: E, Pfe, Pd, Px, GDP, GEO, COMM.

(2) All figures in parentheses are standard errors of the regression coefficients under which they appear.

(3) For definitions of variables, form of the estimating equations, and interpretation of the results, see the text.

(4) The sources of the data are given in table 3–3.

arises from the fact that several variables—Pfe,[11] Pd, and GDP—treated as exogenous in the model are in fact endogenous in the long run. In view of the closeness of the relationship between GDP and E reflected in the highly significant regression coefficients of the GDP variables in regressions (1) to (3), the most potentially serious source of bias would seem to be the misspecification of the GDP variable. This is because simultaneous with the effect of GDP (as the proxy for aggregate capacity) on exports is a very strong relationship in the form of the national income accounting identity going from exports to GDP. Since in many of the LDCs included in the sample, exports are a large part of GDP, the omission of this relationship from the model probably exerts a strong upward bias to the estimate of the coefficient of GDP, the true coefficient being smaller than the estimated one. Due to the unavoidable multicollinearity with other explanatory variables included in the model, such as the CACM variable, certain other regression coefficients could also be affected by the bias in the GDP coefficient.

In order to get some idea of the direction and order of magnitude of these effects on the other coefficients, in general, and on the coefficient of the CACM variable, in particular, we have reestimated regression (3) of table 3-4, assuming the coefficient of GDP to be zero, i.e., dropping GDP from the estimating equation. The result is given in regression (4). In regression (5), we have reintroduced all of the previously dropped variables to see if they would become more significant with the omission of GDP. Indeed, this was found to be the case with respect to Tx and to a lesser extent COMM. Regression (6) is identical to regression (4) except for the inclusion of these two variables. Finally, regression (7) tests the sensitivity of the results to deletion of the EEC and WAR dummy variables. By comparing the results of regressions (4) through (7) with those of regressions (1) through (3), the reader can see that the results are somewhat sensitive to this specification change in the GDP variable. The impact of some variables is increased, while that of others is diminished. Of particular interest here is that the coefficient of the CACM dummy variable is among those whose value and significance are generally increased by the exclusion of the GDP variable.

Therefore, we conclude that the finding of a fairly sizable trade-creating effect of CACM participation from our international cross-section study of comparative export performance is robust in that it is rather insensitive to changes in specification. Experimentation with a simple change in specification of the model to offset the effect of one important source of bias has shown that the true contribution of CACM

---

[11]For an attempt to eliminate the simultaneous equation bias with respect to Pfe by resort to international data for a different time period, see Nugent (1973a).

participation would probably be somewhat higher than the 1.4 percent per annum estimated in regressions (1) to (3).

Even if one were to convert this contribution of the CACM to the export growth rate by the smaller estimate of the efficiency conversion factor of 0.276 obtained in footnote (6) above, it would yield an estimate of the contribution of trade-creation to income growth of more than 0.38 percent per annum. This estimate is almost four times as large as those obtained by the reasonably careful applications of the Balassa approach reported in the previous section. This result must again be regarded as highly tentative, as the various weaknesses mentioned above would have to be overcome before firm conclusions could be reached.

In the meantime, it does offer some reason for believing that by abstracting from the impact of CUs on income growth and indirectly on imports the use of Balassa's method (when properly applied) may seriously understate the amount of trade-creation and its contribution to overall growth derived from CU participation.

3. The Tariff Homogenizing Effect and Its Measurement

In this section we shall attempt quantification of a CU effect that has been previously overlooked: the tariff-homogenizing effect. Not only may CU participation affect the average tariff rate (which, as pointed out above, brings external trade-creation or external trade-suppression, depending on whether or not the average tariff rate is lowered or raised as a result of CU participation), but also it may affect the whole structure of tariffs, including the nature and degree of the dispersion of individual tariff rates around their mean.

If an effect such as this on the dispersion of tariff rates around the mean exists, what is its significance? Intuitively put, the answer to this question is quite simple. Assuming that some price distortions are regarded as necessary, as for example to protect (infant) domestic industry, the number of relative prices distorted and the magnitude of the distortions will be *smaller* the more uniform (or general) the distortions.[12] The welfare cost of any set of price distortions, such as those from tariffs, may thus be expected to increase not only with the average rate of distortion (the average tariff rate) but also with the degree of dispersion of the distortions (tariff rates) among commodities.

If CU participation is likely to affect the tariff structure in such a way as to make tariff rates more uniform among commodities (as will pres-

---

[12]A formal argument to the same effect has been made by Bertrand (1972) and Bertrand and Vanek (1971). Intuitive arguments along the same lines emphasizing policy implications have been made by Little, Scitovsky, and Scott (1970), and Balassa (1971a).

ently be argued), then CU participation would have a positive effect on economic welfare which should be recognized and measured.

It may be reasonable to suppose that any country's tariff structure is a result of both historical accidents and the political power of domestic producers relative to that of domestic consumers in the various sectors of the economy. If this is the case, and if these factors vary significantly from country to country even within a common geographic region, then it would follow that the structure of tariffs would vary considerably from one country to another. If so, intercountry comparisons of tariff rates will probably reveal cases in which one country has a high tariff rate on one commodity and a low one on another, while in another country the reverse is the case.

What would be the effect on their tariff structure of the adoption of a common external tariff among such countries? There is, of course, no single set of rules which potential CU partners must adopt in order to resolve their differences with respect to individual preunion tariff rates and thereby to arrive at a common external tariff structure. However, the guideline followed by the EEC in this respect—namely, to adopt the mean of the existing preunion rates as the common external tariff rate—seems to be a rather natural expedient that has apparently formed the basis of the common external tariff regime in the CACM. If preunion tariff rates differ among commodities and countries, as we have just suggested, and the tariff-averaging procedure for adopting common external tariff rates is employed, as it apparently has been in both the EEC and CACM, CU participation would have the effect of making tariff rates more uniform among commodities.

Let us illustrate this possibility with a simple hypothetical example. Suppose, as shown in case I of table 3–5, there are two countries, 1 and 2, and two commodities of equal importance, A and B. Assume further that the two countries have different tariffs on different commodities but the same average tariff rate of 20 percent. The effect of CU participation would then be to make the tariff rates more homogeneous than

Table 3–5. Hypothetical Tariff Rates (in percent)
Before and After Adoption of a Common External Tariff Regime

	Preunion tariff rates			Common external rates		
	Sector A	Sector B	Average	Sector A	Sector B	Average
Case I						
Country 1	40	0	20	20	20	20
Country 2	0	40	20	20	20	20
Case II						
Country 1	20	20	20	10	30	20
Country 2	0	40	20	10	30	20

the preunion rates (in fact, in this example it would make them perfectly homogeneous). This need not be the case, and indeed case II of the same table illustrates a situation in which the tariff rates of at least one country are made less uniform as a result of CU participation.

Since the tariff-homogenizing effect of CU participation (like most other effects) is not a logical necessity but only a possibility which depends on particular circumstances, our hypothesis of a positive tariff-homogenizing effect can be demonstrated only by empirical testing. Referring to the CACM in particular, using the coefficient of variation (CV), i.e., the standard deviation divided by the mean, as the measure of the degree of dispersion in tariff rates, our hypothesis would be confirmed if and only if postunion tariff rates should be found to be more uniform than preunion tariff rates.

A few remarks about the data and how they were employed are relevant. In order to gain maximum comparability of commodities and their respective tariff rates between and among CACM countries in the preunion period and with respect to those in the postunion period, the classification used has been as disaggregated as possible, namely, distinguishing some 654 commodities at levels varying between 2 and 4 digits. Since it was not possible to find weights appropriate for representing the relative importance of each individual commodity in total imports in the region at the present time, not to mention the additional difficulty of arriving at a set of weights free of the effects of distortions, we have had to settle for testing the sensitivity of the results to alternative sets of weights chosen arbitrarily. Specific tariffs have been converted to their *ad valorem* equivalent on the basis of prices implicit in the value and quantity figures from import statistics. In the relatively few cases where such conversions could not be made, two alternative sets of computations have been carried out: one including those commodities for which ad valorem equivalent tariffs could not be estimated by assigning them zero tariffs, and the other excluding all such items from both preunion and postunion computations.

The results of the CV computations for preunion and postunion tariff rates (that have not been weighted by the overall importance of the commodities) are given in table 3–6. When all commodities are included, the results show that each country achieved some tariff-homogenizing as a result of adoption of the common external tariff rate as a part of CACM participation. In fact, on the average, the CV of the tariff structure would seem to have been cut almost in half. However, these computations are strongly affected by the extremely high CV computed for Honduras, which is directly attributable to the large number of specific tariffs in this country which for lack of data could not be converted to their ad valorem equivalents.

Table 3-6. Coefficients of Variation in Preunion and Postunion Tariff Rates
among 654 Commodities in the CACM

	Including all commodities	Excluding commodities for which ad valorem rates could not be estimated
I. Preunion		
Costa Rica	.819	.800
El Salvador	.537	.456
Guatemala	.584	.583
Honduras	2.524	.629
Nicaragua	.510	.509
Unweighted average for the 5 countries	.995	.596
II. Postunion: the common external rate	.507	.508

Sources: Costa Rica: Ministerio de Economia y Hacienda, *Arancel de Aduanas* (San Jose, 1961). El Salvador: Ministerio de Hacienda, *Tarifa de Aforos* (San Salvador, 1959). Guatemala: *Arancel de Aduanas, Republica de Guatemala* (Guatemala, 1959). Honduras: *Arancel de Aduanas* (Tegucigalpa, 1955). Nicaragua: "Codigo Arancelario de Importaciones," *La Gaceta*, Managua, 1 July 1955. Central America: Secretaria Permanente del Tratado General de Integracion Economica Centroamericana, *Arancel de Aduanas Centro Americano* (Guatemala City, 1965) and modifications of same in 1968.

For this reason the CV calculations of the second column are undoubtedly more representative. Substantial CV reductions as a result of CACM participation are again recorded for Costa Rica, Honduras, and Guatemala. The reduction for Nicaragua is again minimal and El Salvador has even suffered a small increase in its CV. For the region as a whole the reduction in the CV of the tariff structure approaches 0.1 in absolute terms or in relative terms 15 percent of the preunion CV.[13] (These overall results were not seriously affected by the choice of alternative sets of arbitrary commodity weights.)

In order to get some idea of the order of magnitude of the welfare gain that this tariff-homogenizing effect implies, we follow Nugent and Akbar (1971) in applying the three-commodity, general equilibrium model developed in section A1 of chapter 2 in calculating the welfare cost of tariff structures of differing degrees of dispersion.

As noted earlier, this model yields somewhat complicated formulae for the production cost (given in footnote 4 of chapter 2) and for the consumption cost (given in footnote 5 of the same chapter), expressed

---

[13]Elsewhere (Nugent 1973*b*) we have demonstrated that this tariff-homogenizing effect of CU participation is not limited to the CACM case, but has also been achieved by the EEC and, on a limited basis, by the Andean group in Latin America and would be achieved if a common external tariff were adopted in the Arab Common Market. These results give us more confidence that the result reported here for the CACM is neither an aberration nor an odd coincidence.

in terms of a limited number of parameters. Specifically, the production cost was shown to depend on (a) the coefficients determining the curvature of the transformation surface (designated by the parameters L, M, and N in the model) and (b) the tariff rates t_1 on commodity Y and t_2 on commodity Z. Likewise, the consumption cost was shown to depend upon (a) the relative shares of each of the three commodities in total consumption r_x, r_y, and r_z, (b) the elasticity of substitution in consumption, σ and (c) the tariff rates t_1 and t_2. The total welfare cost is simply the sum of the production and consumption costs.

Thus, by choosing values of the tariff rates t_1 and t_2 to reflect differing degrees of dispersion and assuming values of the remaining parameters within what are believed to be their realistic ranges, one can utilize the formulae for production and consumption costs to calculate the welfare cost of tariff structures of differing degrees of dispersion. By comparing alternative calculations, one can determine the magnitude of the welfare gain associated with the degree of tariff homogeneity attained by participation in the CACM.

Nugent and Akbar (1971) have simulated the production and consumption costs of tariff rates of varying mean and degree of dispersion for the same ranges of parameter values used by Johnson (1965a) in his two-commodity model, i.e., L, M, and N varying between 0 and almost 2.0, commodity shares r_i varying between 0.1 and 0.8, and elasticities of substitution varying between 0.5 and 3.0. The number of alternative sets of calculations was very large and the results were, in general, rather sensitive to changes in parameter values. An important exception, however, is the *qualitative* finding that the welfare cost of a tariff structure of given mean but varying degree of dispersion (measured again by the coefficient of variation, CV) increases with the CV. This result was obtained in all alternatives. The *quantitative* impact of a change in CV on welfare cost unfortunately varies rather significantly from case to case. The most representative estimates can be obtained by narrowing the choice of parameter values to a particular set that are thought to be most representative.

On the basis of Johnson's (1966) simulation study showing that the transformation surface is likely to be rather flat (corresponding to values of L, M, and N close to 2.0), we have selected 1.5 as a representative value for each of the curvature coefficients. Further, we have assumed that the long-run elasticity of substitution (in consumption) is unity and that the relative commodity shares (under free trade) are rather similar ($r_x = 0.4$, $r_y = r_z = 0.3$). Finally, since the average tariff rate in the CACM is generally assumed to be somewhere between 20 percent and 40 percent, depending on (1) whether legal tariff rates or implicit rates based on actual tariff collections are used in the calculations, (2) on how the individual commodities are weighted, and (3) the treatment of tariff rates that are available only in specific terms, we have considered alternative average tariff rates between 10 percent and 50 percent.

The specific values we have assumed for the two tariff rates in cases where the individual tariff rates are less homogeneous (and differ from the average) are given in table 3-7, along with the resulting estimates of the total costs of the tariffs assumed in these circumstances. Bearing in mind that the absolute values of the CVs computed from the tariff structures of the Central American countries were generally less than 1.0, the computations in columns A and B of the table are clearly more relevant than those of columns C and D. Comparing the costs of the more homogeneous tariff rates (corresponding to CVs of 0.87) appearing under column A with the respective values for the same average tariff rates but alternative CVs under column B, one can obtain estimates of the impact of a unit change in the coefficient of variation on social costs by the following formula:

$$(3.5) \quad \frac{\text{Social cost of column B} - \text{Social cost of column A}}{\text{CV of column B} \quad - \quad \text{CV of column A}}$$

By substituting the appropriate values from columns A and B of the table into this formula, the following results emerge: with an average tariff rate of 10 percent a unit reduction in CV would increase welfare (measured in terms of national income) by 2.90 percent; with average tariff rates of 20 percent, 30 percent, or 50 percent a reduction in CV of 1.0 would increase welfare by 6.07 percent, 8.69 percent, or 22.00 percent, respectively. If, indeed, the average tariff rate in Central America is between 20 percent and 40 percent, and the overall reduction in the CV of the tariff structure in Central America attributable to CACM participation is (as we have estimated it to be) 0.1, our results would indicate that the tariff-homogenizing effect alone has increased income in the CACM by between 0.6 percent and 1 percent. Assuming a social discount rate of about 15 percent, this one-shot increment in income implies (or rather is equivalent to) a contribution to the annual income growth rate of about 0.1 percent per annum.

The fact that the welfare gain attributable to any given amount of tariff-homogenizing increases with the level of the average tariff provides an additional reason for believing that CUs among countries with high preunion tariff rates are likely to be more beneficial than those among countries with low tariff rates.

The accuracy of these estimates and therefore the validity of any implications derived from them are, of course, limited by (1) the various limitations in the three-commodity, general equilibrium model mentioned in the previous chapter (one of which is the unrealistic assump-

Table 3–7. Welfare Costs (in Terms of % of National Income) of Varying Mean and Coefficient of Variation of Tariff Rates (in %)

Average tariff rate $t_1=t_2$	A		B				C				D			
	Coeff. of variation	Social cost	Tariff rates t_1	t_2	Coeff. of variation	Social cost	Tariff rates t_1	t_2	Coeff. of variation	Social cost	Tariff rates t_1	t_2	Coeff. of variation	Social cost
10	.87	1.13	0	20	1.73	3.63	−10	30	3.10	10.51	−20	40	4.5	20.39
20	.87	4.09	10	30	1.15	5.79	0	40	1.73	10.65	−20	60	3.1	27.23
30	.87	8.19	20	40	1.00	9.32	0	60	1.73	17.87	−20	80	2.6	33.07
50	.87	15.62	30	70	1.05	19.58	0	100	1.73	29.80	–	–	–	–

Notes: (1) The tariff rate on the exportable commodity X is assumed to be zero in all of these computations.

(2) In the case of homogeneous tariff rates (column A), the computations of social cost are identical to those for the corresponding parameters obtained by Johnston (1965a). Indeed, this provides a check on the validity of the computations.

Source: Nugent and Akbar (1971).

tion that all commodities are final goods, thereby avoiding all issues concerning intermediate goods and differences between nominal and effective tariffs), (2) the questionable empirical validity of the assumed parameter values, (3) the fact that the results pertain only to a single source of distortions—tariffs—which in Central America may be partially or even wholly offset by other distortions, such as excise taxes, monopoly power, etc., and (4) data deficiencies (lack of commodity weights) which may affect the CV calculations of the preunion and post-union tariff structures.

Nevertheless, even if not entirely representative, the results of this section indicate that this tariff-homogenizing feature of CU participation that has been completely overlooked in existing studies may be quantitatively as important as the effects that have been captured. Of course, there is nothing in the conventional methods of empirical estimation, such as the Balassa method, that excludes consideration of this effect. The essential feature of this effect is not, however, its effect on aggregate imports (trade-creation) but rather the effect on relative prices which in turn affect the efficiency of producer and consumer allocations. Estimates of changes in overall relationships between imports and income (measured by import shares or elasticities) are likely to be of only secondary and incidental relevance in this respect. More relevant to the measurement of efficiency in this sense would be interindustry and intraindustry changes in the structure of production and consumption, i.e., what is changed with regard to the determination of which items are domestically produced, which items are exported, and which items are imported.

This is illustrative of our basic criticism of the conventional measures. While they do not specifically *a priori* exclude the advantages of economies of scale, intraindustry specialization, efficiency gains, etc., by including only the influence of CU participation directly on trade, it is most improbable that estimates based on such approaches can capture but a small fraction of the total benefits that actually may be derived from CU participation.

4. The Measurement of Other Effects

As we have argued in the previous chapter, many of the conceivably more important effects of CU participation remain difficult to quantify. This conclusion is particularly true with regard to the CACM where there are such obvious gaps in the information that would be required for adequate measurement of economies of scale, x-efficiency, learning-by-doing, and particularly of the portion of such possible economies that might legitimately be attributed to CACM participation.

Even when it has been possible to determine how extensive a certain phenomenon has been in the CACM, it has not generally been possible to obtain an estimate of its contribution to income or to growth of the region. For example, Willmore (1972*b*) applied both of the measures of intraindustry specialization defined in footnote 20 of chapter 2 to sectoral trade data of CACM countries and concluded that according to both measures there was strong evidence of increasing intraindustry specialization subsequent to the CACM's establishment. However, neither Willmore nor anyone else has been able to estimate the contribution to national income attributable to this effect. In part, the gains due to intraindustry specialization may have been captured by the estimates of trade creation either by the Balassa measure or the export performance approach. However, there would seem to be no reason why CU-induced intraindustry specialization would necessarily be confined to specialization across countries which would result in trade-creation. Rather it would seem likely that such benefits would extend to internal intraindustry specialization within countries, which would not normally result in trade creation.

In the same category of effects are the industrialization effects. Two questions arise in this connection. (1) By how much has industrial value added in the CACM increased as a result of CACM participation? (2) What has been the effect of this additional industrial value added to national income and to the growth rate of national income?

The first question is much easier to answer than the second. As had already been mentioned, McClelland (1972) attempted to answer it by calculating the portion of the increase in intraindustry trade that consists of manufactured goods and then multiplying this amount by the value added component of such exports or alternatively as the change in industrial value added directly. Neither attempt was very convincing because no effort was made to separate out that portion of the increased intraregional trade in manufactures or the increase in industrial value added that would have taken place anyway due to increases in income, transport improvements, and other factors not necessarily related to the CACM. The only factors of this sort which McClelland made any attempt to account for were the "integration industry" provision[14] (wherein monopolistic privileges have been granted to those new industries in the region which were accorded "integration industry" status by all five CACM members) and the industrial incentives legislation.[15]

[14]McClelland indicated that this effect could have accounted for 5 percent of the total increase in industrial value added.

[15]He estimated that the industrial incentives may have accounted for 15 percent of the increase in industrial income.

Once again we might suggest that international cross-section studies might provide a better way of separating CU participation effects from other effects than can be obtained from time-series analysis of CU partners themselves. Particularly relevant in this context are the studies of Chenery (1960) and the United Nations (1963), which estimated the amount of industrial value added (V) (in millions of U.S. dollars at 1953 prices) that an individual country would be expected to have on the basis of its per capita income (Y) and population size (P). According to the UN study, for example, the following relationship was obtained from international cross-section data:

$$(3.6) \qquad \log V = -1.637 + 1.369 \log Y + 1.124 \log P$$

This result indicates that a one percent increase in per capita income would raise industrial value added by 1.369 percent, and a one percent increase in population size would raise it by 1.124 percent.

The data for Y and P in terms comparable to those used in the U.N. study (i.e., U.S. dollars and 1953 prices) for the Central American countries are given in the first two columns of table 3–8.

When these values are substituted into the above regression equation, the values for V given in the third column of the table are obtained. These computations represent the "normal" level of industrial value added in the region with and without market unification. As the reader can see, the increase in industrial value added attributable to CU participation amounts to about $125 million, which is about 20 percent of actual industrial value added and a little more than 4 percent of GNP.

By way of qualification it should be emphasized that these results pertain to a certain "normal" pattern observed from the experience of many countries. This pattern may be transferred easily neither to a particular region of the world like Central America, nor to the case of individual countries over time.

The second question (i.e., that concerning the contribution of the increased industrial value added to income and growth), however, is

Table 3–8. Value Added in Manufacturing with and without Integration
(Computed from the U.N.'s Normal Regression Line)

	Per capita income (in U.S. dollars)	Population (in millions)	Value added in mfg. (in millions of U.S. dollars)
1. Costa Rica	360	1.2	89.5
2. El Salvador	240	2.5	117.1
3. Guatemala	260	4.0	221.7
4. Honduras	220	2.0	80.9
5. Nicaragua	300	1.5	89.5
Total			598.7
Central America	265	11.2	724.0

more difficult to answer. This is because such an answer would require a detailed evaluation of the alternative uses to which the resources devoted to industrialization would have been put. This analysis would obviously require that careful distinctions be drawn between those resources that would otherwise be more fully utilized, less fully utilized, or completely unutilized in the alternative uses and that differences in productivity be carefully weighted by the respective quantities of resources in each such category.

However, if the views of Johnson (1965b) and Cooper and Massell (1965) that industrialization, because of its public-good character, is a goal in itself should be accepted, then one may be able to avoid all such complexities arising in the process of converting the measured increase in industrial value added to its efficiency equivalent.

B. MEASUREMENT OF THE NET SUM OF ALL EFFECTS

We have seen that, at best, only several of the many different effects of CU participation, in general, or CACM participation, in particular, are quantifiable on an individual basis. Moreover, most of the methods whereby these individual effects can be measured are subject to biases of unknown magnitude and even direction.

The policy decision as to whether or not to participate in a CU, of course, depends not on the assessment of any one of these effects, but rather on the net benefits of all these effects. Moreover, if one were to proceed to such an overall assessment by adding up all the individual effects, one's efforts would be marred by the overlap between several of these effects which might result in considerable double-counting of benefits.

If one were willing to sacrifice knowledge concerning the degree to which each individual effect contributed to the (net) total effect, one might obtain a quantitative assessment of the overall welfare gain somewhat more directly. Specifically, one might estimate an aggregate production function for CU members from time-series data with dummy variables for the formation of the CU. This is the approach that we shall apply to the CACM in the following paragraphs.

Assuming that the aggregate production function is of Cobb-Douglas form and the customs union is Hicks-neutral, the following relationship may be specified:

$$(3.7) \qquad GNP = A K^{\alpha} L^{\beta} e^{\gamma CU}$$

where K, L, and CU represent capital, labor, and the institution of the CU, respectively. Actually two CU dummy variables, CU_1 and CU_2, with coefficients γ_1 and γ_2, respectively, may be specified in order to distinguish between the once-and-for-all effect (CU_1) representing a shift in the intercept and the gradual or continuous effect (CU_2) representing a shift in the elasticities. Time-series data can then be used to estimate this function—subject, of course, to all the usual problems of time-series analysis: multicollinearity, simultaneous equation bias measurement errors, etc. The coefficients obtained for α and β would be interpreted in the usual way and the coefficients of the CU dummy variables (γ_1, γ_2) would represent the percentage increases in total productivity attributable to the formation of the CU via the once-and-for-all effect and the gradual effects, respectively.

If one wanted to account for the effect of CACM participation on resource formation, such as on labor (L) or on capital (K), one could first estimate the direct effect of CU_1 and CU_2 on these variables and then the indirect effect via the effect of these variables on GNP. Since in the next chapter it shall be seen that the CACM has apparently not had a statistically significant effect on K in CACM members, the possible effect of CU on K and L is ignored at the present in order to concentrate on estimating the direct effects of the CACM on GNP.

Assuming constant returns to scale, an attempt has been made to mitigate the problems of inadequate employment data and multicollinearity among variables by dividing equation (3.7) through by L. This gives:

$$(3.8) \qquad \frac{GNP}{L} = A e^{\gamma_1 CU_1}\, e^{\gamma_2 CU_2} \left(\frac{K}{L}\right)^{\alpha}$$

Almost simultaneous to the institution of the CACM, participating countries have been affected by changes in their international terms of trade, the completion of the externally financed integration highways linking the five Central American countries with modern highways, and perhaps other factors.

Since these factors could have taken place without the institution of the CACM, we have tried to distinguish their effect from that of the CACM itself by adding three additional variables—a dummy variable (R) with an initial value of zero and an additional 1.0 after the completion of each important link in the regional transport system, an index of the international terms of trade (TT) to account for the influence of world market conditions for exports and imports, and time (T) as a proxy for technological changes and the various other factors affecting per capita income which vary with time. The expanded and stochastic version of equation (3.8) is:

$$(3.9) \qquad GNP/L = A(K/L)^{\alpha}\, TT^{\beta}\, e^{\gamma_1 CU_1}\, e^{\gamma_2 CU_2}\, e^{\sigma R}\, e^{\delta T}\, V$$

where V is a random disturbance. The log-linear version of (3.9) is given by:

$$(3.10) \quad \log GNP/L = \log A + E(u) + \alpha \log K/L + \gamma_1 CU_1 + \gamma_2 CU_2$$
$$+ \beta \log TT + \sigma R + \delta T + u^*$$

where $\log V = u$ and $u^* = u - E(u)$ so that $E(u^*)$ becomes zero.[16]

Time-series data (1950–66) for each of the Central American countries and for the region as a whole from appendix A have been used to fit equation (3.10) via ordinary least squares. Since no reliable employment statistics exist, population figures have been used as a proxy for L. Figures on the capital stock (K) have had to be manufactured from a crude estimate of their 1950 values by adding annual increments of net capital formation estimated as the difference between gross capital formation (I) less the product of the assumed rate of depreciation (d) of 0.025 and the lagged capital stock (K_{t-1}). No attempt has been made to adjust either capital stock or labor for changes in effective utilization.

The results with respect to the complete estimating equation are shown as regressions (1) in table 3–9. Following conventional practice, we have subsequently dropped certain variables having regression coefficients with very low T values or the "wrong" sign. However, in order to retain the flavor of an aggregate production function, we have retained the $\log (\frac{K}{L})$ variable, even if it had a low T value. For example, in the result for Central America as a whole, T was dropped from the estimating equation in regression (2) because according to the results of regression (1) it was not significant at the 0.10 level; similarly, R was dropped because the coefficient of R in regression (1) had the "wrong" sign. Since the regression coefficients of regression (2) were all of the expected sign and significant at the 0.10 level (at least), no further modifications were made.

Similarly, in the case of Costa Rica, according to the results of regression (1) $\log TT$, CU_1, R, and T all failed to influence $\log (\frac{GNP}{L})$ significantly and thus all of these variables were omitted from regression (2). On the other hand, $\log (\frac{K}{L})$ was retained in equation (3.2) even though its regression coefficient had been insignificant in regression (1). The rule to retain the $\log (\frac{K}{L})$ variables "despite the results" was

[16]The variable TT, in contrast to the dummy variables, is specified in double logarithmic form. This specification allows one to interpret β as an elasticity of output with respect to prices in the world market and which is invariant with respect to the values the terms of trade indexes take.

Table 3–9. Selected Estimates of Aggregate Production Functions

Central America

(1) $\log$ GNP/L $= 1.52 + .614 \log$ K/L $+ .032 \log$ TT $+ .050$ CU$_2$ $- .012$ R $+ .007$ T
 (1.446) (3.507) (2.304) (5.193) (3.121) (1.023)
 $\bar{R}^2$ = .964 DW = 1.75

(2) $\log$ GNP/L $= 0.04 + .845 \log$ K/L $+ .045 \log$ TT $+ .022$ CU$_1$ $+ .002$ CU$_2$
 (6.802) (4.377) (2.210) (3.210)
 $\bar{R}^2$ = .939 DW = 1.36

Costa Rica

(1) $\log$ GNP/L $= -.40 + .978 \log$ K/L $+ .004 \log$ TT $+ .024$ CU$_1$ $+ .017$ CU$_2$ $+ .024$ R $- .022$ T
 (.967) (.312) (.715) (1.472) (.639) (.793)
 $\bar{R}^2$ = .868 DW = 2.32

(2) $\log$ GNP/L $= 4.23 + .249 \log$ K/L $+ .018$ CU$_2$
 (2.436) (2.636)
 $\bar{R}^2$ = .897 DW = 2.48

El Salvador

(1) $\log$ GNP/L $= 0.73 + .774 \log$ K/L $+ .018 \log$ TT $+ .064$ CU$_1$ $+ .026$ CU$_2$ $- .059$ R $- .001$ T
 (.750) (1.907) (1.493) (2.771) (.160) (.079)
 $\bar{R}^2$ = .630 DW = 2.18

(2) $\log$ GNP/L $= 7.44 + .324 \log$ K/L $+ .015 \log$ TT $+ .017$ CU$_1$ $+ .017$ CU$_2$
 (.063) (1.798) (.532) (1.939)
 $\bar{R}^2$ = .643 DW = 2.05

(3) $\log$ GNP/L $= 3.70 + .285 \log$ K/L $+ .052 \log$ TT $+ .018$ CU$_2$
 (.774) (1.526) (2.025)
 $\bar{R}^2$ = .694 DW = 2.29

Guatemala

(1) $\log$ GNP/L $= 1.38 + .646 \log$ K/L $+ .027 \log$ TT $- .011$ CU$_1$ $+ .019$ CU$_2$ $- .011$ R $+ .005$ T
 (2.238) (2.529) (.616) (2.815) (.621) (1.291)
 $\bar{R}^2$ = .926 DW = 2.42

(2) $\log$ GNP/L $= .59 + .771 \log$ K/L $+ .032 \log$ TT $+ .015$ CU$_2$
 (3.710) (4.083)
 $\bar{R}^2$ = .938 DW = 2.24

Honduras

(1) $\log$ GNP/L $= -10.07 + 2.548 \log$ K/L $- .025 \log$ TT $+ .076$ CU$_1$ $+ .025$ CU$_2$ $+ .015$ R $- .029$ T
 (1.879) (1.422) (1.128) (2.851) (.469) (1.596)
 $\bar{R}^2$ = .817 DW = 1.70

(2) $\log$ GNP/L $= 1.72 + .581 \log$ K/L $+ .013$ CU$_2$
 (3.415) (4.814)
 $\bar{R}^2$ = .864 DW = 1.79

Nicaragua

(1) $\log$ GNP/L $= -9.42 + 2.449 \log$ K/L $+ .029 \log$ TT $+ .136$ CU$_1$ $- .005$ CU$_2$ $+ .044$ R $- .059$ T
 (5.309) (1.905) (2.979) (.409) (1.672) (3.800)
 $\bar{R}^2$ = .919 DW = 3.08

(2) $\log$ GNP/L $= -.35 + .920 \log$ K/L $+ .055 \log$ TT $+ .032$ CU$_1$
 (7.655) (3.841) (1.857)
 $\bar{R}^2$ = .882 DW = 1.95

Notes: (1) Numbers in parentheses indicate T values.

  (2) $\bar{R}^2$ is the coefficient of determination standardized for degrees of freedom.

  (3) DW indicates Durbin-Watson coefficient.

Source: Appendix A (1950–1966 data).

motivated in large part by the suspicion that log $\frac{K}{L}$ and T would be highly correlated and thus that regressions in which both were included could be highly distorted. (This suspicion was generally confirmed by the fact that when T was omitted from the model the regression coefficient of log $(\frac{K}{L})$ generally conformed more closely to *ex ante* expectations and became more significant.)[17]

In the case of El Salvador, regression (2) contained an insignificant regression coefficient pertaining to the CU_1 variable and thus an additional regression—regression (3)—was estimated omitting this variable.

It can readily be seen that the results are rather sensitive to changes in specification. On the basis of these results (and additional experimentation with alternative specifications) we are led to the conclusion that the results are particularly sensitive to the inclusion or exclusion of the time-trend variable (T). Because of the high correlation between log $(\frac{K}{L})$ and T, the regression coefficient of the former variable is particularly sensitive to the changes in specification. However, with a few exceptions (CU_1 in Costa Rica and Nicaragua) the estimates of the customs union impact parameters, γ_1 and γ_2, are rather insensitive to changes in specification.

Referring now to the last regression in every case, i.e., regression (3) in El Salvador and regression (2) in the remaining countries, it can be seen that the log $(\frac{K}{L})$ and log TT variables have exercised significant positive influences on log GNP in Central America as a whole and also in most of the individual countries. Surprisingly enough, neither the integration highway dummy (R) nor time (T) seems to have exerted much if any of their hypothesized positive influences on per capita income.[18]

With the exception of the regression coefficients of CU_2 in El Salvador and CU_1 in Nicaragua (both of which are significant at the 0.10 level), either one, or the other of the CACM dummy variables is sig-

[17]Conversely, experimentation with alternative estimating equations revealed that the coefficient of T is generally positive and statistically significant when log $(\frac{K}{L})$ is excluded.

[18]In the case of T, this negative result is partially attributable to our decision rule to retain log $(\frac{K}{L})$. On the other hand, according to the studies by Bruton (1967), and others, showing that productivity growth seems to have played a much smaller role in overall growth in LDCs than in the developed countries, our finding of negligible technological change should not be considered surprising and therefore should not require explanation. In the case of R, the negative finding may indeed be traceable to the extremely crude method in which the supply of integration highways has been measured.

nificant at the 0.02 level. In all cases these coefficients are positive, indicating a universally positive influence of the CACM on per capita income.

Since the estimates of table 3–9 include two different kinds of CACM dummy variables—one indicating a once-and-for-all effect and the other a continuous effect—in table 3–10 we have converted the former into an equivalent contribution to the annual growth rate, so that the effects can be summed. These estimates are not devoid of possible biases. As pointed out in footnote b of the table, there is good reason to believe that the γ_2 coefficients for Costa Rica, Honduras, and to a lesser extent El Salvador may be biased upward thereby yielding overestimates of the contribution of the CACM to the annual growth rate of per capita income. In view of the high coefficient of determination and insensitivity of the results to changes in specification, the estimate of the contribution of the CACM to the income growth rate in Central America as a whole of 0.6 percent per annum is probably the most reliable and representative of the various estimates.

Given the rather uncertain quality of the data, the paucity of observations, the dubious validity of the particular form (Cobb-Douglas) of the production function,[19] the many other factors influencing long-run

Table 3–10. Increases in per Capita Income Attributable to CACM Participation (%)

	One-shot increase[a] (γ_1)	Contribution to the annual growth rate (γ_2)	Total contribution to the annual growth rate $(.15\gamma_1 + \gamma_2)$
Central America	2.2%	0.2%	0.6%
Costa Rica	–	1.8[b]	1.8
El Salvador	–	1.8[b]	1.8
Guatemala	–	1.5	1.5
Honduras	–	1.3[b]	1.3
Nicaragua	3.2	–	0.4

[a]The one-shot increase has been converted to an annual growth rate by multiplying by 0.15.

[b]Because of (1) the unusually low values of α and also δ obtained for Costa Rica, Honduras and, to a lesser extent, El Salvador and (2) the positive correlation among CU_2 and log $(\frac{K}{L})$ and T, one may suspect that part of the effect of log $(\frac{K}{L})$ and T on log(GNP/L) in these countries is being picked up by γ_2, thereby biasing the estimates of this γ_2 upward and those of α and δ downward.

Source: Table 3–9.

[19]Among the limitations of this form is the very restricted way in which the various kinds and sources of technological change are amalgamated and approximated by the changes in a single parameter. See Nerlove (1965) for an appraisal of the various possible biases arising from this simplification.

economic growth that were omitted from the model, the low coefficient of determination for El Salvador and, to a lesser extent, Honduras, and a fairly serious multicollinearity problem, the necessarily tentative nature of these results can hardly be overemphasized. As new and improved data become available, especially for the period after the de facto withdrawal of Honduras from the CACM, the reliability of such estimates should be enhanced considerably. Moreover, additional data may make it possible to improve upon the method by using a more general type of production function and/or by estimating the entire function for the preunion and postunion periods separately, thereby making it possible to consider and estimate nonneutral effects of CACM participation.[20]

Also it must be admitted that the Central American experience may indeed have been rather special, and thus the results may not easily be generalized to other CUs among LDCs. The apparent success of this CU has been facilitated by very large investments in the transport infrastructure and in the building of regional institutions associated with the CACM (such as the Central American Bank for Economic Integration, the Secretariat of the Common Market, etc.), the bulk of which have been externally financed. Thus, we do not wish to imply that the same results would necessarily be found elsewhere.

[20]See Brown (1966) for an application of this approach.

4 three small-scale econometric models

The purpose of this chapter is to describe, estimate, and provide reduced form solutions for three different versions of the small econometric models of the Central American economies which provide the basis for our simulations, in chapter 5 below, of the potential benefits of coordination of fiscal and monetary policy within the context of the CACM.

The explicit purpose of building the small econometric models is to provide reasonable estimates of the influence of the various macroeconomic policy instruments at the disposal of the governments of the region on each of the most important targets or goals that have been set in the development plans and other official documents.

A. INTRODUCTION

Each of the governments in Central America is apparently committed to the goal of economic development. Each has a development plan or some other document which indicates that it hopes to achieve dramatic increases in per capita income in the next few years, yet each also explicitly or implicitly admits to other goals and constraints, such as income distribution, the stock of international reserves, political stability, the government deficit, and price stability, which may sometimes conflict with the goal of increased per capita income.

One of the most glaring weaknesses of planning in Central America (both at the regional and national levels) and in most other areas of the world has been inability to relate planning goals to the use of specific policy instruments. The result is that what are called "plans" are in fact either dreams about a state of the world the planners like or mere forecasts of what these planners think will transpire.

For small less developed countries, it is true that much depends on factors beyond their control. For example, the outlook for Central American growth depends quite considerably on whether or not other coffee-producing countries uphold the International Coffee Agreement, on what happens to the price of cotton, bananas, sugar, etc., and also on such uncontrollable factors as temperature and rainfall. Fortunately, however, even in Central America economic development is not entirely a game of chance; the influence which governments, by appropriate action, can exert over the destiny of their own economies is considerable. The "boom-bust" pattern that is so obviously an important characteristic of postwar, and undoubtedly also prewar, development in Central America indicates *not* that policy is irrelevant but only that government policy (with possibly a few exceptions) has not succeeded in exerting a stabilizing influence on the growth process. Policy has tended to react passively to exogenous events or even to reinforce the dependence of the economy on external events.

When choices have had to be made between the goals of income growth, income distribution, balance-of-payments security, and price stability, have the choices been efficient? Or, would it have been possible to adopt a better combination of policies so as to attain more satisfactory performance with respect to the various goals? In order for government policy to push the economies up to their production possibility frontiers and from there to move these frontiers outward over time, two things must be done. First, a great deal must be learned about the relationship between each policy instrument at the government's disposal and the more important goals (targets) of development, including the technical substitution possibilities between and among the various instruments on the one hand and goals on the other. Second, the governments must be able to make efficient decisions with respect to the choice of instruments for reaching their desired goals within the confines of what they regard as the political constraints within which they must operate.

This section of our study attempts to make a modest beginning toward the first of these steps by providing several approximations to the relationship between the most important policy instruments— reserve money, government investment, government consumption, import taxes, export taxes, and other taxes (net of transfers)—and each of the more important development goals—income, consumption, investment, the fiscal deficit, and the balance of payments.

The analysis required for estimating the impact of the various policy instruments available to each country on the important target variables (goals) in each of the countries of Central America consists of statistical analysis applied to economic theory. It is economic theory which specifies the form of the direct and indirect relationships between policy instruments and the important target variables. The theoretical specification distinguishes between those variables which need to be explained—endogenous variables—and which include the target variables and those used as explanatory variables: the predetermined variables. Predetermined variables may be of three types: (1) the lagged endogenous variables, e.g., last year's income, (2) policy variables, such as government spending (which may be considered to be determined primarily by noneconomic, political processes and, hence, to be exogenous to the economic system), and (3) other exogenous variables, such as institutions, the passage of time, and external conditions. When a theoretical system provides expressions for each of the endogenous variables in that system in terms of other endogenous and predetermined variables, this system can be solved so as to yield an expression for each endogenous variable in terms of predetermined variables alone. This solution is said to be the "reduced form" of the economic model.

Thus, it can be said that in the reduced form of the *theoretical* model the target variables are the unknowns, i.e., the endogenous variables to be determined, and the policy variables are among the exogenous variables whose values are known or given. In *policy* analysis the roles are reversed: the unknowns, i.e., the variables to be determined, are the values of the policy instruments and the knowns, i.e., the variables that are given, are the target variables. The specification and estimation of the theoretical model, including the derivation of the reduced form solutions, is the subject of the present chapter. Policy analysis is the subject of chapter V below.

B. STRATEGY IN BUILDING THE MODELS

Our task in building the econometric models for each Central American country is to indicate the interrelationships between the most important macroeconomic variables, such as GNP, GDP, Private Consumption, Private Investment, Exports, Imports, the Balance of Payments, and the Government Deficit, and the most important policy instruments— the stock (or alternatively the change in the stock) of reserve money, government consumption, government investment, the tax rates on exports, imports, and expenditure, and also the institution of the CACM—as simply as possible.

One way in which the models were kept as simple as possible was by including only a very limited number of explanatory variables in each structural equation. A second simplification adopted was to specify linear relationships throughout. (In many instances existing theory has demonstrated linear relationships to be more powerful or interesting than nonlinear ones. In other cases, even if the "true" or more interesting relationships are nonlinear ones, linear relationships may provide close approximations within the relevant range of observation. In a few instances, where nonlinear relationships are more commonly used, we have experimented with nonlinear relationships to test for the sensitivity of the results to our use of linear specifications.)[1] A third simplification adopted was to keep the models for each country as similar as possible, thereby not attempting to capture any institutional differences or particular influences that might be important in one or two countries but not in others. A fourth simplification was to estimate the equations strictly in terms of levels, except in special circumstances in which it would seem more reasonable to postulate linear relationships between annual changes in the variables. Thus, we leave it to subsequent researchers to compare these results with those obtained by using nonlinear relationships, more individualized models, and/or by specifying the variables in terms of first differences, percentage changes, or autoregressive transformation schemes.

Another simplification adopted was to exclude all lags of more than one year's duration and to avoid the use of distributed lag functions, even though the latter may be more theoretically satisfying. Aside from the fact that longer lags would reduce the number of observations available, an important justification for this simplification was that on the basis of the high degree of political instability which prevails in the region, the planners' time horizon would seem to be extremely short—one, two, or at the most three years. Strictly speaking, however, this kind of simplification should be made only at the policy stage, not at the specification stage, but one-year lags were generally found to yield results very similar to those based on longer lag specifications.

Intraregional trade and factor movements constitute the link by which the actions of one country in the region affect those of another. They also serve as the principal mechanisms through which the CU effects operate. It is, therefore, important that all such links be specified as carefully and as completely as possible. However, even in this instance some unfortunate simplifications have had to be adopted. Since labor is still quite immobile between countries of the region, and since

---

[1]See Belson (1970) for some experiments with nonlinear forms.

no data on intraregional capital flows are available, we have had to abandon any hope of distinguishing between intraregional and extraregional flows of capital and labor. Again, because of data limitations, the same applies with respect to trade in invisibles. It has been possible to distinguish between intraregional and extraregional flows in the case of visible commodity exports. However, although it would have been preferable to explain these flows in terms of relative prices[2] (as affected by tariffs, taxes, transport costs, and CACM participation), the absence of adequate price data for either individual items or aggregates thereof had made it impossible to explain such movements in terms of relative prices per se.[3] However, some factors affecting relative prices have been included.

For lack of adequate theory, the means to operationalize it, and the data with which to test it and to estimate the parameters, numerous considerations both important to development and particularly characteristic of the region itself, such as income distribution, human capital, entrepreneurial capability, sources of finance, structural considerations, etc. have had to be omitted. The resulting models are of the short-run Keynesian type not unlike the simpler ones that have been used for short-term policy simulations in developed countries. Unfortunately, they thus contain few of the critical constraints to long-run development and provide few (if any) analytic insights of distinction in themselves.[4] They do, however, make it possible to link the targets of one country with the policy instruments of another in a plausible way and thereby fulfill their main purpose: to provide the structural underpinnings for simulating the potential benefits of coordination in macroeconomic policy-making among CACM countries.[5]

[2]Such a procedure has been utilized with some success in the case of the EEC by Resnick (1968) and in both the EEC and EFTA by Resnick and Truman (1972). Both of these studies utilize a simple mark-up theory of price formation which seems to explain the data fairly well. To this author's knowledge these are the only other existing econometric models of a CU.

[3]The structure of and changes in relative prices are said to be the subject of a new program of collaborative research between the Brookings Institution and SIECA.

[4]For interesting, although not necessarily authoritative, views of how econometric models of less developed countries may differ from those of developed countries, see Klein (1965) and Zarembka (1972). For additional examples of econometric models of LDCs, see Adelman and Je (1969), Agarwala (1970), Ayala (1964), Carter (1970), DePrano and Nugent (1966), Dutta and Su (1969), Escuela Nacional de Economia (1970), El Daly (1964), Evans (1968), Halabuk, Kennessey, and Theiss (1965), Islam (1965), Marwah (1969, 1970), Naranjo Villalobos (1970), Narasimham (1956), Nugent (1966), Pavlopoulos (1966), van Rijckeghem (1965), Soonthornsima (1964), Suits (1964), Thorbecke (1969), Thorbecke and Condos (1967), Taylor (1968), United Nations, ECAFE (1964, 1967).

[5]In this respect, the models presented here represent an extremely modest effort for achieving at the level of one very small region of the world what "Project LINK," with an internationally coordinated set of teams with substantial manpower and facilities, is attempting to achieve for the world as a whole. See Ball (1973).

We have actually estimated three different models for each of the Central American countries which shall be referred to as models 1, 2, and 3, respectively. The most important reason for using three different models was to provide the basis for determining the sensitivity of our subsequent calculations of the potential welfare gain from policy coordination at the regional level to changes in specification. However, since decision-makers may be interested directly in the policy-multipliers and other results obtained from these models, the presentation of the results of each alternative model allows any other analyst to make his own subjective choice as to which model he prefers, as well as to see for himself how sensitive the results are to changes in specification. We shall not try to defend any one of the models as being either relatively better than the others, or as being good in an absolute sense. To repeat, we use them mainly for demonstration purposes.

Since model 1 is the mostly highly aggregated, most static and thus the simplest of the three models, we begin our presentation in section C with an exposition of this model. Section D, which is devoted to models 2 and 3, is limited to an exposition of the differences in specification vis-à-vis model 1. In all other respects the three models are identical.

C. EXPOSITION OF MODEL 1

Even with the simplifications mentioned above, the model for each country consists of 17 equations in 17 endogenous variables, 12 exogenous variables, and several lagged endogenous variables. For the CACM as a whole, the entire model consists of more than 80 equations! However, fortunately, 6 of the 17 equations for each country are identities which don't have to be estimated empirically. The symbols and definitions of these variables are listed in table 4-1.

Since the equations are specified in an identical manner for each country, and in order to make the presentation as simple as possible, country subscripts and superscripts and the stochastic error terms will be omitted from the presentation.

Gross Domestic Product

$$(4.1) \qquad GDP = C + I + G + Ex + Ei - Nx - Ni$$

Gross National Product

$$(4.2) \qquad GNP = GDP + TT + NFY$$

Table 4-1. Glossary of Symbols Used in the Econometric and Linear Programming
Models of CACM Countries

A. Endogenous Variables		B. Exogenous Variables	
Symbol	*Variable*	*Symbol*	*Variable*
GDP	Gross Domestic Product	G	Government Consumption
GNP	Gross National Product	Ig	Government Investment
Yd	Disposable Income	RM	Reserve Money
C	Private Consumption	Tn/Nx	Tax Rate on Imports
I	Total Investment (Ip + Ig)	Te/Ex	Tax Rate on Exports
Ip	Gross Private Investment	To/GDP	"Other" Tax Rate
E	Total Exports	Zcm^a	Dummy Variable for Membership in Customs Union
Ex	Extraregional Exports		
Ei	Intraregional Exports		
N	Total Imports	R^a	Dummy Variable for Completion of Integration Highways
Nx	Imports from outside the Region		
Ni	Intraregional Imports	TIME	Time (in years)
K	Capital Stock	TT	Terms of Trade Adjustment
Tn	Import Tax Receipts	NFY	Net Factor Income from Abroad
Te	Export Tax Receipts		
To	Other Tax Receipts net of Transfers from Government to the Private Sector	Nus	Index of United States Imports
		POP	Population
CR	Stock of Credit to the Private Sector	P	Index of Domestic Prices
MS	Money Supply (stock)	C. Other Symbols	
BP	Balance of Payments	*Symbol*	*Definition*
SG	Government Savings		
TNET	Total Tax Receipts net of Transfers to the Private Sector	$\wedge$	over a variable indicates estimate of that variable derived from another equation
		Superscript	indicates country
		C or CR	Costa Rica
		E or ES	El Salvador
		G or GU	Guatemala
		H or HO	Honduras
		N or NI	Nicaragua
		CM or CACM	Central America
		Subscript	t, t-1, indicates time period
		*	indicates desired
		e	indicates expected
		D	before a variable (as in DRM, DMS, DCR) indicates first difference e.g., $(RM_t - RM_{t-1})$, etc.
		LPI	Individual Country Linear Programming Model (without coordination)
		LPC	Collective Central America Linear Programming Model (with coordination)

[a]Because all countries did not join the CACM simultaneously and different integration highways have been completed at different times, the dummy variables *Zcm* and *R* have varied from country to country. See appendix A for the figures used in each case.

According to the national accounting system used in Central America and in much of Latin America, Gross National Product in constant prices is derived from GDP by adding an adjustment for the external terms of trade and net factor income from abroad.

Disposable Income

$$(4.3) \qquad Yd = GNP - Te - Tn - To$$

Note that this definition of disposable income is really quite different from that of personal disposable income which is used in many macroeconomic models in developed countries. This definition was necessitated by lack of data for distinguishing between personal income and business income. Note also that for simplicity *all* taxes (net of government transfers to the private sector) have been subtracted off. With social security and other institutional bases for transfer payments still at a primitive stage in Central America, transfers have been treated as *negative* "other taxes."

Private Consumption

$$(4.4) \qquad C = a_{10} + a_{11} \, Yd + a_{12} \, MS + a_{13} \, TIME$$

Private consumption is hypothesized to depend mainly on the level of disposable income, but perhaps also on wealth and various demographic and institutional factors for which *TIME* may be a good proxy. *MS* includes only the most highly liquid forms of wealth, but nevertheless, as *MS* rises, there should be less desire to stockpile additional assets and hence consumption should rise. Hence, both a_{11} and a_{12} should be positive and a_{13} could be either positive or negative. (We would have liked to include distribution of income in the consumption function, but the absence of data on either functional or size distribution of income precluded this.)

Private Investment. In small market economies subject to rather strong business cycles, as in Central America, one would expect investors to plan their capital expenditures (investment which is a flow term) in such a way that at any point in time their capital stock (K) is a proportion (V) of their expected sales (S^e), where the desired proportion V would be identified by least cost conditions.

$$(4.5a) \qquad K^*_t = V \, S^e_t$$

In a world of rather abrupt business cycles and shifts in tax policies, sales expectations might be based largely on the GNP of the previous period (GNP_{t-1}).[6] (Government spending would probably be excluded from private investor decisions on the grounds that government is geared to the requirements of public services.)

(4.5b) $S_t^c = (1 + W) GNP_{t-1}$

where W is the expected rate of growth in spending potential and dis-hoarding.

The investor knows that when time period t is reached, the previous period's capital stock will have depreciated at a rate d, and he must make capital expenditures at such a rate as to make up the difference between the depreciated value of the capital stock at the beginning of the period and his desired capital stock at the end of the period.

(4.5c) $Ip_t = Z [K_t^* - \left(\dfrac{1}{1+d}\right) K_{t-1}] = ZV (1+W) GNP_{t-1}$

$- \dfrac{Z}{1+d} K_{t-1}$

where Z is an adjustment factor depending on the time-phasing of un-completed investment projects and desired or undesired inventories.

Planned or desired investment spending, however, might be disturbed by supply conditions such as credit restrictions or the influence of CU participation on foreign investment.

When these modifications are made in (4.5c), we obtain:

(4.5) $Ip = a_{20} + a_{21} GNP_{t-1} + a_{22} K_{t-1} + a_{23} TIME$

$+ a_{24} Zcm + a_{25} CR$

An alternative and somewhat more general expression is the Koyck transformation of the distributed lag function in which

(4.5′) $Ip = a_{20} + a_{21} GNP_{t-1} + a_{22} K_{t-1} + a_{23} Zcm + a_{24} CR$

$+ a_{25} TIME + a_{26} Ip_{t-1}$

Extraregional Exports. Exports of the Central American countries would seem to depend on foreign demand (measured by Nus), the tax rate on exports, credit conditions, CU participation (which might have a deleterious effect on the relative price of extraregional exports and hence on the profitability of exports), and several other factors, such as marketing capability, which might vary with time.

[6]Note that this is a slightly shorter lag than the eighteen months that seems typical for the United States, but this would seem reasonable in view of the greater political instability typical of the region and hence the need to react quickly to changing conditions.

(4.6) $Ex = a_{30} + a_{31} Nus + a_{32}Te/Ex + a_{33}CR + a_{34}TIME$

$+ a_{35}Zcm$

Intraregional Exports. Exports of any country i to the other member countries Ei would depend on intraregional imports of those countries, credit conditions in the exporting country i, the existence of paved roads between country i and its neighbors, and finally other factors affecting competitiveness that might vary with time.

(4.7) $Ei^i = a_{40} + a_{41} \sum_{\substack{j=1 \\ j \neq i}}^{4} Ni^j + a_{42}CR^i + a_{43} R^i + a_{44}TIME$

Extraregional Imports

(4.8) $Nx = a_{50} + a_{51}GNP + a_{52}Tn/Nx + a_{53}Zcm + a_{54}CR$

$+ a_{55}R + a_{56}TIME$

Equation (4.8) represents the view that imports from the rest of the world would depend upon income, the tax rate on these imports, credit conditions, and the trade diversion effect of CU participation and the integration highway system.

Intraregional Imports. Similarly intraregional imports would be influenced primarily by income, credit conditions, the existence of the CU, the existence of paved highways between the importing country and its neighbors, and various other factors associated with time.

(4.9) $Ni = a_{60} + a_{61}GNP + a_{62}Zcm + a_{63}CR + a_{64}R$

$+ a_{65}TIME$

Capital Stock

(4.10) $K_t = \left(\dfrac{1}{1+d}\right)K_{t-1} + Ip_t + Ig_t$

Tax Receipts

(4.11a) $Tn = Nx \cdot Tn/Nx$, by definition

However, (4.11a) is a nonlinear relationship. In order to keep the model linear, this nonlinear relationship was approximated by the following linear one:

(4.11) $\qquad$ $Tn = a_{70} + a_{71} Nx + a_{72} Tn/Nx$

Similarly the other nonlinear tax relationships were approximated by the following linear ones:

(4.12) $\qquad$ $Te = a_{80} + a_{81} Ex + a_{82} Te/Ex$

(4.13) $\qquad$ $To = a_{90} + a_{91} GDP + a_{92} To/GDP$

Money and Credit. The money supply is determined by the stock of reserve money which is assumed to be a policy instrument. The stock of loans to the private sector is proportional to the money supply (including deposits at commercial banks); however, this proportionality factor might change over time as financial institutions and regulations change.

(4.14) $\qquad$ $CR = b_{10} + b_{11} MS + b_{12} TIME$

(4.15) $\qquad$ $MS = b_{20} + b_{21} RM + b_{22} TIME$

Balance of Payments

(4.16) $\qquad$ $BP = Ex + Ei - Nx - Ni + TT + NFY$

Note that *BP* is not the entire balance of payments, since capital movements are not included.

Government Savings (the Fiscal Balance)

(4.17) $\qquad$ $SG = Tn + Te + To - G - Ig$

D. REVISIONS IN MODEL 1: MODELS 2 AND 3

Since export performance would seem to have played an extremely important role in explaining the cyclical swings in economic activity as well as the long-run growth and capital formation in Central America, it was considered desirable to disaggregate the aggregate GNP_{t-1} variable in the investment equations into income from exports (E_{t-1}) and other income $(GNP_{t-1} - E_{t-1})$. Second, we have specified the financial variable so as to treat the net change in reserve money (DRM), instead of the stock of reserve money (RM), as the policy instrument. The revised versions of equations (4.14) and (4.15) are:

(4.15a) $\qquad$ $MS = b_{20} + b_{21} MS_{t-1} + b_{22} DRM + b_{23} TIME$

(4.14a) $\qquad$ $CR = b_{10} + b_{11} CR_{t-1} + b_{12} D\hat{M}S$

A third change is that the impact of credit on all of the real variables, such as investment, imports, and exports, is felt through the change in stock (or the flow) of credit to the private sector rather than through the stock of credit.

The incorporation of these three changes in specification into the remainder of model 1 constitutes model 2. With these changes model 2 should contain more in the way of dynamic feedbacks than model 1.

Model 3 attempts to incorporate into the model an additional dynamic adjustment process, this time in the all-important linking variable intraindustry imports (Ni). The alternative specification of Ni is as follows:

(4.9a) $Ni = a_{60} + a_{61}Ni_{t-1} + a_{62} (\widehat{GDP} - GDP_{t-1})$

$+ a_{63}Zcm + a_{64}R$

E. ESTIMATION PROCEDURE: CRITERIA

Equations (4.1)–(4.17) in each of the three models comprise a system of seventeen equations in seventeen endogenous variables which, barring linear dependencies or inconsistencies between equations, is a determinate system capable of being solved.

However, this system of equations contains a number of feedbacks. For example, Yd affects C in the consumption function, but C is also a large part of GDP via the GDP accounting identity, equation (4.1), and, after subtractions are made for NFY, TT, and taxes, C is also a large part of Yd. If the coefficients of equation (4.4) above, including the coefficient a_{11} of Yd, were estimated directly by ordinary least squares, without taking this feedback effect into account, the estimate of a_{11} would be biased upward. To avoid this kind of bias in estimating the coefficients of the equations in a highly aggregative model of this kind in which endogenous variables appear on the right side, we have used two-stage least squares as the estimation procedure throughout the analysis.

Unfortunately, as econometricians are painfully aware, this kind of problem is only one of a number of pitfalls and dangers plaguing the use of simple procedures such as direct least squares or even two-stage least squares. Since the textbooks on econometrics are full of examples of such dangers, we shall not go into these difficulties or what can be done about them here. However, we owe the reader, at least, some warning about the most serious kinds of dangers in the present results. These would seem to be:

1) The small sample bias. (All equations in the model have been estimated upon the basis of only sixteen observations—the annual

observations 1951–66 given for each country in appendix A. With an estimation based on such a short period of time, serious doubts can be raised about the stability of the model's parameters in years beyond those of the sample.)

2) Measurement errors or errors-in-variables problems. (The time-series data for the earlier years of this period have been taken rather unquestioningly from an earlier publication of SIECA [1965] which has been updated with revisions on the basis of published and unpublished data from the central bank of each country, SIECA and AID/ROCAP. Systematic measurement errors can result in biased estimates of the model's coefficients.)

3) Multicollinearity due to strong time trends in most of the series used in the model. (Multicollinearity can make the results very sensitive to the way in which the model is specified.)

4) Possible correlation of the error terms (not shown in the above presentation) with the predetermined variables. (This problem is particularly likely to arise when some of the variables treated as pre-determined in the estimating equations are in fact endogenous or lagged endogenous variables, as in equations (4.5), (4.14), and (4.15). It can lead to bias in the estimates of the regression coefficients.)

5) Existence of autocorrelation in the error terms due to the omission of other systematic influences from our estimating equations, persistent errors in measurement, etc. (This problem undoubtedly arises in several equations due to the use of data obtained from different sources and the deliberate attempt to include only a minimum number of explanatory variables. Unless additional procedures are undertaken to adjust for this shortcoming the resulting regression coefficients will no longer be minimum variance estimates.)

Although we have tried to mitigate the influence of type (3) and (4) errors by careful specification and by experimentation with alternative forms, the results unfortunately remain rather sensitive to alternative specifications. We have tried to limit type (5) errors by the use of Durbin-Watson statistics as one of our criteria in selecting which sets of estimates to choose, but, as will be seen in section G below, in some cases (especially the monetary equations) we have used certain equations even though the Durbin-Watson statistics did not fall within the "nonrejection bounds."[7]

---

[7]According to the tables prepared by Durbin and Watson (1951) the following numbers represent cut-off values in interpreting the significance of the values of the Durbin-Watson coefficient (DW) computed in the regressions reported later in the chapter.

Number of Explanatory Variables in the Estimating Equation

	1	2	3	4	5
DW_L	1.08	0.95	0.82	0.69	0.56
DW_U	1.36	1.54	1.75	1.97	2.21

The reader should be particularly aware of these deficiencies in interpreting the standard errors and $\bar{R}^2$ that will be reported below. (The ordinary significance tests break down when small samples are used and the error terms are autocorrelated.) Additional problems are suggested in the use of dummy variables for essentially nonquantifiable magnitudes.[8]

Following conventional practice we have rejected forms in which the regression coefficients had the "wrong" signs or were of the "correct" signs but were smaller than their standard errors.[9]

Due to the relationship between intraregional exports (Ei) for country i and intraregional imports (Ni) of the other member countries, the simultaneous blocs in the models are actually all interdependent and, presumably, would have to be estimated simultaneously by two-stage least squares. However, since this particular feedback (of Ei on GDP and eventually on Ni, etc.) has been very small historically and, because with the limited number of observations available, a simultaneous treatment would require the use of principal components analysis in order to make *any* estimate of the relevant coefficients, we have treated the intraregional imports of other CACM countries,

the $\sum\limits_{\substack{j=1 \\ j\neq i}}^{4} N_i^j$ in equation (4.7) above, as an *exogenous* variable.

This makes each country-model independent in the sense that the parameters of each country can be estimated separately. Furthermore, the model for each country breaks down into a series of recursive blocs which can be estimated in order. Thus, we can start with equation (4.15) which has only one variable—an *exogenous* variable—on the right side. It is a "reduced form" equation; as such it can be estimated directly by least squares. Using the estimates of MS from (4.15), the credit equation (4.14) can be estimated by least squares, since the error terms (which we have, for simplicity, not shown) of (4.14) and (4.15) will be independent of each other. Estimates of credit (CR) can thus be used in order to estimate equations (4.5), (4.6), and (4.7). Estimates of Ex from (4.6) can then be used to estimate Te in (4.12); estimates

---

When $DW < DW_L$, the hypothesis that the error terms are serially independent would have to be rejected (at the 0.05 level).

When $DW > DW_U$, the hypothesis that the error terms are serially independent is not rejected.

When $DW_L < DW < DW_U$, the outcome of the test is in doubt.

[8]For a fascinating discussion of these and other problems, see Basmann (1971).

[9]For an interesting investigation of possible biases introduced by the two-step procedure, see Lovell and Prescott (1968). In exceptional cases we have included a variable if its coefficient was no larger than its standard error, if it was a policy variable, and/or if estimation of alternative forms showed the results to be relatively stable.

of Ip can be used to estimate K via (4.10). Estimates of Ip, Ex, Ei, Te, CR, and MS together, can be used to estimate the remaining equations (4.1), (4.2), (4.3), (4.4), (4.8), (4.9), (4.11), and (4.13)—which make up the simultaneous bloc referred to above—simultaneously.

The causal flow is from reserve money to money supply and credit, which, along with tax policies, lagged variables, and the CU and integration roads dummy variables, determine investment and exports. In turn, exports, investment, money supply, credit, the two dummy variables, government spending and tax policies, and the exogenous influences of the terms of trade and net factor income from abroad, taken together, simultaneously determine the values for GDP, GNP, Yd, C, Nx, Ni, Tn, To, BP, and SG. If, in fact, the intraregional imports of other member countries, Ni^j, $j \neq i$, were treated as an endogenous variable in the Ei equation of country i, Ei would also be a part of the simultaneous bloc in each country, and all these simultaneous blocs would be interrelated, making one extremely large bloc influenced by virtually *all* the predetermined variables in *all* the countries.

In the longer run, however, there is greater interdependence in the system as some of the endogenous variables, namely, those that appear as lagged endogenous variables in explaining current values of the same or other endogenous variables, begin to exert influence on the values of the endogenous variables in the system in the next period. Thus, GNP and K in year t help determine the value of Ip in year $t + 1$. This links the exogenous variables in year t to the endogenous variables in year $t + 1$.

Moreover, in models 2 and 3 the temporal interdependence is increased by the addition of transformations of distributed lag-type functions in the money supply, credit, and intraregional import equations. These dynamic features make the solutions of the systems depend not only on values of the exogenous variables but also on initial conditions. Each of the single-year models for models 1, 2, and 3 can be extended so as to include most of the dynamic feedbacks by rewriting an identical set of the seventeen equations, updating the time subscripts by one period. The lagged endogenous variables in the second-period equations now correspond to the endogenous variables in the first-period equations.

F. SOME ADDITIONAL QUALIFICATIONS AND LIMITATIONS IN THE MODELS

Considering the short-term nature of the models and their expressed purpose of showing the tradeoffs between various policy instruments and planning targets (especially those between and among countries), the most important shortcomings of the models are probably the following:

1) the exclusion of the price variables (for reasons given above);[10]

2) the treatment of reserve money (RM) as a monetary policy instrument and thus as an exogenous policy variable, whereas, in reality it is probably the result of an endogenous money supply function;[11]

3) the fairly simplistic and aggregative treatment of intraregional trade variables;[12] and

4) the omission of income distribution and of its effects on the macroeconomic variables.[13]

Also the way in which the integration highway system was measured (as a dummy variable whose value is increased by one following each important link in the system) leaves a lot to be desired. More ideally one would like to measure the incidence of the integration highways by their effect on the cost of transport within the region.[14]

Finally, the reader is reminded of the numerous simplifications (discussed in section B above) that have been adopted, the limited number of observations, the uncertain quality and perhaps inconsistency of the data, and the relatively strong correlation of all variables over time, which gives rise to a fairly severe multicollinearity problem. Clearly, in such circumstances, further testing would be necessary before the specific results reported here could be regarded with confidence.

Nevertheless, because of the rather consistently high coefficients of determination adjusted for degrees of freedom ($\bar{R}^2$) and the fairly general confirmation of *a priori* expectations about the direction of the

---

[10]The overall price level has remained remarkably constant in several countries of the region; while on the one hand this has made it difficult to estimate behavioral relationships involving price movements, on the other hand, it offers circumstantial evidence suggesting that price stability has been an important aim of economic policy and, thus, that its omission is an important shortcoming that should be overcome in future research.

[11]A more appropriate specification might have designated as the monetary policy instruments purer, policy variables such as rediscount rates, reserve ratios, credit ceilings, etc., but these would be extremely hard to quantify, given the frequency with which they change and the inevitable changes over time in their relative effectiveness.

[12]In view of the crucial role which intraregional trade and capital movements play in the increasing interdependence of the CACM countries, it is hoped that eventually sufficient data will become available to introduce the whole matrix of trade and capital flows in the model instead of only the aggregate intraregional commodity imports and exports, as at present.

[13]Indeed one might suspect that the composition of a government macroeconomic policy package does affect income distribution, which not only enters into the social welfare function (as a "goal" or "target variable") but also indirectly affects the other elements of the social welfare function—balance of payments, employment, income growth, and, even more indirectly, the fiscal balance and the rate of inflation.

[14]Gabriel Siri of SIECA is reported to be working on estimates of the average transport cost reduction brought about by each new road in the area.

effects, the results appear to be sufficiently representative to suggest that the subsequent policy simulations may be of some practical interest.

Moreover, considering that the main purpose of the models is for simulating the potential gains of policy coordination at the regional level and that all three models will be used in order to test the sensitivity of the overall results to changes in specification, parameter values, etc., these qualifications would not seem to detract substantially from the achievement of their limited objective.

G. ESTIMATES OF THE STRUCTURAL EQUATIONS OF MODELS 1, 2, AND 3

Results for the forms of the equations selected for use in model 1 are presented by country, in alphabetical order in tables 4–2 through 4–6 below. Corresponding results for model 2 are presented in tables 4–7 through 4–11, and for model 3 for Guatemala and Nicaragua in tables 4–12 and 4–13. (For the other three countries models 2 and 3 are identical.) The reader is referred back to table 4–1 for the definitions of symbols and terms used.

All coefficients have been estimated by two-stage least squares and the criteria outlined in section E have been employed in eliminating variables or choosing preferred forms for inclusion in the model. In the presentation of all our results the numbers in parentheses indicate standard errors of the regression coefficients, $\bar{R}^2$ indicates the coefficient of determination adjusted for degrees of freedom, and DW indicates the Durbin-Watson statistic. The remaining equations (not shown in these results) are the identities, i.e., equations (4.1), (4.2), (4.3), (4.10), (4.16), and (4.17), which are, of course, the same for all countries.

Since the form of the three models and the kinds of variables included in them are rather similar, we shall discuss the results collectively. The most important feature of these results is the significance of the most important policy instruments. We shall begin our discussion with a brief review of the policy effects incorporated in the models.

Export taxes are generally shown to have a strongly depressing effect on exports in each of the countries of the region. This is in spite of the fact that a substantial portion of the export taxes collected are derived from coffee exports, which are largely administered on a quota basis by the International Coffee Agreement. As one might have suspected, the effect of changes in export tax rates is stronger in those countries where export taxes on other commodities, such as lumber, shrimp, bananas, and cotton, are significant than in those countries where the export

Table 4–2. Estimates of model 1 for Costa Rica

Equation no.	Equation	$\bar{R}^2$	DW
(4.15)	$MS = 3.3850 + 1.3931\ RM + .00076\ TIME$ $\quad\quad\quad (.2727) \quad\quad (.00039)$	.9793	0.60
(4.14)	A credit equation for Costa Rica was not estimated because a consistent series on credit to the private sector could not be obtained. MS was used in place of CR elsewhere in the model.		
(4.5)	$Ip = -5.6292 + .2285\ GNP_{t-1} - .0373K_{t-1} + .00085\ Zcm + .1282\ \widehat{MS}$ $\quad\quad\quad\quad (.1712) \quad\quad\quad (.0620) \quad\quad (.00760) \quad\quad (.7128)$	.8066	2.77
(4.6)	$Ex = 60.8291 + .4482\ \widehat{MS} + .00419\ TIME - 942.4532\ Te/Ex$ $\quad\quad\quad\quad (.6016) \quad\quad (.00162) \quad\quad (231.9681)$	.9347	2.89
(4.7)	$Ei = -8.5048 + .2187\ \widehat{MS} + .2276\ \sum_{\substack{j=1\\j\neq CR}}^{4} Ni_j - .00123\ TIME$ $\quad\quad\quad\quad (.1760) \quad\quad (.0196) \quad\quad\quad\quad (.00050)$	.9514	1.44
(4.12)	$Te = -3.2133 + .0394\ \widehat{Ex} + 83.1108\ Te/Ex$ $\quad\quad\quad\quad (.0039) \quad\quad (10.4210)$	.9452	1.83
(4.4)	$C = 2.5152 + .8783\ \widehat{Yd}$ $\quad\quad\quad\quad (.0158)$	.9978	1.98
(4.8)	$Nx = 26.9702 + .1502\ \widehat{GNP} - 148.4491\ Tn/Nx + 1.2018\ \widehat{MS} - .0087\ RCR - .00376\ Zcm$ $\quad\quad\quad\quad (.1254) \quad\quad (42.8029) \quad\quad\quad\quad (.8408) \quad\quad (.0058) \quad\quad (.00742)$	.9361	2.23
(4.9)	$Ni = -53.7455 + .2056\ \widehat{GNP} + .0007\ Zcm - .0035\ TIME$ $\quad\quad\quad\quad (.0929) \quad\quad (.0038) \quad\quad (.0019)$	.7158	1.25
(4.11)	$Tn = -28.8671 + .2655\ \widehat{Nx} + 111.3581\ Tn/Nx$ $\quad\quad\quad\quad (.0161) \quad\quad (6.1096)$	.9852	2.17
(4.13)	$To = -31.23 + .0700\ GDP + 446.9741\ To/GDP$ $\quad\quad\quad\quad (.0027) \quad\quad (45.3244)$	.9847	1.13

Table 4–3. Estimates of Model 1 for El Salvador

Equation no.	Equation	$\bar{R}^2$	DW
(4.15)	$MS = 32.2528 + \underset{(.1155)}{.8167}\ RM$	.7656	0.56
(4.14)	$CR = -242.5528 + \underset{(.8688)}{4.2036}\ \widehat{MS}$	.6000	0.40
(4.5)	$Ip = -18.7532 + \underset{(.0406)}{.08424}\ GNP_{t-1} + \underset{(.1118)}{.2398}\ \widehat{CR}$	.8260	2.62
(4.6)	$Ex = 60.1061 + \underset{(.00109)}{.00388}\ TIME - \underset{(44.8092)}{120.7129}\ Te/Ex + \underset{(.1035)}{.2086}\ \widehat{CR}$	.9517	1.82
(4.7)	$Ei = -6.0016 + \underset{(.0589)}{.2393}\ \sum_{\substack{j=1 \\ j\neq ES}}^{4} N_i^j + \underset{(.00095)}{.00323}\ RES + \underset{(.0456)}{.0952}\ \widehat{CR}$	.9893	1.87
(4.12)	$Te = -8.7862 + \underset{(.0191)}{.1041}\ \widehat{Ex} + \underset{(8.2004)}{75.5921}\ Te/Ex$	.8806	1.42
(4.4)	$C = -24.5543 + \underset{(.0292)}{.9482}\ \widehat{Yd}$	.9859	2.28
(4.8)	$Nx = 42.5555 + \underset{(.0699)}{.2253}\ \widehat{GNP} - \underset{(82.3796)}{362.1296}\ Tn/Nx + \underset{(.0018)}{.00355}\ TIME - \underset{(.0036)}{.00712}\ R^{ES} - \underset{(.0062)}{.0156}\ Zcm$	.9704	2.90
(4.9)	$Ni = -35.0259 + \underset{(.0290)}{.04241}\ \widehat{GNP} + \underset{(.0035)}{.00456}\ Zcm + \underset{(.0760)}{.23203}\ \widehat{CR}$	.9362	2.23
(4.11)	$Tn = -18.1019 + \underset{(.0084)}{.13585}\ \widehat{Nx} + \underset{(8.2242)}{130.3632}\ Tn/Nx$	.9518	2.58
(4.13)	$To = -30.3851 + \underset{(.0016)}{.0528}\ \widehat{GDP} + \underset{(35.8836)}{586.6096}\ To/GDP$	.9944	2.00

Table 4-4. Estimates of Model 1 for Guatemala

Equation no.	Equation	$\bar{R}^2$	DW
(4.15)	$MS = 4.0405 + 1.0508\ RM + .00102\ TIME$ $\qquad\qquad\ (.1364)\qquad\ (.00063)$	.9817	0.85
(4.14)	$CR = -79.1256 + 1.53472\ \widehat{MS}$ $\qquad\qquad\qquad\ (.13201)$	.8994	0.74
(4.5)	$Ip = 16.7037 + .1984\ GNP_{t-1} + .4115\ \widehat{CR} - .0931K_{t-1} + .1682\ Ip_{t-1}$ $\qquad\qquad\ (.1434)\qquad\qquad\ (.2177)\qquad (.0642)\qquad\ (.1307)$	.8826	1.41
(4.6)	$Ex = 28.9505 + .1738\ \widehat{CR} + .7697\ Nus - 128.4933\ Te/Ex$ $\qquad\qquad\ (.1442)\qquad (.2274)\qquad\ (50.3480)$	.9645	2.71
(4.7)	$Ei = -2.9825 + .0678\ \widehat{CR} + .4119\ \sum\limits_{j=1}^{4}\ Ni_{\,j \neq GU} - .00087\ TIME$ $\qquad\qquad\ (.0572)\qquad (.0316)$ $\qquad\qquad\qquad\qquad\qquad\qquad\qquad\qquad\ (.00047)$	.9763	2.83
(4.12)	$Te = -4.7403 + .0545\ \widehat{Ex} + 83.9677\ Te/Ex$ $\qquad\qquad\ (.0161)\qquad\ (9.2291)$	.9125	0.35
(4.4)	$C = -1.4844 + .9172\ \widehat{Yd}$ $\qquad\qquad\ (.0262)$	.9879	1.55
(4.8)	$Nx = -24.2722 + .1889\ \widehat{GNP} - 129.3026\ Tn/Nx + .3000\ \widehat{CR} - .0092\ RGU - .0211\ Zcm$ $\qquad\qquad\ (.0590)\qquad\ (62.0848)\qquad\qquad (.2249)\qquad (.0045)\qquad\ (.0092)$	.9687	2.20
(4.9)	$Ni = -64.2834 + .0952\ \widehat{GNP} - .0025\ TIME + .0017\ Zcm + .0051\ RGU$ $\qquad\qquad\ (.0406)\qquad\ (.0015)\qquad\ (.0038)\qquad (.0023)$	.9139	1.46
(4.11)	$Tn = -38.1619 + .2330\ \widehat{Nx} + 156.5781\ Tn/Nx$ $\qquad\qquad\ (.0356)\qquad\ (24.7353)$	.7375	0.85
(4.13)	$To = -48.3473 + .0495\ \widehat{GDP} + 972.7516\ To/GDP$ $\qquad\qquad\ (.0020)\qquad\ (59.0644)$	.9815	0.78

Table 4–5. Estimates of Model 1 for Honduras

Equation no.	Equation	$\bar{R}^2$	DW
(4.15)	MS = −.6561 + 1.1792 RM + .00062 TIME (.1174)　　　(.00007)	.9553	1.11
(4.14)	A credit equation for Honduras was not estimated because a consistent series on credit to the private sector could not be obtained. MS was used in place of CR elsewhere in the model		
(4.5)	Ip = 206.5832 + .3274 GNP$_{t-1}$ + .6122 $\widehat{MS}$ − .4879 K$_{t-1}$ + .01141 TIME 　　　　(.1889)　　　　(.6743)　　(.2522)　　(.0072)	.4873	2.39
(4.6)	Ex = 74.3115 + .4394 $\widehat{MS}$ + .00709 TIME −3363.2751 Te/Ex −.01789 Zcm 　　　(.2245)　　(.00325)　　　(457.5516)　　(.005221)	.9533	2.08
(4.7)	Ei = 3.8373 + .1045 $\sum_{j=1}^{4}$ Ni $_{j\neq HO}$ + .00169 RHO 　　　　(.0121)　　　　　　　　(.00053)	.9536	2.34
(4.12)	Te = −1.4851 + .0205 $\widehat{Ex}$ + 72.80273 Te/Ex 　　　　(.0015)　　(4.8642)	.9688	2.21
(4.4)	C = 4.0073 + .8608 $\widehat{Yd}$ 　　　(.0262)	.9863	1.12
(4.8)	Nx = −15.9851 + .3718 $\widehat{GNP}$ − 109.3410 Tn/Nx − .00260 TIME − .00511 Zcm 　　　　(.1021)　　(41.5851)　　　(.0015)　　(.0023)	.9306	2.38
(4.9)	Ni = −99.4189 + .3574 $\widehat{GNP}$ − .00409 TIME + .00096 R^{HO} + .2398 $\widehat{MS}$ 　　　　(.0482)　　(.0007)　　(.00016)　　(.2102)	.9599	1.75
(4.11)	Tn = −13.5383 + .1926 $\widehat{Nx}$ + 70.5236 Tn/Nx 　　　　(.0123)　　(4.8492)	.9671	2.29
(4.13)	To = −20.0757 + .04761 $\widehat{GDP}$ + 424.3270 To/GDP 　　　　(.0015)　　(19.1819)	.9899	2.11

Table 4–6. Estimates of Model 1 for Nicaragua

Equation no.	Equation	$\bar{R}^2$	DW
(4.15)	$MS = -1.5986 + 1.6368\ RM$ $\qquad\qquad\quad (.0577)$	.9914	0.99
(4.14)	$CR = 9.4731 + .7656\ \widehat{MS} + .00187\ TIME$ $\qquad\qquad\ (.3672) \qquad\quad (.00104)$	.7494	0.53
(4.5)	$Ip = -2.9111 + .1560\ GNP_{t-1} - .1014\ K_{t-1} + 1.0239\ \widehat{CR}$ $\qquad\qquad\quad (.0849) \qquad\quad (.0420) \qquad (.2919)$	.8659	1.27
(4.6)	$Ex = -40.2147 + .1646\ Nus + 9.9968\ Te/Ex + 1.9504\ \widehat{CR} - .01128\ Zcm$ $\qquad\qquad\quad (.32513)\ (148.8680) \qquad (.8232) \qquad\quad (.01626)$	.9148	1.84
(4.7)	$Ei = 1.8636 + .13865 \displaystyle\sum_{j=1}^{4} Ni\ j{\neq}NI - .00037\ TIME$ $\qquad\qquad\ (.01263)\ \ j=1 \qquad\qquad\quad (.00011)$	.9461	1.53
(4.12)	$Te = -1.2861 + .01337\ \widehat{Ex} + 72.59837\ Te/Ex$ $\qquad\qquad\quad (.00459) \qquad\ (6.06263)$	.9311	0.93
(4.4)	$C = -6.4748 + .8941\ \widehat{Yd}$ $\qquad\qquad\ (.0414)$	.9690	1.79
(4.8)	$Nx = -20.3157 + .43161\ \widehat{GNP} - 149.79536\ Tn/Nx - 0.01130\ Zcm$ $\qquad\qquad\quad (.03280) \qquad\quad (40.83579) \qquad\qquad (.00593)$	.9823	2.05
(4.9)	$Ni = -40.6429 + .16855\ \widehat{GNP} - 0.01238\ TIME$ $\qquad\qquad\quad (.04530) \qquad\quad (.00077)$	.7614	0.62
(4.11)	$Tn = -19.4982 + 96.4912\ Tn/Nx + .1854\ \widehat{Nx}$ $\qquad\qquad\quad (13.1945) \qquad\quad (.0187)$	.941	0.97
(4.13)	$To = -21.2054 + 469.6716\ To/GDP + .04604\ GDP$ $\qquad\qquad\quad (29.0988) \qquad\qquad (.00222)$	.994	2.20

Table 4-7. Estimates of Model 2 for Costa Rica

Equation no.	Equation	R^2	DW
(4.15)	$MS = -3.0888 + 1.0503\,MS_{t-1} + 1.7020\,DRM$ $(.0348)\quad(.2694)$	.9845	2.22
(4.5)	$Ip = -5.7345 + .21766\,E_{t-1} + .13045\,(GNP - E_{t-1})_{t-1} + 1.42116\,(\widehat{MS} - MS)_{t-1}$ $(.18216)\quad(.06075)\quad(.76469)$	.8173	2.43
(4.6)	$Ex = .1864 + .2361\,Nus - 974.0280\,Te/Ex - .0069\,Zcm + 1.5629\,\widehat{MS}$ $(.2023)\quad(344.9951)\quad(.0082)\quad(.5240)$	.8636	2.17
(4.7)	$Ei = .7337 + .22455\,\sum_{j=1}^{4} Ni_{j \neq CR} - .00062\,TIME$ $(.01986)\quad(.00018)$	.9495	1.10
(4.12)	$Te = -3.2486 + .04004\,\widehat{Ex} + 82.42361\,Te/Ex$ $(.00443)\quad(11.45361)$	.9344	2.05
(4.4)	$C = 2.9994 + .87696\,\widehat{Yd}$ $(.02270)$	.9900	1.56
(4.8)	$Nx = 47.9442 + .26101\,\widehat{GDP} - 100.43567\,Tn/Nx + .47323\,(MS - MS_{t-1}) - .0158\,R^{CR}$ $(.03845)\quad(50.34543)\quad(.93645)\quad(.00789)$		
(4.9)	$Ni = -8.6345 + .02829\,\widehat{GDP} + .00494\,Zcm$ $(.01291)\quad(.00393)$	.6576	0.88
(4.11)	$Tn = -28.9953 + .26712\,\widehat{Nx} + 111.11381\,Tn/Nx$ $(.01916)\quad(7.19585)$	.9876	1.80
(4.13)	$To = -31.2453 + .07012\,\widehat{GDP} + 446.20695\,To/GDP$ $(.00253)\quad(41.82829)$	.9870	1.18

Table 4–8. Estimates of Model 2 for El Salvador

Equation no.	Equation	$\bar{R}^2$	DW
(4.15)	$MS = -1.4185 + 1.0574\ MS_{t-1} + 1.3561\ DRM - .00046\ TIME$ $(.1273)\qquad (.00026)$	.9326	1.94
(4.14)	$CR = -60.5226 + .8622\ CR_{t-1} + .9934\ \widehat{DMS}$ $(.4157)\qquad (.3467)$	.9651	2.01
(4.5)	$Ip = 5.1799 + .31083\ E_{t-1} + .02753\ (GNP_{t-1}-E_{t-1}) + .55813\ (\widehat{CR}-CR_{t-1})$ $(.08122)\qquad (.05990)\qquad\qquad (.34007)$	.83629	2.53
(4.6)	$Ex = 72.3771 + .29612\ Nus - 162.30784\ Te/Ex + .02425\ Zcm + .90775\ (\widehat{CR}-CR_{t-1})$ $(.15584)\qquad (57.9556)\qquad (.00776)\qquad (.46658)$	.9379	1.91
(4.7)	$Ei = 1.1963 + .36265 \sum_{j=1}^{4} Ni_{j\neq ES} + .10256\ (\widehat{CR}-CR_{t-1}) + .00352\ R^{ES}$ $(.05664)\qquad\qquad (.12676)\qquad\qquad (.00147)$	.9856	1.40
(4.12)	$Te = -6.8579 + .09163\ \widehat{Ex} + 70.93335\ Te/Ex$ $(.02428)\qquad (10.38419)$	.8130	1.01
(4.4)	$C = -24.0431 + .94728\ \widehat{Yd}$ $(.05214)$	.9564	2.57
(4.8)	$Nx = 11.5721 + .34147\ \widehat{GDP} - 336.18552\ Tn/Nx - .00709\ R^{ES} - .02083\ Zcm$ $(.07007)\qquad (102.97639)\qquad (.00706)\qquad (.01166)$	.8962	2.32
(4.9)	$Ni = -1.6386 + .00448\ \widehat{GDP} + .61174\ (\widehat{CR}-CR_{t-1}) + .00439\ Zcm + .00860\ R^{ES}$ $(.03907)\qquad (.24857)\qquad\qquad (.00559)\qquad (.00333)$	.9073	2.18
(4.11)	$Tn = -18.0944 + .13582\ \widehat{Nx} + 130.34325\ Tn/Nx$ $(.14189)\qquad (15.83954)$	.8653	2.54
(4.13)	$To = -30.3857 + .05264\ \widehat{GDP} + 585.15181\ To/GDP$ $(.00273)\qquad (61.99088)$	.9832	2.16

Table 4–9. Estimates of Model 2 for Guatemala

Equation no.	Equation	$\bar{R}^2$	DW
(4.15)	$MS = .7177 + .9991\ MS_{t-1} + 1.0763\ DRM$ $\qquad\quad (.0333) \qquad\qquad (.1365)$	.9845	2.22
(4.14)	$CR = -16.9452 + .9808\ CR_{t-1} + .3330\ \widehat{DMS}$ $\qquad\qquad\quad (.0866) \qquad\qquad (.1277)$	.9894	2.00
(4.5)	$Ip = 2.0874 + .33847\ E_{t-1} + .26182\ (GNP_{t-1} - E_{t-1}) - .10659\ K_{t-1}$ $\qquad\qquad (.20117) \qquad (.18823) \qquad\qquad\qquad\qquad (.07458)$ $\qquad + 2.59041\ (\widehat{CR}-CR_{t-1}) + .00255\ Zcm$ $\qquad\quad (1.19937) \qquad\qquad\qquad (.01135)$	.8809	1.23
(4.6)	$Ex = 18.6289 + .95348\ Nus - 119.32324\ Te/Ex + .39650\ (\widehat{CR}-CR_{t-1})$ $\qquad\qquad (.15924) \qquad\quad (54.72643) \qquad\qquad (.76002)$	.9611	2.53
(4.7)	$Ei = -1.8497 + .42690\ \sum\limits_{\substack{j=1 \\ j\neq GU}}^{4} Ni - .00039\ TIME$ $\qquad\qquad (.02932) \qquad\qquad\qquad\quad (.00024)$	.9755	2.80
(4.12)	$Te = -4.6424 + .05394\ \widehat{Ex} + 83.69091\ Te/Ex$ $\qquad\qquad (.01640) \qquad\quad (9.39262)$	.9101	0.33
(4.4)	$C = -.7405 + .91633\ \widehat{Yd}$ $\qquad\qquad (.03076)$	.9834	1.53
(4.8)	$Nx = 5.6184 + .17099\ \widehat{GDP} - 167.01937\ Tn/Nx + 2.18477\ (\widehat{CR}-CR_{t-1})$ $\qquad\qquad (.02742) \qquad\quad (48.38199) \qquad\qquad (.66850)$ $\qquad - .00791\ RGU - .01778\ Zcm$ $\qquad\quad (.00363) \qquad\quad (.00729)$	.9787	2.35
(4.9)	$Ni = -20.6596 + .02764\ \widehat{GDP} + .00012\ Zcm + .00656\ RGU$ $\qquad\qquad (.01032) \qquad\quad (.00404) \qquad (.00226)$	.9003	1.17
(4.11)	$Tn = -39.8481 + .23918\ \widehat{Nx} + 160.33771\ Tn/Nx$ $\qquad\qquad (.03203) \qquad\quad (22.23104)$	.7873	1.03
(4.13)	$To = -48.4209 + .04960\ \widehat{GDP} + 972.95531\ To/GDP$ $\qquad\qquad (.00203) \qquad\quad (59.27217)$	.9813	1.13

Table 4–10. Estimates of Model 2 for Honduras

Equation no.	Equation	$\bar{R}^2$	DW
(4.15)	$MS = -.0026 + 1.0180\ MS_{t-1} + 1.0523\ DRM$ $\quad\quad\quad\quad (.0632) \quad\quad\quad (.1194)$	.9541	2.31
(4.5)	$Ip = 31.1927 + .29626\ GNP_{t-1} - .11715\ K_{t-1} + .00641\ Zcm$ $\quad\quad\quad\quad (.16209) \quad\quad\quad (.07200) \quad\quad (.00504)$	.4932	2.50
(4.6)	$Ex = 25.8914 + .7738\ Nus - 1680.9401\ Te/Ex - .00718\ Zcm$ $\quad\quad\quad\quad (.0640) \quad (221.4493) \quad\quad\quad (.00410)$	.9533	2.08
(4.7)	$Ei = 3.8373 + .1045 \sum_{j=1}^{4} Ni^j\ j{\neq}HO + .00169\ RHO$ $\quad\quad\quad\quad (.0121) \quad\quad\quad\quad\quad\quad (.00053)$	.9534	2.34
(4.12)	$Te = -1.4753 + .0204\ \widehat{Ex} + 72.8556\ Te/Ex$ $\quad\quad\quad\quad (.0015) \quad\quad (4.8642)$	.9688	2.21
(4.4)	$C = 6.2286 + .85421\ \widehat{Yd}$ $\quad\quad\quad\quad (.04859)$	.9536	1.70
(4.8)	$Nx = 34.4689 + .19961\ \widehat{GDP} - 161.34008\ Tn/Nx + .15454\ (\widehat{MS}-MS_{t-1})$ $\quad\quad\quad\quad (.03106) \quad\quad\ (39.32143) \quad\quad\quad (.42517)$ $\quad\quad\quad -.00421\ Zcm$ $\quad\quad\quad\ (.00443)$	.8779	2.28
(4.9)	$Ni = -50.3924 + .16662\ \widehat{GDP} + .00647\ Zcm - .00748\ RHO$ $\quad\quad\quad\quad (.00460) \quad\quad\quad (.00460) \quad\quad (.00317)$	.8567	1.27
(4.11)	$Tn = -13.5117 + .19226\ \widehat{Nx} + 70.51986\ Tn/Nx$ $\quad\quad\quad\quad (.01538) \quad\quad (5.97679)$	.9501	2.17
(4.13)	$To = -20.1791 + .04787\ \widehat{GDP} + 424.4849\ To/GDP$ $\quad\quad\quad\quad (.00179) \quad\quad\quad (23.24655)$	.9852	2.55

Table 4–11. Estimates of Model 2 for Nicaragua

Equation no.	Equation	$\bar{R}^2$	DW
(4.15)	$MS = -.4598 + 1.0199\ MS_{t-1} + 1.4380\ DRM$ $\quad\quad\quad\quad (.0392)\quad\quad\quad (.1820)$	.9812	1.65
(4.14)	$CR = -8.1686 + .6886\ CR_{t-1} + .6828\ \widehat{DMS}$ $\quad\quad\quad\quad\quad (.1116)\quad\quad\quad (.1469)$	.9520	1.67
(4.5)	$Ip = 5.4471 + .42279\ E_{t-1} + .18406\ (GNP_{t-1}-E_{t-1}) - .07438\ K_{t-1}$ $\quad\quad\quad\quad\quad (.12343)\quad\quad (.07521)\quad\quad\quad\quad\quad\quad (.03645)$ $\quad\quad\quad + .84906\ (\widehat{CR}-CR_{t-1})$ $\quad\quad\quad\quad\quad (.29324)$	.8934	2.17
(4.6)	$Ex = -22.2747 + .98283\ Nus - 17.3859\ Te/Ex + .68335\ (\widehat{CR}-CR_{t-1})$ $\quad\quad\quad\quad\quad\quad (.16131)\quad\quad\quad (186.2493)\quad\quad\quad\quad (.81006)$	.8685	1.39
(4.7)	$Ei = 1.8636 + .13865\ \sum\limits_{j=1}^{4}\ Ni^{j}_{\ j\neq NI} - .00039\ TIME$ $\quad\quad\quad\quad\quad (.01263)\quad\quad\quad\quad\quad\quad\quad (.00011)$	.9461	1.53
(4.12)	$Te = -1.2320 + 0.01292\ \widehat{Ex} + 72.17996\ Te/Ex$ $\quad\quad\quad\quad\quad\quad (.00098)\quad\quad\quad (2.45564)$	.9237	0.83
(4.4)	$C = 7.1108 + .89612\ \widehat{Yd}$ $\quad\quad\quad\quad\quad (.04089)$	.9570	2.02
(4.8)	$Nx = 14.4268 + .38612\ \widehat{GDP} - 241.79798\ Tn/Nx - .01789\ Zcm$ $\quad\quad\quad\quad\quad\quad (.02852)\quad\quad (37.63315)\quad\quad\quad\quad (.00585)$	.9844	1.52
(4.9)	$Ni = -40.8941 + .13449\ \widehat{GDP} - .01878\ Zcm + .99923\ (\widehat{CR}-CR_{t-1})$ $\quad\quad\quad\quad\quad\quad (.01737)\quad\quad (.00492)\quad\quad\quad (.26117)$	.9116	1.05
(4.11)	$Tn = -16.3318 + .17109\ \widehat{Nx} + 88.02393\ Tn/Nx$ $\quad\quad\quad\quad\quad\quad (.02762)\quad\quad (19.42521)$	.7168	0.70
(4.13)	$To = -21.1493 + .04685\ \widehat{GDP} + 462.14952\ To/GDP$ $\quad\quad\quad\quad\quad\quad (.00261)\quad\quad (33.76884)$	.9914	2.14

Table 4-12. Estimates of Model 3 for Guatemala

Equation no.	Equation	$\bar{R}^2$	DW
(4.4)	$C = -1.7084 + .91745\ \widehat{Yd}$ $\quad\quad\quad\ (.02309)$	.9906	1.49
(4.8)	$Nx = 10.8908 + .16470\ \widehat{GDP} - 170.23482\ Tn/Nx + 2.28779\ (\widehat{CR}-CR_{t-1})$ $\quad\quad\quad\quad\quad (50.81224)\quad\quad\quad (.69611)$ $\quad\quad -.00760\ RGU - .01676\ Zcm$ $\quad\quad\ (.00381)\quad\quad (.00760)$	.9764	2.15
(4.9)	$Ni = -.6578 + 1.02411\ Ni_{t-1} + .03962\ \widehat{GDP}-GDP_{t-1} + .00241\ Zcm$ $\quad\quad\quad\quad (.09334)\quad\quad (.03046)\quad\quad\quad\quad (.00198)$	.9684	2.04
(4.11)	$Tn = -40.6733 + .24218\ \widehat{Nx} + 162.17758\ Tn/Nx$ $\quad\quad\quad\quad (.03027)\quad\quad (22.21212)$	.7911	0.91
(4.13)	$To = -48.3920 + .04957\ \widehat{GDP} + 972.87539\ To/GDP$ $\quad\quad\quad\quad (.00191)\quad\quad (55.85946)$	.9834	0.84

Note: Other equations are identical to those of model 2.

Table 4-13. Estimates of Model 3 for Nicaragua

Equation no.	Equation	$\bar{R}^2$	DW
(4.4)	$C = -6.4808 + .89410\ \widehat{Yd}$ $\qquad\qquad (.03971)$	.9712	1.98
(4.8)	$Nx = 17.4950 + .37726\ \widehat{GDP} - 243.36165\ Tn/Nx - .01659\ Zcm$ $\qquad\qquad (.02060) \qquad\quad (28.19818) \qquad\quad (.00431)$	.9912	2.43
(4.9)	$Ni = -1.2924 + 1.38959\ Ni_{t-1}$ $\qquad\qquad (.26453)$	.9780	2.61
(4.11)	$Tn = -17.7316 + .17741\ \widehat{Nx} + 91.76706\ Tn/Nx$ $\qquad\qquad (.02361) \qquad\quad (16.63060)$	.7907	0.82
(4.13)	$To = -21.1926 + .04622\ \widehat{GDP} + 467.96013\ To/GDP$ $\qquad\qquad (.00232) \qquad\quad (30.27070)$	.9930	2.81

Note: Other equations are indentical to those of model 2.

taxes are almost entirely on coffee. Our estimates indicate that an increase in the export tax rate of one percent (in absolute terms) in Honduras would lower exports (in constant prices of 1962) by at least 16 million dollars! In the other countries the effect seems to be smaller, but nevertheless not insignificant. Tariffs on extraregional imports inhibit imports from outside Central America significantly in all countries for all models. Income and sales taxes cut down on the real value of disposable income and hence limit consumption in real terms.

The effects of government spending can be seen only in the results of the reduced form equations of each model and thus will be discussed later. Suffice it to say that the government spending multipliers were always positive, but in a number of countries were significantly less than one. This is a somewhat different result than is usually obtained by similar models in advanced countries, but is reasonable in view of the high marginal propensity to import and other "leakages" that are characteristic of small LDCs.

Monetary policy, which in model 1 is measured by the RM variable and in models 2 and 3 by DRT, is the dominant influence on money and credit. In model 1, the stock of credit (or money) has had an effect on exports in all countries and in models 2 and 3 the flow of credit DRM has had a positive effect on exports in all countries except Honduras. Similarly, financial factors have had an important direct influence on imports in all countries except Nicaragua and, of course, they have had an indirect influence on imports through their effect on income in all countries. An effect of monetary policy on private investment has been revealed in all countries. However, it must be admitted that in a number of cases the influence of money or credit on these variables is not statistically significant (at the 0.10 level). The reason why the influence of monetary policy may not have been as significant as the effects of the instruments of fiscal policy may lie in the fact that the allocations of the total stock of credit may be changed from year to year, and thus the aggregate stock may not be a very good measure for the relevant credit variable. One might suspect that more disaggregated data on credit allocations would give better fits.

The establishment of the CACM does not seem to have had a significant effect on the level of private investment in any of the Central American economies, although the results of model 2 provide some indication that such an effect may have been felt in Guatemala and Honduras. It is more likely, however, that this effect would only occur with a lag, and thus it is quite possible that further study and more recent data (e.g., table 1–4) would show that investment may have been induced to a greater extent than indicated by our results. There is some indication that the CACM has had a detrimental effect on extraregional exports from Honduras, Nicaragua, and possibly Costa Rica, but in no case does this effect seem to have been large. However, the greatest effect has been in creating more trade within the Central American region. In general, these results are consistent with those we obtained for the CU dummy variables in the aggregate production functions reported in chapter 3 above.

A third feature of the models presented here is that because of the fact that investment in all models and several other variables in models 2 and 3 are directly affected by lagged endogenous variables, and thereby almost all the endogenous variables are *indirectly* affected by such variables, the model allows one to analyze the effects of the policy instruments not only on the variables of the current period but also on those of future periods. Since, in the formation of the model, no lags of greater than one year were employed, most of these dynamic interconnections between policy instruments and other variables will have begun to be felt within two years. For this reason, and in order to keep the model as simple as possible and not to extend it beyond its admittedly short-run capabilities, we have expanded the model so as to include only two periods (years).

Finally, and this was of course the purpose of building the models in the first place, through the influence of the various policy instruments on the intraregional trade variables the influences of any one country's policy instruments are also transmitted to each of the other countries in the region. The policy effects will be revealed more clearly in the following section dealing with the policy multipliers obtained from the reduced-form solutions.

H. COMPLETE SOLUTIONS TO THE MODELS

Each of the three models consists of 17 equations per country (except for Costa Rica and Honduras, which lack credit equations and thus have only 16) which, when expanded to include two years, makes 34 equations. These systems of 34 equations per country can alternatively be treated as separate models or can be fitted together to make one big model for Central America, consisting of 34×5 or 170 equations. Adding the following identities for each of the two periods yields a complete system for each model consisting of 176 equations.[15]

---

[15]As Jean Waelbroeck has kindly pointed out, were it not for the presence of transport costs, two additional equations (one for each year) requiring intraregional imports to be equal to intraregional exports, i.e., $N_i^{CR} + N_i^{ES} + N_i^{GU} + N_i^{HO} + N_i^{NI} = E_i^{CR} + E_i^{ES} + E_i^{GU} + E_i^{HO} + E_i^{NI}$, could have been specified as a way or precluding the

(4.171-2)
$$GDP^{CACM} = GDP^{CR} + GDP^{ES} + GDP^{GU}$$
$$+ GDP^{HO} + GDP^{NI}$$

(4.173-4)
$$C^{CACM} = C^{CR} + C^{ES} + C^{GU} + C^{HO} + C^{NI}$$

(4.175-6)
$$I^{CACM} = I^{CR} + I^{ES} + I^{GU} + I^{HO} + I^{NI}$$

for each year t and $t + 1$

This system of 176 equations is of the form:

$$\text{(a)} \quad IY = AY + BX$$

where Y is the vector of 176 endogenous variables and X is a vector of 98 predetermined variables and a constant term. A and B are matrices of dimensions 176×176 and 176×99, respectively. The solution to this system is given by:

$$\text{(b)} \quad Y = (1 - A)^{-1} BX$$

This system of equations may be called the reduced form of the model because each of the 176 endogenous variables contained in Y is expressed as a linear function of the 99 predetermined variables *only*. (The constant term is treated as a "variable" whose value is fixed at 1.0.)

When the necessary calculations are carried out on the A and B matrices[16] from any of the three models whose results were reported above, a 176×99 set of reduced-form coefficients is obtained. Such a matrix of coefficients expresses in quantitative terms the impacts of each of the 99 predetermined variables on each of the 176 endogenous variables. Since many of the endogenous variables are of only secondary interest, and since a number of the predetermined variables are not policy instruments, there is no need to present the entire matrix of reduced-form coefficients.

For present purposes we shall confine most of our attention to the effects of the various policy instruments on the most important economic variables—GDP, C, BP, and SG—of each of the two periods. These effects are often referred to as the *policy multipliers*, a generalization of the familiar "*investment multiplier*," which can be derived from a naive Keynesian macroeconomic model and expresses the direct and indirect effects of investment on national income.

---

possibility of inconsistency in this respect. Fortunately, after allowing for transport costs the results have turned out to be relatively consistent, without the inclusion of such a constraint.

[16]The calculations are (1) to subtract the 176×176 A matrix from the 176×176 I matrix to get a 176×176 $(I - A)$ matrix, (2) to invert this matrix, and (3) to post-multiply it by the 176×99 B matrix. The resulting $(I - A)^{-1} B$ matrix is 176×99.

We shall illustrate the method as well as the kind of results we have obtained by presenting results obtained from the complete reduced-form solution to model 2. In order to keep the size of the tables within manageable limits, we shall confine our attention to the impacts of the five policy instruments (Te/Ex, Tn/Nx, To/GDP, G or Ig and DRM) of year t on only the three most important target variables (GNP, BP, and SG) in years t and $t + 1$. The impact multipliers expressing the effect of one percent changes in export tax rates, import tax rates, and "other" tax rates on each of the target variables are shown in tables 4-14, 4-15, and 4-16, respectively. The impact multipliers of government expenditures and the change in reserve money (DRM) are given in tables 4-17 and 4-18. Finally, for comparison purposes, we show the impact multipliers of the terms of trade (TT) and net factor income from abroad (NFY) in table 4-19.

Although the primary impact of changes in the policy instruments are felt in the country in which the action is taken, it should be clear from these results that the policy changes do have very substantial effects in the other countries of the CACM. It is not surprising to find out that the spreading effects on the other countries tend to be greater in the case of Honduras and Nicaragua, the countries with the greatest intraregional deficits.

It is the short-term nature of our models which is responsible for the result that export taxes and other taxes are generally harmful, while import duties are beneficial. The reader is warned not to be duped into thinking that import duties are beneficial. Indeed, the results reported in chapter 3 above indicate that the tariffs, especially unequal ones, have probably imposed substantial welfare losses that have been only partially alleviated by CACM participation. The finding here of the opposite effect is the result of the way our models work. Import taxes in the short run deter imports and, since imports are a subtraction from income in the GDP accounting identity, raise income and almost everything else, including the fiscal balance and international reserves. The rise in income in the country initiating the action raises imports from the other CACM members, raising exports and hence income and eventually investment in these countries.

Another result that these tables reveal is that the impact of any of these policy changes is not confined to a single time period. Indeed, in many instances the lagged effects of the policy changes are almost as great as the immediate effects. In the case of the change in the reserve money instrument the lagged effect is stronger than the simultaneous effect. This result is attributable to the importance of the lag operators in the monetary equations of model 2.

"Long-run" policy multipliers, which could be derived from the equilibrium or "steady-state" solution of the model in which all lagged

Table 4-14. The Effects in Millions of C.A. Pesos at 1962 Prices of a 1% Increase in the Export Tax Rate (Te/Ex) via Model 2

Country & variable affected	Country in which action is taken	Costa Rica	El Salvador	Guatemala	Honduras	Nicaragua
Central America						
GNPt		−20.2491	−4.4170	−5.4515	−42.3138	−1.5340
GNPt+1		−7.4965	−1.2195	−4.3085	−29.1828	−0.7103
Costa Rica						
GNPt		−18.9406	−0.0090	−0.0642	−2.1829	−0.0682
SGt		−2.2144	−0.0013	−0.0090	−0.3053	−0.0095
BPt		−4.2724	−0.0022	−0.0158	−0.5363	−0.0168
GNPt+1		−6.2294	−0.0059	−0.0728	−1.9208	−0.0464
SGt+1		−0.8711	−0.0008	−0.0102	−0.2690	−0.0065
BPt+1		1.7909	0.0001	−0.0065	−0.0853	−0.0007
El Salvador						
GNPt		−0.4315	−4.3756	−0.1137	−3.8624	−0.1207
SGt		−0.0427	0.1273	−0.0113	−0.3825	−0.0119
BPt		−0.0632	−0.1101	−0.0167	−0.5660	−0.0177
GNPt+1		−0.3122	−1.1801	−0.1301	−3.4407	−0.0835
SGt+1		−0.0309	−0.1169	−0.0129	−0.3407	−0.0083
BPt+1		0.0263	0.4076	−0.0001	0.1411	0.0079
Guatemala						
GNPt		−0.6656	−0.0246	−5.2179	−5.9586	−0.1862
SGt		−0.0602	−0.0022	0.3003	−0.5392	−0.0168
BPt		−0.1109	−0.0041	−0.1614	−0.9927	−0.0310
GNPt+1		−0.7708	−0.0271	−4.0336	−7.8975	−0.2096
SGt+1		−0.0698	−0.0025	−0.3650	−0.7147	−0.0190
BPt+1		0.0655	0.0026	0.7955	0.4201	0.0193
Honduras						
GNPt		−0.1019	−0.0038	−0.0268	−29.3295	−0.0285
SGt		−0.0088	−0.0003	−0.0023	−2.1439	−0.0025
BPt		−0.0224	−0.0008	−0.0059	−6.1073	−0.0063
GNPt+1		−0.0893	−0.0031	−0.0348	−14.9114	−0.0241
SGt+1		−0.0077	−0.0003	−0.0030	−1.2861	−0.0021
BPt+1		0.0106	0.0004	0.0003	5.4167	0.0032
Nicaragua						
GNPt		−0.1095	−0.0040	−0.0289	−0.9803	−1.1305
SGt		−0.0124	−0.0005	−0.0033	−0.1107	0.5919
BPt		−0.0224	−0.0008	−0.0059	−0.2010	0.4130
GNPt+1		−0.0948	−0.0033	−0.0371	−1.0124	−0.3467
SGt+1		−0.0107	−0.0004	−0.0042	−0.1143	−0.0391
BPt+1		0.0197	0.0008	0.0027	0.1426	0.1789

variables are equated with unlagged variables, are not presented because the long-run multiplier and, indeed, the whole concept of a steady-state were thought to be totally irrelevant to short or even medium-term policy decisions in Central America.[17]

[17]Such a procedure might, however, be of interest in the determination of the customs union effect, the full impact of which will clearly not be realized in one, two, or even six years.

The reader should be reminded that all the policy multipliers and the various implications of these results are explicitly based on the results of model 2. However, by comparing the policy multipliers presented in tables 4–14 through 4–18 for model 2 with the corresponding multipliers for models 1 and 3 in appendix B (tables B–1–A through B–1–F and B–2–A through B–2–F, respectively), it can be seen that the same general pattern of the results is obtained with these models. There are, of course, differences in the sizes of the various multipliers.

Table 4–15. The Effects in Millions of C.A. Pesos at 1962 Prices of a 1% Increase in Import Duty Rates (Tn/Nx) via Model 2

Country & variable affected	Country in which action is taken	Costa Rica	El Salvador	Guatemala	Honduras	Nicaragua
Central America						
GNPt		0.5306	5.2486	1.6259	3.1503	3.7474
GNPt+1		0.1519	0.3287	1.2092	2.1727	1.5451
Costa Rica						
GNPt		0.4963	0.0107	0.0192	0.1625	0.1666
SGt		0.9123	0.0015	0.0027	0.0227	0.0233
BPt		0.8611	0.0027	0.0047	0.0399	0.0409
GNPt+1		0.1216	0.0047	0.0208	0.1430	0.1050
SGt+1		0.0170	0.0007	0.0029	0.0200	0.0147
BPt+1		−0.0349	−0.0007	0.0017	0.0063	−0.0037
El Salvador						
GNPt		0.0113	5.1994	0.0340	0.2876	0.2948
SGt		0.0011	1.3617	0.0034	0.0285	0.0292
BPt		0.0017	1.5640	0.0050	0.0421	0.0432
GNPt+1		0.0072	0.2924	0.0372	0.2562	0.1890
SGt+1		0.0007	0.0290	0.0037	0.0254	0.0187
BPt+1		−0.0008	−0.1005	−0.0002	−0.0105	−0.0216
Guatemala						
GNPt		0.0174	0.0292	1.5563	0.4436	0.4547
SGt		0.0016	0.0026	1.3447	0.0401	0.0412
BPt		0.0029	0.0049	1.3624	0.0739	0.0758
GNPt+1		0.0187	0.0260	1.1305	0.5880	0.4891
SGt+1		0.0017	0.0023	0.1023	0.0532	0.0443
BPt+1		−0.0020	−0.0042	−0.2229	−0.0313	−0.0510
Honduras						
GNPt		0.0027	0.0045	0.0080	2.1836	0.0696
SGt		0.0002	0.0004	0.0007	0.5833	0.0060
BPt		0.0006	0.0010	0.0018	0.8166	0.0153
GNPt+1		0.0021	0.0027	0.0101	1.1101	0.0553
SGt+1		0.0002	0.0002	0.0009	0.0958	0.0048
BPt+1		−0.0003	−0.0007	−0.0002	−0.4033	−0.0085
Nicaragua						
GNPt		0.0029	0.0048	0.0086	0.0730	2.7617
SGt		0.0030	0.0005	0.0010	0.0082	0.7784
BPt		0.0006	0.0010	0.0018	0.0150	0.9844
GNPt+1		0.0022	0.0029	0.0107	0.0754	0.7069
SGt+1		0.0003	0.0003	0.0012	0.0085	0.0798
BPt+1		−0.0006	−0.0011	−0.0009	−0.0106	−0.3644

For example, an increase in the export tax rate of Guatemala of one percent (in absolute terms) would lower the GNP of Central America as a whole in the current year (year t) by 5.45 million C.A. pesos and that of the next year (year $t + 1$) by 4.31 million C.A. pesos according to table 4–14, which is based on model 2; alternatively according to appendix table B–1–A based on model 1, the same policy change would lower GNP of Central America in years t and $t + 1$ by 5.16 and 2.56, respectively; similarly, according to appendix table B–2–A based on

Table 4–16. The Effects in Millions of C.A. Pesos at 1962 Prices of a 1% Increase in "Other" Tax Rates (To/GDP) via Model 2

Country & variable affected	Country in which action is taken Costa Rica	El Salvador	Guatemala	Honduras	Nicaragua
Central America					
GNPt	−7.8288	−11.3658	−25.5651	−8.9522	−7.7602
GNPt+1	−2.2412	−0.7118	−19.0131	−6.1741	−3.1997
Costa Rica					
GNPt	−7.3229	−0.0232	−0.3013	−0.4618	−0.3450
SGt	3.4380	−0.0032	−0.0421	−0.0646	−0.0482
BPt	2.1140	−0.0057	−0.0740	−0.1135	−0.0848
GNPt+1	−1.7938	−0.0103	−0.3276	−0.4064	−0.2173
SGt+1	−0.2509	−0.0014	−0.0459	−0.0569	−0.0304
BPt+1	0.5156	0.0016	−0.0271	−0.0180	0.0077
El Salvador					
GNPt	−0.1668	−11.2593	−0.5332	−0.8172	−0.6104
SGt	−0.0165	4.7366	−0.0528	−0.0809	−0.0604
BPt	−0.0244	3.8932	−0.0781	−0.1197	−0.0894
GNPt+1	−0.1067	−0.6332	−0.5854	−0.7280	−0.3912
SGt+1	−0.0106	−0.0627	−0.0580	−0.0721	−0.0387
BPt+1	0.0122	0.2177	0.0033	0.0298	0.0446
Guatemala					
GNPt	−0.2573	−0.0632	−24.4694	−1.2606	−0.9417
SGt	−0.0233	−0.0057	7.5151	−0.1141	−0.0852
BPt	−0.0429	−0.0105	4.8390	−0.2100	−0.1569
GNPt+1	−0.2760	−0.0562	−17.7749	−1.6708	−1.0128
SGt+1	−0.0250	−0.0051	−1.6086	−0.1512	−0.0917
BPt+1	0.0289	0.0091	3.5047	0.0889	0.1056
Honduras					
GNPt	−0.0394	−0.0097	−0.1259	−6.2051	−0.1441
SGt	−0.0034	−0.0008	−0.0109	3.7097	−0.0124
BPt	−0.0086	−0.0021	−0.0276	2.2642	−0.0316
GNPt+1	−0.0312	−0.0059	−0.1570	−3.1547	−0.1144
SGt+1	−0.0027	−0.0005	−0.0136	−0.2721	−0.0099
BPt+1	0.0048	0.0016	0.0027	1.1460	0.0176
Nicaragua					
GNPt	−0.0423	−0.0104	−0.1353	−0.2074	−5.7190
SGt	−0.0048	−0.0018	−0.0153	−0.0234	3.9758
BPt	−0.0087	−0.0021	−0.0277	−0.0445	2.9687
GNPt+1	−0.0331	−0.0062	−0.1678	−0.2142	−1.4639
SGt+1	−0.0037	−0.0007	−0.0187	−0.0242	−0.1653
BPt+1	0.0083	0.0024	0.0139	0.0302	0.7545

Table 4-17. The Effects in Millions of C.A. Pesos at 1962 Prices of 1 Million C.A. Peso Increase in Government Expenditure (G or Ig) via Model 2

Country & variable affected	Country in which action is taken	Costa Rica	El Salvador	Guatemala	Honduras	Nicaragua
Central America						
GNPt		2.00	2.05	2.87	2.47	1.87
GNPt+1		0.57	0.13	2.13	1.70	0.77
Costa Rica						
GNPt		1.87	–	0.03	0.13	0.08
SGt		−0.74	–	–	0.02	0.01
BPt		−0.54	–	–	0.03	0.02
GNPt+1		0.46	–	0.04	0.11	0.05
SGt+1		0.06	–	–	0.02	–
BPt+1		−0.13	–	–	–	–
El Salvador						
GNPt		0.04	2.03	0.06	0.23	0.15
SGt		–	−0.80	–	0.02	0.01
BPt		–	−0.70	–	0.03	0.02
GNPt+1		0.03	0.11	0.07	0.20	0.09
SGt+1		–	0.01	–	0.02	0.01
BPt+1		–	−0.04	–	−0.01	−0.01
Guatemala						
GNPt		0.08	0.01	2.74.	0.35	0.23
SGt		–	–	−0.75	0.03	0.02
BPt		0.01	–	−0.54	0.06	0.04
GNPt+1		0.07	0.01	1.99	0.46	0.24
SGt+1		0.01	–	0.18	0.04	0.02
BPt+1		−0.01	–	−0.39	−0.02	−0.03
Honduras						
GNPt		0.01	–	0.01	1.71	0.03
SGt		–	–	–	−0.85	–
BPt		–	–	–	−0.62	–
GNPt+1		0.01	–	0.02	0.87	0.03
SGt+1		–	–	–	0.07	–
BPt+1		–	–	–	−0.32	–
Nicaragua						
GNPt		0.01	–	0.02	0.06	1.38
SGt		–	–	–	0.01	−0.84
BPt		–	–	–	0.01	−0.72
GNPt+1		0.01	–	0.02	0.06	0.35
SGt+1		–	–	–	0.01	0.04
BPt+1		0.01	–	–	−0.01	−0.18

model 3, the effect on GNP of Central America in the same two years would be 5.50 and 4.59, respectively.

In some cases, the multipliers vary to a larger extent, depending on the model, as can be seen in the case of the monetary policy instrument by comparing tables 4-18, B-1-E, and B-2-E. However, in this case it should be recalled that the definition of the policy instrument—RM in model 1, and DRM in models 2 and 3—is not the same and thus greater differences in multipliers should not seem surprising.

Table 4-18. The Effects in Millions of C.A. Pesos at 1962 Prices of a One Million C.A. Peso Increase in Reserve Money (DRM) via Model 2

Country & variable affected	Country in which action is taken	Costa Rica	El Salvador	Guatemala	Honduras	Nicaragua
Central America						
GNPt		7.99	4.23	0.31	−0.47	3.59
GNPt+1		8.29	6.08	0.25	−0.33	4.70
Costa Rica						
GNPt		7.47	0.38	–	−0.02	0.48
SGt		1.37	0.05	–	–	0.07
BPt		−0.30	0.09	–	–	0.12
GNPt+1		7.44	0.50	–	−0.02	0.55
SGt+1		1.16	0.07	–	–	0.08
BPt+1		0.61	0.06	–	–	0.05
El Salvador						
GNPt		0.17	2.47	–	−0.04	0.86
SGt		0.02	0.36	–	–	0.08
BPt		0.02	−0.28	–	–	0.13
GNPt+1		0.24	3.20	–	−0.04	0.98
SGt+1		0.02	0.42	–	–	0.10
BPt+1		0.01	−0.58	–	–	–
Guatemala						
GNPt		0.26	1.05	0.30	−0.07	1.32
SGt		0.02	0.09	0.22	−0.01	0.12
BPt		0.04	0.17	−0.70	−0.01	0.22
GNPt+1		0.48	1.84	0.23	−0.09	2.08
SGt+1		0.04	0.16	0.19	−0.01	0.19
GPt+1		–	–	−0.60	–	−0.04
Honduras						
GNPt		0.04	0.16	–	−0.32	0.20
SGt		–	0.01	–	–	0.02
BPt		–	0.04	–	−0.04	0.04
GNPt+1		0.06	0.24	–	−0.17	0.26
SGt+1		–	0.02	–	−0.01	0.02
BPt+1		–	–	–	0.06	–
Nicaragua						
GNPt		0.04	0.17	–	−0.01	0.73
SGt		–	0.02	–	–	0.09
BPt		–	0.04	–	–	−0.68
GNPt+1		0.07	0.25	–	−0.01	0.84
SGt+1		0.01	0.03	–	–	0.10
BPt+1		–	−0.01	–	–	−0.65

To a large extent, there is no particular pattern to the differences, the differences simply representing a moderate degree of sensitivity to the changes in specification. There is, however, one rather consistent difference—the intercountry policy multipliers are somewhat smaller in model 3 than in models 1 and 2.[18] Thus, while from tables 4-17 and appendix table B-1-D it can be seen that an increase of government

[18]Note that Nicaragua's policies have no effect on other countries in model 3.

spending in year t in Guatemala of 1.0 C.A. pesos raises GNP of Costa Rica in years t and $t + 1$, respectively, by 0.03 and 0.04 C.A. pesos according to model 2, and by 0.09 and 0.08 C.A. pesos according to model 1, from table B–2–D according to model 3, the corresponding increases are no larger than 0.00 and 0.01. This difference is attributable to the different way in which intraregional imports were handled in model 3 as opposed to models 1 and 2. However, since the main dif-

Table 4–19. The Effects in Millions of C.A. Pesos at 1962 Prices of a One Million C.A. Peso Increase in the Adjustment for Terms of Trade or Net Factor Income from Abroad (TT) or (NFY) via Model 2

Country & variable affected	Country in which action is taken	Costa Rica	El Salvador	Guatemala	Honduras	Nicaragua
Central America						
GNPt		2.75	2.94	3.63	3.11	2.79
GNPt+1		0.76	0.18	2.71	2.19	1.15
Costa Rica						
GNPt		2.64	–	0.03	0.11	0.12
SGt		0.23	–	–	0.02	0.02
BPt		0.53	–	–	0.03	0.03
GNPt+1		0.65	–	0.04	0.13	0.08
SGt+1		0.09	–	–	0.02	0.01
BPt+1		–0.19	–	–	0.01	–
El Salvador						
GNPt		0.04	2.92	0.05	0.19	0.22
SGt		–	0.19	–	0.02	0.02
BPt		–	0.33	–	0.03	0.03
GNPt+1		0.03	0.16	0.08	0.24	0.14
SGt+1		–	0.02	–	0.02	0.01
BPt+1		–	–0.06	–	–	–0.02
Guatemala						
GNPt		0.06	0.01	3.51	0.28	0.34
SGt		–	–	–0.23	0.03	0.03
BPt		0.01	–	–0.50	0.05	0.05
GNPt+1		0.07	0.01	2.55	0.50	0.37
SGt+1		0.01	–	0.23	0.04	0.03
BPt+1		0.01	–	–0.51	–	–0.04
Honduras						
GNPt		0.01	–	0.01	2.46	0.05
SGt		–	–	–	0.13	–
BPt		–	–	–	0.47	0.01
GNPt+1		0.01	–	0.02	1.25	0.04
SGt+1		–	–	–	0.11	–
BPt+1		–	–	–	–0.46	–
Nicaragua						
GNPt		0.01	–	0.01	0.05	2.05
SGt		–	–	–	0.01	0.12
BPt		–	–	–	0.01	0.32
GNPt+1		0.01	–	0.02	0.07	0.53
SGt+1		–	–	–	0.01	0.06
BPt+1		–	–	–	–	–0.27

ference in this case is that of delay in the timing of the effects, i.e., shifting the incidence from year t to year $t + 1$, $t + 2$, etc., the differences observed are more apparent than real.

I. TESTING THE MODELS

Our main purpose in presenting each of the above models or their results was to provide the basis for simulating the potential gains in welfare attributable to policy coordination in Central America and to determine the sensitivity of the results to changes in model specification.

However, both for that purpose and for purposes of drawing explicit policy conclusions from the results presented above, it is useful to get some idea of the empirical relevance of the models.

We shall not attempt formal tests of the models against either serious or naive alternative hypotheses. Rather, following conventional practice, we have provided two bases for a cursory evaluation of the present models.

First, in appendix tables B–3, B–4, and B–5, are presented the historical forecasts of each of the seventeen endogenous variables for each of the five countries of models 1, 2, and 3, respectively, for the period 1951–66. These "forecasts" have been obtained by multiplying the values of each of the predetermined variables (presented in appendix tables A–1 through A–5) by the appropriate set of coefficients from the reduced-form solutions (derived from the results of tables 4–2 through 4–13 above and from which the policy multipliers discussed above have been drawn). Naturally, these forecasts are not really predictions, as the data points used in making the forecasts were not independent of the parameters of the models.[19]

Second, since 1967 data were not used in estimating the model, we have presented in table 4–20 true forecasts of several of the most crucial variables for that year, alongside the actual values (according to the preliminary figures presented in appendix A). These forecasts have been obtained by exactly the same means as the historical "forecasts," except that preliminary 1967 figures for the predetermined variables (given in appendix A) have been used.

Turning first to the historical forecasts, by comparing the forecasts of models 1, 2, and 3, that are given in appendix tables B–3, B–4, and B–5, respectively, with the corresponding data series in appendix A, it can be seen that models 1, 2, and 3 provide predictions of the endog-

---

[19]The same data were used for estimating the parameters of the models, thereby biasing the forecast values toward the actual value.

Table 4-20. Comparative Forecasts for 1967

	Variable	Acual 1967 vaiue	Forecasts Via model 1	Via model 2	Via model 3
Costa Rica	GNP	658.0	630.0	669.4	660.6
	C	490.7	462.3	487.6	488.5
	Ip	95.1	99.1	103.7	103.7
	SG	−35.0	−24.4	−18.2	−18.1
	BP	−43.4	−62.3	−52.8	−52.5
El Salvador	GNP	831.5	860.8	837.0	839.2
	C	686.3	703.4	682.2	284.1
	Ip	92.4	106.7	100.9	100.9
	SG	−1.5	−2.2	−3.9	−3.7
	BP	−38.5	−44.6	−41.4	−41.1
Guatemala	GNP	1321.3	1367.7	1374.9	1402.7
	C	1067.3	1149.9	1156.0	1163.4
	Ip	183.1	182.7	178.8	178.8
	SG	−36.7	−24.4	−24.2	−12.9
	BP	−65.8	−51.7	−46.7	−26.2
Honduras	GNP	538.0	542.9	556.4	556.9
	C	424.0	424.1	433.9	434.3
	Ip	60.1	56.5	58.4	58.4
	SG	−17.3	−15.5	−14.6	−14.6
	BP	−16.4	−8.0	−6.3	−6.1
Nicaragua	GNP	506.3	481.7	503.2	445.1
	C	413.4	375.6	391.3	344.9
	Ip	81.1	81.3	81.1	81.1
	SG	−25.2	−26.2	−22.0	−28.6
	BP	−68.8	−35.7	−29.9	−41.6
Central America	GNP	3855.1	3883.0	3940.9	3944.4
	C	3081.7	3115.2	3151.1	3145.2

enous variables that, although quite different from each other, are always of the correct order of magnitude. This demonstrates that the three models differ considerably from one another and yet that each model is empirically relevant to the Central American region.

The percentage errors of forecast vary from variable to variable, from year to year, and from model to model. Nevertheless, it is possible to make a few generalizations:

1) The forecast errors for GNP are almost always less than 10 percent and frequently are less than one percent. In almost every case, the larger errors can be traced to unusually large discrepancies between predicted and actual extraregional exports and/or private investment.[20]

2) The percentage errors in some of the larger variables, such as money, credit, and capital, are usually very small.

[20]These are variables which are typically rather volatile and depend to a large extent on external forces and subjective and qualitative elements that are difficult to quantify.

3) The percentage errors in the balance-of-payments variables (BP) which incorporate the errors in a number of different equations are usually very large, even though the absolute discrepancies may be fairly small. (Nevertheless, the year-to-year patterns of these variables are fairly representative of the actual patterns.) On the other hand, errors in the tax variables and in SG are generally very small in relative, as well as absolute, terms.

4) The ability of the models to "predict" cyclical swings in GNP and periodic crises in the balance of payments and the fiscal position varies from model to model. Models 2 and 3 generally perform better in this regard than model 1. Referring specifically to model 2, cyclical troughs or slowdowns are correctly predicted in 1955, 1961, and 1964 for Costa Rica; 1954, 1955, 1958–59 for El Salvador; 1954–55 and 1958 for Guatemala; 1953–55 and 1960 for Honduras; and 1958 for Nicaragua. However, the model erred in predicting that 1962 would have been a depression year in El Salvador; 1960 a recession year in Guatemala; and it exaggerated several of the slumps in the region, especially that of 1957 in Nicaragua. Although not very accurate in predicting the balance-of-payments surplus or deficit, the model correctly "predicted" the larger crises in the balance of payments in each country; i.e., 1965, 1966 in Costa Rica, 1959–60 and the late 1960s in El Salvador, 1955–58 and 1965 in Guatemala, 1954 and 1963–64 in Honduras, and 1954–56, 1958 and 1964–66 in Nicaragua.[21]

We turn now to the 1967 forecasts shown in table 4–20 for a few of these same variables. To facilitate comparisons, the forecasted values from each of the three models are given side-by-side along with the actual values. Once again, some of the variables are more accurately predicted by one model, others by another. We shall leave it up to the reader to conduct his own test and choose his own model. In each case the predictive ability of the model for 1967 (one year beyond the date used in estimating the model) is not significantly different from that demonstrated by the historical "forecasts" for the 1951–66 period. Thus, there is no evidence to suggest that the model is less relevant to present-day Central America than it was for the 1950s and early 1960s.

A thorough comparative evaluation of the models would require the specification of a set of weights expressing the relative importance of each of the endogenous variables. Such an activity, however, would hardly seem relevant and appropriate in the present circumstances in which we are using the three different models for simulation and sen-

---

[21]The reader should be reminded that our definition of the balance-of-payments variable (BP), i.e., equation (4.16) above, does not correspond to the conventional definition.

sitivity analysis. The above comparisons are based upon the several variables—GNP, *BP*, *SG*—which we subjectively have felt to be most important in the present context.

Eventually, as alternative models of a similar nature become available, it may be possible to carry out more meaningful comparisons by comparing the forecasts of serious alternative models with those of the present models. Certainly, the errors of forecast observed in both sets of comparisons are large enough to urge caution, if not total disrespect, upon anyone—academician, businessman, or policy-maker—who would like to draw specific conclusions from any of the present models. Any important private or public decisions should be based on much more careful and detailed investigations. Nevertheless, the errors are small enough to give us reason to believe that each of the models is sufficiently different and yet sufficiently realistic so that collectively they may provide a satisfactory basis for simulating the potential welfare gains attributable to policy coordination. Should the reader feel that the errors of forecast seem excessive compared to those he may have seen in models for other countries, he should be reminded that the present models start more or less from scratch, treating only truly exogenous phenomena as given, whereas many of the other models that have been developed and which may have yielded generally smaller percentage errors of forecast, have treated as given such important, though difficult to predict, variables as exports and investment.

5 a quantitative assessment of the potential welfare gains from policy coordination at the regional level

Once the complete (reduced-form) solutions to the two-year versions of models 1, 2, and 3 are obtained, which, as discussed above, explain the values that each of the endogenous variables take on for each of two years t and $t + 1$ in terms only of policy instruments and other predetermined variables, we can turn the analysis around to draw our policy implications.

In Tinbergenian terms the economic variables, which previously have been treated as the endogenous variables (or unknowns in the system of equations), can be designated as target variables (the values of which can be specified by the policy-maker), and the policy instruments (which were previously treated as exogenous variables) become the endogenous variables (or unknowns) to be solved for.

Tinbergen (1952) distinguished between fixed targets (e.g., income must equal 100 in year t) and flexible targets (e.g., income should be maximized in year t). He also emphasized the relationship between the number of targets and number of instruments. In the fixed-target case an equal number of targets and instruments generally implies a unique solution. If the number of instruments is less than the number of targets, there will normally be no solution. To obtain a feasible solution, one either has to dispose of targets or add instruments to create equality between the numbers of instruments and of targets.

In the case of flexible targets and in the case of fixed targets with more instruments than targets, a number of solutions will generally be possible and one or more maximizing criteria can be adopted as a means of choosing among solutions. Tinbergen developed the concept of an efficiency coefficient (representing the impact on the target of a one-unit increase in the instrument) and briefly treated methods for comparing the efficiency of different policies, and for handling inconsistency between short-term and long-term policies or targets. Nevertheless, the stress of his work has been more on counting instruments and targets and on fixed-target problems, than on methods of maximizing with respect to flexible targets. Hansen (1958) showed that dynamic systems, such as the two-year versions of the models developed in the previous chapter, can be handled without greater difficulty.

In his major extensions of and contributions to the theory of economic policy, Theil (1964, 1965) concentrated on flexible-target problems. The use of flexible targets eliminates concern for the mechanical process of counting variables, instruments, etc., and allows the policy-maker to retain all relevant targets without having to discard some in order to preserve the needed equality between instruments and targets. However, since Theil's flexible target (preference) function is a quadratic function of targets and instruments in which one minimizes the sum of the weighted squares of deviations of instruments and targets from desired levels, the spirit of Theil's method is still very close to that of fixed targets. Furthermore, this approach has the unfortunate quality of treating positive and negative deviations from the stated values as equally undesirable. However, in general, it seems likely that preferences are likely to be asymmetric, i.e., people will prefer more income to less income, etc.

Fox, Sengupta, and Thorbecke (1966) have managed to mitigate some of these shortcomings, but their approach is based upon the presumption that the model-builder would be able to extract the exact weights which the planners attach to each different goal, i.e., a complete specification of the planner's welfare function. It is our contention that, even if it were possible to interview the policy-makers in depth, to examine their written and oral pronouncements in detail, or to study their past decisions in respect to the circumstances within which these decisions were made (as if to derive their "revealed preferences"), it is highly doubtful that the model-builder would be able to come up with any particular welfare specification that the policy-makers would be willing to stick with regardless of the consequences. The policy-maker is not only likely to be unable to reveal all the subtleties of his welfare function, but he is likely not to want to reveal them, even if he could, for fear that the model-builder might subsequently show him that rationally he should do something that he really doesn't want to do.

Therefore, it would seem that policy models must be used in such a way as to provide the policy-makers with more useful and comprehensive results without requiring full disclosure of their welfare function. The policy-maker should be shown not only the relation of individual targets to individual goals or the substitutability of one instrument for another, as has become customary, but also the possibility-trade-offs between each of his different goals.[1] What is needed is a complete set (a whole matrix as it were) of possibility-trade-offs which would allow the policy-maker to study the implications of all the alternatives before him in terms of different combinations of goal satisfaction and instrument manipulation. Knowing the *possibility*-trade-offs between instruments and goals among instruments themselves *and* between and among the different goals, the policy-maker would then be able to select that policy package which equates the demonstrated possibility-trade-offs with his own subjective *desirability*-trade-offs.

A. PROCEDURE

Let us suppose that we wish to demonstrate to an individual policy-maker in any individual country in the CACM the possibility trade-offs available to him. For simplicity we shall outline as follows the procedure in terms of a single country, thereby avoiding the need to use country subscripts:

First, we arbitrarily pick one goal, e.g., GDP in the country, as the single (flexible) target to be maximized,

(5.1)   GDP = Maximum

Second, we set appropriate constraints on each of the other welfare goals in the country

(5.2) $C \geqq C \text{ min}$

(5.3) $I \geqq I \text{ min}$

---

[1]In an interesting paper, Alfred H. Conrad (1968) emphasized the importance of this task and offered his assessment that it could be accomplished. Nugent and DePrano (1966) developed the specific methods for obtaining a set of such trade-offs that will be employed here.

(5.4) $\qquad$ $BP \geq BP\ min$

(5.5) $\qquad$ $SG \geq Sg\ min$

Third, we include the trade-offs between instruments and targets for the particular country obtainable from the reduced-form solutions to the models in chapter 4:

$$(5.6) \qquad GDP = C_{10} + C_{11}\frac{Te}{Ex} + C_{12}\frac{Tn}{Nx} + C_{13}\frac{To}{GDP} + C_{14}RM$$

$$+ C_{15}G + C_{16}Ig$$

$$(5.7) \qquad C = C_{20} + C_{21}\frac{Te}{Ex} + C_{22}\frac{Tn}{Nx} + C_{23}\frac{To}{GDP} + C_{24}RM$$

$$+ C_{25}G + C_{26}Ig$$

$$(5.8) \qquad I = C_{30} + C_{31}\frac{Te}{Ex} + C_{32}\frac{Tn}{Nx} + C_{33}\frac{To}{GDP} + C_{34}RM$$

$$+ C_{35}G + C_{36}Ig$$

$$(5.9) \qquad BP = C_{40} + C_{41}\frac{Te}{Ex} + C_{42}\frac{Tn}{Nx} + C_{43}\frac{To}{GDP} + C_{44}RM$$

$$+ C_{45}G + C_{46}Ig$$

$$(5.10) \qquad SG = C_{50} + C_{51}\frac{Te}{Ex} + C_{52}\frac{Tn}{Nx} + C_{53}\frac{To}{GDP} + C_{54}RM$$

$$+ C_{55}G + C_{56}Ig$$

Estimates of the C_{ij} coefficients can be obtained from the reduced-form solutions to the model. Thus for model 2, estimates of the coefficients for all countries have already been given in tables 4–14 to 4–19.[2] For any individual country, the actual (or, alternatively, the optimal) values of the policy instruments of all other countries as well as those of the other predetermined variables can be multiplied by the corresponding reduced-form coefficients and then combined with the constant term in what might be called a consolidated version of the reduced-form solution. This step in the specification of the policy model is common also to the Tinbergen and Theil approaches.

Fourth, we impose upper and lower bounds on each of the policy instruments so as to represent political constraints on extreme policy

---

[2]Alternatively, estimates of the coefficients for models 1 and 3 can be found in appendix tables B–1 and B–2, respectively.

changes. The particular upper and lower bounds chosen reflect either maximum positive and negative year-to-year changes or maximum positive and negative deviations from the historical trends in the policy variables—whichever seems most appropriate in the particular country under consideration.

$$(5.11) \quad \frac{Te}{Ex} \geq \frac{Te}{Ex} \text{ Min} \qquad (5.17) \quad \frac{Te}{Ex} \leq \frac{Te}{Ex} \text{ Max}$$

$$(5.12) \quad \frac{Tn}{Nx} \geq \frac{Tn}{Nx} \text{ Min} \qquad (5.18) \quad \frac{Tn}{Nx} \leq \frac{Tn}{Nx} \text{ Max}$$

$$(5.13) \quad \frac{To}{GDP} \geq \frac{To}{GDP} \text{ Min} \qquad (5.19) \quad \frac{To}{GDP} \leq \frac{To}{GDP} \text{ Max}$$

$$(5.14) \quad RM \geq RM \text{ Min} \qquad (5.20) \quad RM \leq RM \text{ Max}$$

$$(5.15) \quad G \geq G \text{ Min} \qquad (5.21) \quad G \leq G \text{ Max}$$

$$(5.16) \quad Ig \geq Ig \text{ Min} \qquad (5.22) \quad Ig \leq Ig \text{ Max}$$

Since all of the variables can be scaled (and the constraints and equations changed accordingly), one can add nonnegativity constraints on each of the target and instrument variables. This gives to the system of equations and inequalities (5.1) to (5.22) the form of a linear programming model.

$$\text{Max} \quad CX$$
$$[I - A] \quad X \leq B$$
$$X \geq O$$

The "dual" of the above "primal" linear programming formulation has the following form:

$$\text{Min} \quad PB'$$
$$P[I - A]' \geq C'$$
$$P \geq O$$

The linear programming form offers the great advantage that solutions to both the primal and the dual can be obtained easily and quickly. If there exists a feasible solution to either the primal or the dual problem, there generally exists an infinite number of solutions from which an optimal solution can be chosen. From the primal solution we can obtain the optimal policy package (X), as well as the maximum welfare attainable (CX), given the constraints. From the dual solution we obtain the shadow prices (P) representing the cost in terms of welfare of tightening each particular constraint by one unit. The way our system has been formulated, it is the shadow prices that provide both the trade-offs between each limitation on each policy instrument and the welfare criterion (GDP) and the trade-offs between each other welfare goal (C, I, BP, and SG) and GDP. Since all the shadow prices are relative prices, and since all are relative to the same standard (in this case GDP), ratios of the different shadow prices of the different constraints can also be calculated. Thereby, a whole matrix of all the possible trade-offs between each policy instrument and welfare goal and each and every other policy instrument and welfare goal can easily be obtained. These trade-offs are the *possibility*-trade-offs. With knowledge about the *possibility*-trade-offs, the policy-maker can choose the optimal policy mix by matching the possibility-trade-offs with his *desirability*-trade-offs. (It has frequently been found in linear and quadratic programming problems that the shadow prices are less sensitive to change in specification and constraints than are the primal problem solutions. In such cases they may be considered more reliable).[3]

Similarly, the reduced-form solutions and constraints with respect both to the welfare goals and to the policy instruments given by (5.1) to (5.22) for any individual country can be fitted together with those of the other members of the CACM with coefficients obtainable from the complete reduced-form solutions from chapter 4. The logical criterion function for the resulting combined linear programming model for Central America as a whole is maximization of regional GDP as defined in equations (4.171-2) in chapter 4 above. Primal problem solutions in this case give the optimal policy package and attainable values of the various goals for each of the countries when policy decisions for the different countries are made simultaneously, i.e., are completely co-ordinated, and the dual solution will now contain all the possibility-trade-offs not only within each country but also between countries. By comparing the possibility-trade-offs and regional and national GDP and other goal attainment levels obtained from autonomous national decision-making models on the one hand and the regionalized coordi-nated decision-making model on the other hand, one can obtain a quan-titative estimate of the benefits of harmonization or coordination in the sense defined above.

The essence of our procedure for estimating the potential benefits of policy coordination consists of making just such comparisons—of the welfare achievable under the traditional pattern of autonomous decision-making at the national level with that achievable under complete policy

---

[3]However, as Westphal (1971) pointed out, it may be difficult to interpret shadow prices unambiguously in situations where the primal problem includes various kinds of side constraints.

coordination at the regional level—for each of two different sets of assumptions about the nature of the political feasibility and secondary target constraints.

The reader familiar with the literature in economics concerning developmental externalities and planning may recall that a similar approach was used some time ago by Chenery (1959) in demonstrating the advantage of coordinating investment decisions with and without the existence of economies of scale. While Chenery's approach failed to differentiate between the advantages of coordination of investment and those of perfect information, in our application of the procedure we shall make such a distinction as will be explained shortly.

It should be recalled that the number of instruments is vital both to the fixed-target approaches and to flexible-target approaches. In the former the number of instruments must be equal to the number of targets, if a unique solution to the policy problem is to be obtained. In the latter approach (including the present generalization thereof), the greater the number of instruments the greater will be the flexibility that the planner has in selecting his trade-offs.

What does economic integration do to the number of policy instruments available to any member country? Judging from recent events in Central America, the commitment to participate in the CACM seems to imply a sacrifice in autonomous discretion in the use of certain of the most important policy instruments—tariff policy and exchange-rate policy. For example, one policy instrument whose use seems to be greatly restricted by participation in the CACM is the exchange rate. Guatemala, Honduras, and El Salvador have never used the exchange-rate instrument in recent years and thus may never have missed the liberty of using it. For the other two countries, however, Nicaragua and Costa Rica—which have generally followed more expansionary monetary and fiscal policies and offset their relatively more inflationary effects as far as the balance of payments is concerned with occasional devaluations—and particularly for Costa Rica, which, as shown in tables 1-1 and 1-4, has come to face increasingly serious deficits in its trade and balance of payments, the inability to use this instrument may have imposed substantial social costs. As early as 1967, Costa Rica attempted to devaluate but was told by its CACM partners that it could not do so, at least with respect to intraregional transactions. This resulted in a dual exchange rate for a certain period of time, i.e., a higher number of colones per dollar on extraregional transactions than for intraregional ones, but since the IMF would not permit this, eventually the dual exchange rate was reunified at the pre-1967 rate. As an attempt to offset, avoid, or at least postpone the increasing crunch of the balance-of-payments deficit, Costa Rica has apparently gone into the business of borrowing from foreign commercial banks and even into the dubious practice of attracting "hot money" from troubled financial organizations, such as Investors Overseas Services. Certainly, these alternative stop-gap measures have been less desirable than devaluation, especially as far as long-run development is concerned. Therefore, for a country like Costa Rica, the commitment to economic integration has involved an unknown amount of welfare loss due to the constraints on the use of its policy instruments that have been imposed on it by its partners. The magnitude of that loss for Costa Rica (and Nicaragua) would depend on the comparative advantage that a policy package *in*cluding exchange rate policy would have over a policy package *ex*cluding exchange rate policy in satisfying the socioeconomic goals of these particular countries, given the resource, behavioral, and other constraints within which they must operate.

Of course, the other advantages of CU participation on static and dynamic efficiency, resource availability, etc. within the economic sphere, as we have already seen in chapter 3, can and evidently have offset the loss in potential welfare that may be implied by the reduction in terms of policy flexibility. Indeed, we have already calculated the net benefits of CU participation to be quite substantial. In Central America the reduction in policy flexibility as a result of union seems to have been small—at least in most of the countries of the region.

However, there would not seem to be any inherent reason why participation in a CU should necessarily lead to less flexibility and hence lower welfare. Indeed, by appropriate coordination among countries it would seem conceivable that a greater amount of flexibility could be achieved.

The issue is indeed a much broader one than the single example given above indicates; it involves the much discussed but often ambiguous terms of "harmonization" or "coordination" of policy within an integrated area. Ambiguity in the meaning of these terms stems from the fact that many different definitions are possible. To avoid such ambiguity, we shall define harmonization as the regionalized coordination of policies.[4]

Our purpose will be to demonstrate the advantage of harmonization in this sense over the alternative "traditional" model of nonharmonized national decision-making. We shall restrict ourselves to a comparison

---

[4]Another common definition of harmonization is tax rate and/or subsidy equalization among member countries. The desirability of this kind of harmonization is a matter of some controversy (Balassa 1961), but the same argument presented above in terms of the benefits derived from the effect of a common external tariff on the variation in the degree of distortion from commodity to commodity would presumably be applicable to harmonization of indirect tax rates.

of welfare achievable under a system in which all policies are determined in a centralized manner at the regional level and one in which each country's policies are determined centrally at the national level. (Other interesting comparisons, such as between decentralized and centralized decision-making at the national level, or comparisons between policy planning with a short-run time horizon and that with a long-run planning horizon, will not be attempted in this study, but could easily be undertaken by the interested reader with the analytical framework provided here.) If the benefits of regionalized planning turn out to be negligible, it would indeed be difficult to make a strong case for harmonization in the sense of our definition. If, on the other hand, the benefits turn out to be considerable, policy-makers must be shown the cost that their societies would have to pay if they remain unwilling to coordinate. The conclusions should also hold, although to a lesser extent, for any other form of coordination in between the extremes of centralized decision-making and completely decentralized decision-making.

It should be admitted that "regionalized coordination of policy decisions" is not an unambiguous phrase in itself. Each of the member countries has its own welfare function (goals), and the concept of decision-making at the regional level presumes that the different national objectives must be weighted in some way so as to add up to a regional preference function (or a set of goals with regionally set priorities). It is, of course, quite likely that the resulting optimal policy mix would be quite sensitive to the particular weights assigned to each country's objectives. However, we shall argue that in our case the use of a common objective, such as maximization of regional GDP (which implies an equal weighting of a dollar's worth of GDP in every country) subject to side constraints of various kinds reflecting desired equity, the limits of political feasibility, and other welfare goals, reveals substantial benefits to regional coordination of policy that remain fairly stable no matter which model or which set of constraints is used.

It must also be pointed out that the task of estimating the benefits of policy coordination, while conceptually quite simple, is not an easy one. Moreover, virtually no studies of this sort have ever been attempted.[5]

[5]Two recent studies by Cooper (1968, 1969) attempt to provide the theoretical foundation for such an approach. Cooper concentrates on the dynamics of policy adjustment in the decentralized context and also investigates different degrees of coordination, which are issues well beyond the scope of this study. The quantitative results presented in the latter paper are basically hypothetical. A particularly interesting result, and one which suggests that any results should be used with caution, is the sensitivity of the comparisons between coordinated and uncoordinated policy solutions to changes in certain parameters in the model relating policies to economic variables. The potential benefits of policy coordination have also been discussed by Tinbergen (1963) but never estimated.

B. DETAILED DESCRIPTION OF METHODS USED

We shall return now to describe how we implemented the step-by-step procedure outlined for the single-country case in equations (5.1)–(5.22) above.

In each case, we have chosen to maximize the present value of GDP_t and GDP_{t+1} which at a zero rate of discount is simply $GDP_t + GDP_{t+1}$ where $t = 1967$ and $t + 1 = 1968$. The lower bounds on the secondary welfare goals (Yd, C, Ip, MS, SG, and BP) have been set for both 1967 and 1968 at their actual 1967 levels (given by the 1967 entries for the respective variables in the data shown in appendix A). In the Central American regional model the objective was to maximize GDP^{CACM} subject to the additional constraints on GDP in each country, such that GDP in each country could be no lower than the actual 1967 values.

From the complete reduced-form solutions to each of the models we have arrived at consolidated versions of the reduced forms by multiplying the reduced-form coefficients of the nonpolicy instrument exogenous variables (i.e., the coefficients TT_i, NFY_i, N_{us}, $\sum_{j=1}^{4} Ni_{j \neq i}^{j}$, R^t, $TIME$, Zcm) and those of the appropriate lagged endogenous variables (i.e., in model 1 the coefficients of GNP_{t-1}, $[GNP_{1966}]$, K_{t-1} and I_{t-1} and in models 2 and 3 also of E_{t-1}, MS_{t-1}, CR_{t-1} and Ni_{t-1}), in the former instance by the actual 1967 and 1968 levels of the exogenous variables and in the latter cases by the 1966 values of these endogenous variables. Naturally, the variable $\sum_{j=1}^{4} Ni_{j \neq 1}^{j}$ is exogenous only in the case of the individual country models. In the regional Central American model, in which all policies of all countries are determined simultaneously, all of the Ni^j variables are endogenous.

Then from the resulting consolidated reduced-form matrix (expressing the relationship of each of the policy instruments on each of the endogenous variables in the system) we select only those rows corresponding to endogenous variables in which we are particularly interested. Thus, several of the less important variables, such as credit, tax revenue collected (by type), etc., can be eliminated for simplicity. This consolidated and abbreviated reduced-form matrix has the form $Y^* = (I - A)^{*-1} B^* X^* + C$, where the stars indicate the designated portions of the vectors and matrices of the original Y, X vectors and $(I - A)$ and B matrices from the complete models.

For the upper and lower bounds on the policy instruments which represented the fourth step in our procedure, we have used the following rules:

Public Expenditure and Reserve Money Variables (G, Ig, and RM)

1) Lower bounds: the actual 1967 values (from appendix A) for both years t and $t + 1$.

2) Upper bounds: for year t (1967) the actual 1967 value plus the largest historical one-year increase; for year $t + 1$ (1968) the actual 1967 value plus twice the largest historical single-year increase.

In models 2 and 3 the change in reserve money (DRM) is the policy instrument. The lower bound was the lowest historical increase in reserve money and the upper bound was the largest historical increase.

Tax Rate Variables ($\frac{Te}{Ex}$, $\frac{Tn}{Nx}$, and $\frac{To}{GDP}$)

1) Lower bounds: zero for $\frac{Te}{Ex}$, $\frac{To}{GDP}$, and 0.10 for $\frac{Tn}{Nx}$

2) Upper bounds: the highest historical rate

Since the latter set of constraints, i.e., the upper and lower bounds on the tax rate variables, were thought to be intentionally but unrealistically loose, we decided to experiment with another alternative set of bounds that would be considerably tighter than these. This alternative set of bounds is henceforth referred to as "Type 2" bounds as opposed to the original looser bounds identified as "Type 1" bounds.

The major difference is that the *lower* bounds on $\frac{Tn}{Nx}$ were *lower* in the Type 2 set than in the Type 1 set. The Type 1 bounds are given in table 5–1 and the Type 2 bounds in table 5–2.

This completes the procedure. After these calculations, adjustments, and additions, we have versions of models 1, 2, and 3 for each individual country and for Central America as a whole that are of the linear programming form described above. The advantage of this linear programming form lies in the power of the solutions provided: on the one hand, a set of relative shadow prices representing the possibility-trade-offs between each and every policy instrument and each and every target, and on the other hand, the optimal values of the policy instruments and the maximum attainable levels of the targets. Our present objective is to compare the welfare obtainable when complete coordination of policies is possible among countries of the region (utilizing the full Central America model) with that obtainable when no coordination of policy among CACM members is possible (utilizing the separate national models). Therefore, we shall confine our attention to the primal problem solutions—the optimal values of the policy instruments and especially of the target variables.

Table 5-1. Type 1 Bounds for 1967 and 1968

	Target variable	Lower bounds 1967-68	Instrument variable	Lower bounds 1967-68	Upper bounds 1967	Upper bounds 1968
Costa Rica	GDP	673.4	G	101.9	120.0	140.0
	Yd	557.0	Ig	29.0	37.0	45.0
	C	490.7	RM	61.2	72.0	83.0
	Ip	95.1	DRM	0	15.0	15.0
	MS	114.7	Te/Ex	0	5.2	5.2
	SG	−35.0	Tn/Nx	20	35.0	35.0
	BP	−43.4	To/GDP	0	8.2	8.2
El Salvador	GDP	830.7	G	65.3	71.0	77.0
	Yd	744.0	Ig	26.0	40.0	54.0
	C	686.3	RM	101.0	116.0	131.0
	Ip	92.4	DRM	0	15.0	15.0
	MS	104.0	Te/Ex	0	29.0	29.0
	SG	−32.2	Tn/Nx	10	20.5	20.5
	BP	−38.5	To/GDP	0	7.6	7.6
Guatemala	GDP	1372.4	G	99.8	120.0	124.0
	Yd	1221.3	Ig	36.9	50.0	65.0
	C	1067.3	RM	132.4	145.0	158.0
	Ip	183.1	DRM	0	11.0	11.0
	MS	156.6	Te/Ex	0	26.5	26.5
	SG	−36.7	Tn/Nx	10	31.0	31.0
	BP	−65.8	To/GDP	0	5.8	5.8
Honduras	GDP	561.4	G	53.7	62.0	70.0
	Yd	485.0	Ig	16.6	25.0	32.0
	C	424.0	RM	36.1	41.0	46.0
	Ip	60.1	DRM	0.9	4.4	4.4
	MS	52.0	Te/Ex	0	2.8	2.8
	SG	−17.3	Tn/Nx	10	25.6	25.6
	BP	−16.4	To/GDP	0	6.0	6.0
Nicaragua	GDP	547.3	G	53.6	59.0	64.0
	Yd	450.9	Ig	27.0	32.0	37.0
	C	413.4	RM	41.4	50.0	58.0
	Ip	81.1	DRM	0	8.0	8.0
	MS	67.0	Te/Ex	0	9.0	9.0
	SG	−25.2	Tn/Nx	10.0	29.5	29.5
	BP	−68.8	To/GDP	0	6.3	6.3

Source: Rules presented in text and data presented in appendix A.

C. RESULTS

Using model 1 in the way we have just described, with Type 1 bounds for Central America as a whole, we obtain from the optimal primal solution to the linear programming model the values for 1967 and 1968 given in the first two columns (i.e., the columns indicated "LPC unadjusted") of table 5-3. The optimal solutions for the individual country models are given in the fourth pair of columns (i.e., the columns indicated "LPI unadjusted"). Note that in all cases the values of the GDP and

Table 5-2. Type 2 Bounds for Instrument Variables for 1967 and 1968

Country	Variable	Lower bounds 1967-68	Upper bounds 1967	1968	Variable	Lower bounds 1967-68	Upper bounds 1967-68
Costa Rica	G	101.9	120	140	Te/Ex	0	5.2
	Ig	29.0	37	45	Tn/Nx	20	31.0
	DRM	0	15	15	To/GDP	0	8.2
El Salvador	G	65.3	71	77	Te/Ex	7.7	29.0
	Ig	26.0	40	54	Tn/Nx	10.0	15.0
	DRM	0	20	20	To/GDP	0	7.6
Guatemala	G	99.8	112	124	Te/Ex	2.4	26.5
	Ig	36.9	50	65	Tn/Nx	10.0	12.6
	DRM	0	11	11	To/GDP	0	5.8
Honduras	G	53.7	62	70	Te/Ex	0.5	2.8
	Ig	16.6	25	32	Tn/Nx	10.0	18.4
	DRM	0.9	4.4	4.4	To/GDP	0	6.0
Nicaragua	G	53.6	59.0	64.0	Te/Ex	0	9.0
	Ig	27	32	37	Tn/Nx	10	15.0
	DRM	0	25	25	To/GDP	0	6.3

Note: All other bounds are identical to those indicated by Type 1 bounds in table 5-1.

most of the other target variables are larger in the Central America model (in which the policies of all countries are determined simultaneously) than in the single-country model (in which the policies of each country are determined separately). Similarly, the optimal solutions to the target variables from the Central America model and the individual-country models are presented in the first and fourth pairs of columns, respectively, in tables 5-4 and 5-5 when Type 1 bounds are applied to models 2 and 3, respectively. In these cases, the Central America solutions are not always better than the individual-country solutions.

However, the difference in these two sets of optimal solution values is not only attributable to different approaches to policy determination but also the estimation errors in the intraregional import equations (Ni)—the only equations treated differently in the aggregate Central America model and in the individual-country models. The reader will recall that Ni variables of the other countries are treated as exogenous variables in the individual-country models but are, of course, endogenous in the aggregate Central America model. In the former set of models no estimation error is involved, whereas, in the latter model estimation error is introduced. In order to account for this difference in treatment we have computed the difference in the values of the constant terms in the consolidated and abbreviated reduced-form equations attributable to this source. We have then adjusted the original constant terms in the individual country models upward by the extent to

Table 5–3. Optimal Solutions for Model 1 with Type 1 Bounds

| | Comparison 1 | | | | | | Comparison 2 | | | |
| | LPC Unadjusted | | LPI Adjusted | | LPI (adjusted & perfect information) | | LPI Unadjusted | | LPC Adjusted | |
	1967	1968	1967	1968	1967	1968	1967	1968	1967	1968
GDPCR	795.0	853.2	709.7	763.8	686.0	779.5	725.3	780.2	811.3	871.2
CCR	594.2	615.0	508.7	547.2	491.7	559.4	524.3	557.9	595.6	627.4
IPCR	100.1	175.2	100.1	124.8	100.1	119.6	100.1	128.3	100.1	178.9
SGCR	-32.9	8.5	-20.9	-1.3	-18.8	3.1	-23.1	0.5	-35.0	10.2
BPCR	-43.4	-43.4	-43.4	-43.4	-43.4	-43.4	-43.4	-43.4	-43.4	-43.4
GDPE	1089.9	1169.4	976.3	1007.0	985.0	1049.5	1025.5	1067.3	1144.0	1184.0
CE	899.1	961.0	805.3	820.7	824.7	847.8	854.5	872.8	953.3	1012.3
IPE	119.0	155.3	119.0	135.3	119.0	141.3	119.0	143.6	119.0	157.1
SGE	5.6	38.5	11.7	26.1	10.7	30.1	8.0	31.5	1.5	40.2
BPE	-38.5	-38.5	-38.5	-38.5	-38.5	-38.5	-38.5	-38.5	-38.5	-38.5
GDPG	1667.6	1917.6	1551.9	1742.6	1585.8	1759.6	1594.1	1808.3	1714.6	1985.8
CG	1366.3	1548.3	1260.0	1441.0	1290.2	1455.1	1298.8	1494.8	1409.4	1607.2
IPG	141.1	193.3	141.1	170.4	141.1	177.1	141.1	178.8	141.1	195.9
SGG	-36.7	-13.9	-36.7	-27.1	-36.7	-21.7	-36.7	-23.6	-36.7	-9.9
BPG	-52.8	-65.8	-62.4	-65.8	-59.6	-65.8	-58.9	-65.8	-49.0	-65.8
GDPH	654.2	701.2	627.6	665.9	630.0	669.8	647.4	689.0	673.9	724.8
CH	486.9	521.8	466.9	496.2	467.7	499.2	481.1	512.6	504.0	538.8
IPH	65.1	101.6	65.1	83.2	65.1	84.0	65.1	89.7	65.1	108.0
SGH	-17.3	-9.2	-17.3	-13.8	-17.3	-13.5	-17.3	-10.0	-17.3	-5.5
BPH	-3.3	-16.4	-6.5	-16.4	-6.2	-16.4	-4.2	-16.4	-0.5	-16.4
GDPN	624.5	709.5	603.7	677.4	614.2	690.4	606.5	681.4	629.0	713.9
CN	460.9	526.5	437.8	497.8	447.1	508.7	440.3	501.4	460.4	530.4
IPN	92.3	126.0	92.3	127.8	92.3	129.4	92.3	116.5	92.3	141.2
SGN	-25.2	-25.2	-25.2	-25.2	-25.2	-25.2	-25.2	-25.2	-25.2	-25.2
BPN	-35.7	-45.4	-38.4	-45.0	-37.3	-45.3	-38.1	-45.0	-35.7	-45.1
GDPCM	4831.2	5351.0	4469.2	4856.7	4595.2	4948.8	4598.8	5026.2	4972.9	5524.2
CCM	3807.4	4172.6	3478.7	3802.9	3596.7	3901.5	3599.0	3939.5	3922.6	4315.8

Table 5–4. Optimal Solutions for Model 2 with Type 1 Bounds

| | LPC Unadjusted | | Comparison 1 | | | | Comparison 2 | | | | | |
| | | | LPI Adjusted | | LPI (adjusted & perfect information) | | LPI Unadjusted | | LPC Adjusted | | LPI (unadjusted & perfect information) | |
	1967	1968	1967	1968	1967	1968	1967	1968	1967	1968	1967	1968
GDPCR	946.5	1185.5	870.0	1092.4	885.2	1129.8	944.6	1146.1	1012.8	1239.4	950.8	1183.6
CCR	690.8	860.1	632.1	790.1	636.7	818.3	688.9	830.4	757.7	900.4	695.1	858.6
IPCR	136.7	187.9	136.7	177.8	136.7	178.7	136.7	187.6	136.7	197.8	136.7	188.5
SGCR	-10.2	17.2	-2.0	17.0	-2.6	13.1	-10.0	21.1	-19.5	21.4	-10.8	18.1
BPCR	-43.4	-43.4	-43.4	-43.4	-43.4	-43.4	-43.4	-43.4	-43.4	-43.4	-43.4	-43.4
GDPE	1004.3	1135.6	952.7	1049.3	952.0	1084.0	1009.9	1097.2	1062.4	1184.1	1009.2	1131.9
CE	830.8	926.2	799.7	874.1	799.0	908.9	856.4	914.9	889.7	967.7	856.2	949.7
IPE	101.0	130.6	101.0	124.1	101.0	124.1	101.0	131.3	101.0	137.9	101.0	131.2
SGE	-9.1	15.1	-7.4	11.6	-7.3	9.6	-10.6	16.5	-12.4	20.2	-10.5	14.5
BPE	-38.5	-38.5	-38.5	-38.5	-38.5	-38.5	-38.5	-38.5,	-38.5	-38.5	-38.5	-38.5
GDPG	1650.0	2139.8	1600.5	2081.3	1592.2	2048.0	1666.9	2153.9	1720.9	2206.6	1657.6	2133.6
CG	1349.6	1774.0	1304.1	1718.5	1296.5	1698.1	1365.0	1788.1	1414.7	1830.0	1356.5	1769.1
IPG	128.8	199.0	128.8	186.8	128.8	185.0	128.8	203.8	128.8	219.3	128.8	201.2
SGG	-36.7	-29.5	-36.7	-36.7	-36.7	-36.7	-36.7	-26.0	-36.7	-14.4	-36.7	-26.9
BPG	-41.5	-65.8	-48.1	-65.8	-49.7	-65.8	-40.1	-65.8	-35.5	-65.8	-40.9	-65.8
GDPH	665.6	815.1	660.1	804.0	657.0	802.6	669.8	816.2	675.6	828.0	666.6	814.8
CH	497.3	613.3	492.9	604.7	490.5	603.6	500.5	614.2	505.1	623.5	498.1	618.2
IPH	63.4	96.2	63.4	89.6	63.4	93.7	63.4	97.4	63.4	99.0	63.4	96.5
SGH	-17.3	-17.3	-17.3	-17.3	-17.3	-17.3	-17.3	-17.3	-17.3	-17.3	-17.3	-17.3
BPH	1.9	-11.1	1.1	-11.0	0.7	-10.3	2.4	-12.1	3.2	-12.5	2.0	-11.4
GDPN	626.2	741.1	621.9	733.9	622.3	737.8	617.2	735.8	621.9	743.3	617.6	739.6
CN	458.3	555.4	454.5	548.9	454.8	552.4	450.3	550.6	454.5	557.4	450.6	554.1
IPN	90.0	113.1	90.0	111.7	90.0	111.8	90.0	111.5	90.0	113.0	90.0	111.6
SGN	-25.2	-25.2	-25.2	-25.2	-25.2	-25.2	-25.2	-25.2	-25.2	-25.2	-25.2	-25.2
BPN	-34.1	-46.0	-34.6	-45.3	-34.5	-45.1	-35.0	-44.9	-34.6	-45.7	-35.0	-44.6
GDPCM	4891.9	6021.7	4705.2	5760.9	4708.7	5802.2	4908.4	5949.2	5093.6	6073.6	4901.8	6003.5
CCM	3826.9	4728.9	3683.3	4536.3	3677.5	4581.3	3861.1	4698.2	4021.0	4879.1	3856.5	4744.7

Table 5–5. Optimal Solutions for Model 3 with Type 1 Bounds

| | Comparison 1 | | | | | | Comparison 2 | | | |
| | LPC Unadjusted | | LPI Adjusted | | LPI (adjusted & perfect information) | | LPI Unadjusted | | LPC Adjusted | |
	1967	1968	1967	1968	1967	1968	1967	1968	1967	1968
GDPCR	933.7	1156.9	881.9	1102.2	870.1	1108.4	944.6	1146.1	996.1	1199.7
CCR	678.0	838.5	633.8	797.5	624.9	802.2	688.9	830.4	741.0	870.5
IPCR	136.7	185.9	136.7	173.1	136.7	176.3	136.7	187.6	136.7	195.2
SGCR	-8.4	18.2	-2.2	16.3	-1.0	16.8	-10.0	21.1	-17.3	23.1
BPCR	-43.4	-43.4	-43.4	-43.4	-43.4	-43.4	-43.4	-43.4	-43.4	-43.4
GDPE	985.9	1096.3	955.8	1062.8	934.5	1073.2	1009.9	1097.2	1040.2	1129.5
CE	813.2	892.7	802.8	887.2	781.5	900.4	856.8	914.9	867.5	921.1
IPE	101.0	128.3	101.0	124.5	101.0	121.9	101.0	131.3	101.0	135.1
SGE	-8.1	14.7	-7.5	11.3	-6.4	7.9	-10.6	16.5	-11.1	20.0
BPE	-38.5	-38.5	-38.5	-38.5	-38.5	-38.5	-38.5	-38.5	-38.5	-38.5
GDPG	1778.8	2365.4	1760.9	2328.1	1760.9	2355.5	1662.6	2073.2	1682.2	2107.6
CG	1468.4	1956.1	1452.0	1933.6	1452.0	1956.4	1361.8	1720.6	1379.8	1723.3
IPG	128.8	233.3	128.8	228.2	128.8	228.2	128.8	202.7	128.8	208.3
SGG	-36.7	-10.3	-36.7	-13.4	-36.7	-15.7	-36.7	-19.7	-36.7	-14.4
BPG	-31.5	-65.8	-33.0	-65.8	-33.0	-65.8	-41.1	-65.8	-39.5	-65.8
GDPH	662.2	805.6	660.7	805.2	653.7	798.9	669.8	816.2	671.3	818.5
CH	494.6	605.9	493.4	605.4	487.9	600.7	500.5	614.2	501.7	616.9
IPH	63.4	94.2	63.4	89.8	63.4	92.8	63.4	97.4	63.4	97.8
SGH	-17.3	-17.3	-17.3	-17.3	-17.3	-17.3	-17.3	-17.3	-17.3	-17.3
BPH	1.4	-11.4	0.3	-9.9	0.3	-9.8	2.4	-12.1	2.6	-12.8
GDPN	602.5	728.1	596.4	719.5	589.8	713.5	609.7	737.6	615.8	756.0
CN	436.7	543.1	428.7	535.4	425.4	530.1	443.2	551.6	448.6	559.1
IPN	90.0	107.9	90.0	106.1	90.0	104.1	90.0	110.1	90.0	111.9
SGN	-25.2	-25.2	-25.2	-25.2	-25.2	-25.2	-25.2	-25.2	-25.2	-25.2
BPN	-36.2	-41.5	-36.8	-40.6	-37.5	-39.2	-35.4	-42.7	-34.8	-43.7
GDPCM	4963.1	6152.3	4855.7	6017.8	4809.0	6049.5	4896.6	5870.3	5005.6	6011.3
CCM	3890.9	4836.5	3810.7	4759.1	3771.7	4789.8	3851.2	4631.7	3938.6	4686.9

which the Central America model was overestimating each endogenous variable and downward by the extent to which the model was underestimating each endogenous variable. Conversely, the opposite set of adjustments can be made in the constant terms of the Central America model to make the results comparable with the unadjusted individual-country solutions.[6] The optimal solutions obtained from the adjusted individual-country models are now given in the second pair of columns (those indicated by "LPI Adjusted") in each of the tables. Similarly, the optimal solutions obtained from the adjusted Central America model are now given in the fifth pair of columns (those indicated by "LPC Adjusted") in each of these tables.

The solution values for the target variables from the first and second pairs of columns are now comparable, in as much as the effect of estimation error in the Ni equations has now been accounted for. Similarly, and for the same reasons, the fourth and fifth pairs of columns are comparable. As the reader can easily see, without exception when full coordination of policies among countries is possible (as in the Central America model) higher targets are achievable than when no such coordination is possible.

However, it is still possible that our comparisons yield an overestimate of the true benefit from regional coordination of macroeconomic policies in Central America. This is because the individual-country optimizations were computed without the benefit of knowledge about the optimal policy decisions in the other countries, whereas complete coordination of policy in the Central America model was sufficient to provide perfect information. One might wonder how much better the individual countries might have been able to do with respect to their goals if they had perfect information about what the other countries would be doing at the optimum. We have recalculated the individual-country model maximizations under conditions where each individual country knows the optimal solutions of the other individual countries[7] by plugging optimal values of $\sum_{j=1}^{4} Ni_{j\neq1}^{j}$ (instead of *actual* values)

---

[6]The need for such an adjustment would have been alleviated to some extent if, as pointed out in footnote 15 of chapter 4, a constraint guaranteeing equality between intraregional imports and exports had been imposed.

[7]This adjustment may still be incomplete. Logically, a complex and iterative tâtonnement process would be involved whereby observed differences between the *assumed* optimal solutions of other countries and the *computed* optimal solutions of other countries would be introduced into a new set of assumed optimal solutions, and a subsequent set of optimal solutions would be computed. The process could and presumably should be repeated until (hopefully) convergence is reached. This iterative process was not followed because the initial differences between the assumed and computed optimal solutions were very small.

into the reduced-form coefficients in arriving at the values of the constant terms in the consolidated and abbreviated reduced forms. The resulting constant terms can either be left alone (unadjusted) or can be adjusted to account for estimation error in the Ni terms as before. The sets of optimal solutions for the individual-country models resulting from the latter operation to models 1, 2, and 3 are shown in the third pair of columns (indicated "LPI Adjusted and Perfect Information") in tables 5-3, 5-4, and 5-5, respectively. The former alternative (leaving the terms unadjusted) was utilized only in model 2. The set of optimal solutions computed in this case is shown in the sixth and last pair of columns (indicated "LPI Unadjusted and Perfect Information") of table 5-4. These columns are comparable with the fifth pair of columns, i.e. ("LPC Adjusted") while the third pair of columns ("LPI Adjusted and Perfect Information") are comparable to the first pair ("LPC Unadjusted").

The reader can easily see that the provision of perfect information generally brings the noncoordinated policy model (the individual-country model) solutions somewhat closer to those of the complete coordination of policy model (the Central America model) especially in the case of model 1. However, the effect of perfect information is not generally very large—accounting for only a small fraction of the differences between the comparable solutions obtained under complete coordination of policy and in the absence of such coordination.

The same procedures that were employed with respect to the looser Type 1 bounds in obtaining the results recorded in tables 5-3, 5-4, and 5-5 have been employed with respect to models 1, 2, and 3 and Type 2 bounds in tables 5-6, 5-7, and 5-8, respectively. Since the adjustment for perfect information in the individual-country models did not seem to make much difference in the case of the Type 1 bounds for models 2 and 3 and since the results in the case of Type 2 bounds for model 1 paralleled the results obtained for model 1 with Type 1 bounds, this adjustment was not carried out in tables 5-7 and 5-8.

The percentage increases in GDP in the current year attributable to policy coordination (based on the results of tables 5-3 through 5-8) are summarized in table 5-9. In a few cases, there are sizable variations in the estimates for an individual country depending on which model was used, which type of bounds, and which type of comparison. For example, in El Salvador the range of estimates of the GDP gain goes all the way from a low of 2 percent in the case of model 3 with Type 2 bounds and "comparison 1" to about 12 percent in the case of model 1 with Type 1 bounds and "comparison 2." In other countries, however, the results are far less sensitive to such changes and in some countries the results are remarkably stable. The estimates tend to be

Table 5–6. Optimal Solutions for Model 1 with Type 2 Bounds

	Comparison 1						Comparison 2			
	LPC Unadjusted		LPI Adjusted		LPI (adjusted & perfect information)		LPI Unadjusted		LPC Adjusted	
	1967	1968	1967	1968	1967	1968	1967	1968	1967	1968
GDPCR	745.7	822.6	691.2	765.7	infeasibility		707.0	782.1	766.6	844.5
CCR	544.7	597.3	491.7	554.8	encountered		506.9	565.5	565.6	612.4
IPCR	100.1	162.3	109.8	119.0	in solution		100.1	122.6	100.1	167.1
SGCR	-25.9	-1.9	-18.9	-8.1	for Costa Rica		-20.5	-6.4	-30.6	0.5
BPCR	-43.4	-43.4	-43.4	-43.4			-43.4	-43.4	-43.4	-43.4
GDPE	938.3	1005.7	863.2	891.5	875.6	933.5	916.4	951.4	993.8	1027.6
CE	761.3	818.8	695.7	720.4	715.6	747.2	745.4	772.1	820.6	876.2
IPE	119.0	135.8	115.5	120.1	118.8	125.9	119.0	128.2	119.0	142.1
SGE	13.1	26.7	14.2	16.4	16.4	20.2	13.9	21.7	8.8	32.7
BPE	-38.5	-38.5	-38.5	-38.5	-38.5	-38.5	-38.5	-38.5	-38.5	-38.5
GDPG	1555.2	1761.9	1471.0	1648.1	1512.6	1665.1	1520.9	1712.8	1603.4	1838.8
CG	1263.1	1424.9	1185.9	1366.4	1224.1	1378.8	1231.7	1424.8	1307.4	1488.9
IPG	141.1	171.0	137.8	154.1	141.1	162.7	141.1	164.2	141.1	173.8
SGG	-36.7	-25.0	-36.7	-36.7	-36.7	-29.3	-36.7	-31.8	-36.7	-21.2
BPG	-62.1	-65.8	-65.8	-65.8	-65.7	-65.8	-65.0	-65.8	-58.1	-65.8
GDPH	620.6	661.2	598.0	632.0	600.4	636.0	617.9	655.1	641.1	685.7
CH	463.5	494.6	447.6	473.6	448.4	476.6	461.5	490.0	478.0	512.2
IPH	65.1	93.7	65.1	76.0	65.1	76.5	65.1	80.0	65.1	98.6
SGH	-17.3	-12.7	-17.3	-17.3	-17.3	-17.3	-17.3	-16.0	-17.3	-10.7
BPH	-7.0	-16.4	-9.6	-16.4	-9.3	-16.4	-7.4	-16.4	-4.7	-16.4
GDPN	586.1	660.6	572.4	640.3	583.4	652.8	575.6	644.0	590.0	666.9
CN	426.5	482.8	413.4	464.6	419.6	475.1	413.4	467.9	430.0	488.4
IPN	92.3	131.8	92.3	123.3	92.3	124.6	92.3	123.5	92.3	135.6
SGN	-25.2	-25.2	-25.2	-25.2	-25.2	-25.2	-25.2	-25.2	-25.2	-25.2
BPN	-39.8	-44.5	-41.3	-44.5	-40.6	-44.6	-41.3	-44.3	-39.3	-44.5
GDPCM	4445.8	4912.0	4195.8	4577.6	see note	above	4337.8	4745.4	4595.1	5108.0
CCM	3559.0	3818.4	3234.3	3579.8			3358.0	3720.4	3601.5	3977.9

Table 5-7. Optimal Solutions for Model 2 with Type 2 Bounds

	Comparison 1				Comparison 2			
	LPC Unadjusted		LPI Adjusted		LPI Unadjusted		LPC Adjusted	
	1967	1968	1967	1968	1967	1968	1967	1968
GDPCR	936.9	1184.6	856.1	1078.5	930.7	1132.2	1003.0	1239.2
CCR	707.3	862.4	624.6	782.6	675.1	822.8	747.3	903.3
IPCR	136.7	186.7	136.7	176.0	136.7	185.8	136.7	196.6
SGCR	−12.5	15.7	−0.9	16.2	−8.0	20.3	−18.1	19.9
BPCR	−43.4	−43.4	−43.4	−43.4	−43.4	−43.4	−43.4	−43.4
GDPE	923.3	1070.4	870.9	974.6	928.0	1022.6	981.8	1119.8
CE	746.8	869.9	714.1	796.1	771.3	836.9	805.3	912.1
IPE	101.0	134.1	104.8	127.5	104.8	134.7	104.8	141.4
SGE	−0.7	21.8	1.1	19.3	−2.0	24.2	−3.9	26.8
BPE	−38.5	−38.5	−38.5	−38.5	−38.5	−38.5	−38.5	−38.5
GDPG	1551.8	1991.2	1490.0	1869.1	1550.1	1933.1	1613.9	2082.5
CG	1259.5	1635.9	1202.9	1524.1	1258.1	1582.7	1316.6	1745.1
IPG	136.8	179.3	139.0	169.0	130.9	174.4	128.8	191.1
SGG	−36.7	−36.7	−36.7	−36.7	−36.7	−36.7	−36.7	−34.9
BPG	−57.6	−65.8	−65.1	−65.8	−51.9	−65.8	−44.5	−65.8
GDPH	627.2	758.3	619.2	740.2	628.9	752.5	637.1	771.4
CH	469.5	571.3	463.3	557.2	470.9	566.8	477.3	581.5
IPH	63.4	85.5	63.4	78.2	63.4	86.0	63.4	88.3
SGH	−17.3	−17.3	−17.3	−17.3	−17.3	−17.3	−17.3	−17.3
BPH	−2.8	−7.6	−3.9	−7.6	−2.6	−8.8	−1.5	−9.0
GDPN	583.0	697.5	579.8	692.5	575.1	694.4	578.5	700.0
CN	420.1	516.3	417.6	511.8	413.9	513.5	416.6	518.5
IPN	90.0	130.9	90.0	129.9	90.0	129.7	90.0	130.8
SGN	−25.2	−25.2	−25.2	−25.2	−25.2	−25.2	−25.2	−25.2
BPN	−52.7	−68.3	−53.0	−67.8	−53.4	−67.4	−53.1	−68.0
GDPCM	4622.1	4943.7	4416.0	5354.9	4612.8	5534.8	4814.3	5141.4
CCM	3603.3	4455.8	3422.5	4171.8	3589.3	4322.7	3763.1	4660.5

somewhat larger according to model 1 than according to models 2 or 3. This, however, is largely attributable to the more direct response to policy changes postulated in this model relative to models 2 and 3, where lags in response were utilized to a greater degree. Thus, as noted above, smaller estimates of gains from policy coordination according to models 2 and 3 relative to model 1 in the current period may be made up for by greater gains in future periods.

However, the most striking feature of the results is the stability of the results for Central America as a whole, as well as of the relative position of the different countries. The overall potential gains from policy coordination for the region as a whole appear to be quite sizable— from 2 percent to 7 percent of the region's GDP. These benefits would be distributed somewhat unevenly, the smaller countries, like Costa Rica and El Salvador, generally benefiting more than the larger ones, like Guatemala, unless the smaller ones are not in a position to take advantage of export opportunities within the region.

Table 5-8. Optimal Solutions for Model 3 with Type 2 Bounds

| | Comparison 1 | | | | Comparison 2 | | | |
| | LPC Unadjusted | | LPI Adjusted | | LPI Unadjusted | | LPC Adjusted | |
	1967	1968	1967	1968	1967	1968	1967	1968
GDPCR	913.5	1138.4	868.0	1088.4	888.3	1051.7	975.9	1181.2
CCR	660.8	827.5	626.3	790.0	642.7	763.5	720.8	859.5
IPCR	136.7	183.1	136.7	171.3	127.0	168.7	136.7	192.4
SGCR	−6.0	17.0	−1.2	15.5	−13.2	11.6	−14.4	21.9
BPCR	−43.4	−43.4	−43.4	−43.4	−43.4	−43.4	−43.4	−43.4
GDPE	891.1	1006.9	874.0	988.1	891.1	978.5	945.4	1040.2
CE	718.7	815.8	717.2	809.2	738.1	803.0	769.0	844.2
IPE	104.8	130.0	104.8	127.9	101.0	124.5	104.8	136.9
SGE	0.9	20.7	1.0	19.0	−3.9	15.9	−1.9	26.0
BPE	−38.5	−38.5	−38.5	−38.5	−38.5	−38.5	−38.5	−38.5
GDPG	1654.0	2166.6	1641.7	2161.4	1543.6	1905.9	1557.5	1908.8
CG	1353.9	1790.6	1342.6	1812.9	1252.7	1558.7	1265.4	1559.8
IPG	128.8	200.0	128.8	196.5	129.0	171.2	128.8	175.0
SGG	−36.7	−28.7	−36.7	−34.3	−36.7	−36.7	−36.7	−32.8
BPG	−41.8	−65.8	−42.9	−65.8	−51.1	−65.8	−49.8	−65.8
GDPH	621.0	742.4	619.8	741.4	628.9	752.5	630.1	753.5
CH	464.7	558.9	463.8	557.8	470.9	566.8	471.8	567.2
IPH	63.4	82.7	63.4	78.3	63.4	86.8	63.4	87.3
SGH	−17.3	−17.3	−17.3	−17.3	−17.3	−17.3	−17.3	−17.3
BPH	−3.7	−7.9	−3.8	−6.5	−2.6	−8.8	−2.5	−9.3
GDPN	579.7	738.0	575.5	732.9	589.6	750.8	593.2	765.8
CN	417.1	552.0	413.4	547.4	425.2	563.4	428.4	567.9
IPN	90.0	129.4	90.0	128.4	90.0	132.3	90.0	133.3
SGN	−25.2	−25.2	−25.2	−25.2	−25.2	−25.2	−25.2	−25.2
BPN	−52.7	−62.0	−52.8	−61.5	−51.7	−63.5	−51.4	−64.1
GDPCM	4659.3	5792.4	4579.0	5712.2	4541.5	5439.4	4702.1	5637.4
CCM	3615.2	4544.8	3563.3	4517.3	3529.6	4255.4	3655.4	4395.4

Table 5-9. Percentage Increases in GDP Attributable to Regional Coordination of Macroeconomic Policies in Central America in Year t (%)

| | Model: Bounds Type: | Model 1 | | Model 2 | | Model 3 | |
		Type 1	Type 2	Type 1	Type 2	Type 1	Type 2
Costa Rica		12–14%	7%	6–7%	8%	6%	6–10%
El Salvador		10–12	6	5	6	4–6	2–5
Guatemala		5–7	3	4	4	2	1–6
Honduras		−1–5	3–4	1	1.3	0.2–1.5	0.4
Nicaragua		1–3	0.5–2.0	0.7	.5	1–1.5	0.7
Central America		5–7	3.5	3.5	4	2.5–3.5	2–4

Source: Tables 5-2 through 5-8.

In order to give the reader a feel for how the higher incomes are generated when policies are coordinated, we present in table 5-10 the optimal policy solutions for the coordinated case "LPC Adjusted" side-by-side with those for the uncoordinated case "LPI Unadjusted" for model 1 with Type 1 bounds for years t (1967) and $t + 1$ (1968). The pattern of the results obtained from the other models or sets of bounds is sufficiently similar that the results shown in table 5-10 may be considered fairly representative of all the results.

How can these alternative optimal policy solutions be characterized? Coordination of policies generally makes it possible for each individual

Table 5-10. Comparisons of Optimal Policies between "LPC Adjusted" and "LPI Unadjusted" Solutions Using Model 1 with Type 1 Bounds

Country	Variable	Solution values			
		1967		1968	
		LPC Adjusted	LPI Unadjusted	LPC Adjusted	LPI Unadjusted
CR					
	G	116.8	101.9	101.9	101.9
	Ig	37.0	37.0	29.0	29.0
	RM	70.6	72.0	70.1	70.1
	Te/Ex	0	0.7	0	0
	Tn/Nx	35.0	35.0	35.0	35.0
	To/GDP	5.1	5.8	8.1	8.2
ES					
	G	71.0	65.3	70.6	65.3
	Ig	40.0	26.0	26.0	26.0
	RM	116.0	116.0	131.0	123.3
	Te/Ex	0	0	0	0
	Tn/Nx	20.5	20.5	20.5	20.5
	To/GDP	5.2	4.4	7.6	7.6
GU					
	G	112.0	112.0	124.0	109.9
	Ig	50.0	50.0	65.0	36.9
	RM	145.0	145.0	132.4	132.4
	Te/Ex	0	0	0	0
	Tn/Nx	31.0	31.0	31.0	31.0
	To/GDP	1.2	2.3	4.0	0
HO					
	G	62.0	62.0	53.9	68.1
	Ig	25.0	25.0	32.0	16.6
	RM	41.0	41.0	46.0	46.0
	Te/Ex	0	0	0	0
	Tn/Nx	25.6	25.6	25.6	25.6
	To/GDP	4.8	5.9	6.0	6.0
NI					
	G	59.0	59.0	64.0	64.0
	Ig	32.0	32.0	37.0	37.0
	RM	50.0	50.0	58.0	58.0
	Te/Ex	9.0	9.0	9.0	9.04
	Tn/Nx	29.5	29.5	29.5	29.5
	To/GDP	1.8	2.4	1.5	2.4

country to adopt more expansionary policies than it would be able to adopt in the absence of coordination. These more expansionary policies raise exports and indirectly investment and income, etc. For example, coordination makes it possible for Costa Rica to follow more expansionary spending policies (higher G and Ig) and to lower its export and "other tax" rates (Te/Ex and To/GDP, respectively) in return for a slightly less expansionary monetary policy (RM). El Salvador is able to increase government spending in the current period (t) and money supply in year $t + 1$ at the cost of a slightly higher "other tax" rate To/GDP. Similarly, Guatemala is able to trade off an increase in the "other tax" rate in year $t + 1$ for a reduction in the "other tax" rate in year t and an increase in government spending in year $t + 1$. Honduras is able to reduce its "other tax" rate in year t and to raise government spending in year $t + 1$. Finally, Nicaragua is able to reduce its "other tax" rate in year t and lower its export tax rate in year $t + 1$.

What these solutions reflect is that the greater flexibility derived from a simultaneous solution to the policy instruments of all countries allows the countries to trade off slack in some of the less-binding resources or constraints for additional flexibility in some of the more-binding ones. For example, the shadow prices obtained from the dual solution for the individual-country version of model 1 with Type 1 bounds (corresponding to the primal solution designated as LPI in table 5–10) reveal that the balance-of-payments constraint (BP) is the dominant constraint when Costa Rica determines its policies autonomously, without the cooperation of the other Central American countries. In the shadow-price solutions for the corresponding LPC model, which incorporates complete coordination of policies among countries, there is no longer a single dominant constraint. More of the constraints are binding simultaneously. In other countries different constraints are binding. For example, in the case of Guatemala in model 1, without coordination it is the government savings constraint (SG) which is binding. However, in all cases the impact of coordination is the same: the various policy changes outlined above between the uncoordinated and coordinated policy versions serve to substitute more intensive use of the less constrained variables for less intensive use of or greater availability of the more constrained variables, in the process allowing incomes to rise.

Since intraregional trade provides the vital link between the individual-country models, and because trade continues to play a very important role in the Central American countries, we present in sections A and B, respectively, of table 5–11 the optimal solutions with respect to the trade variables attainable without coordination and those attainable with coordination.

Table 5-11. Measurement of Trade-Creation Attributable to Policy Coordination (Based on Model 1 with Type 1 Bounds)

A. Without Coordination (LPI Unadjusted)					
	Costa Rica	El Salvador	Guatemala	Honduras	Nicaragua	Central America
1967 Values						
Ex	177.3	186.8	218.6	202.5	183.3	968.5
Ei	37.1	77.4	75.8	25.3	19.1	234.7
E	214.4	264.2	294.4	227.8	202.4	1203.2
Nx	209.3	222.9	234.6	138.7	168.2	973.3
Ni	33.1	90.6	57.5	70.0	31.2	282.4
N	242.4	313.5	292.1	208.7	199.4	1256.1
1968 Values						
Ex	187.7	196.0	250.8	212.5	214.0	1061.0
Ei	41.1	88.1	80.4	28.4	23.6	261.6
E	228.8	284.1	331.2	240.9	237.6	1322.6
Nx	215.1	236.1	269.0	151.6	202.1	1073.9
Ni	40.6	88.3	75.2	72.3	33.0	309.4
N	255.7	324.4	344.2	223.9	235.1	1383.3

B. With Coordination (LPC Adjusted)					
	Costa Rica	El Salvador	Guatemala	Honduras	Nicaragua	Central America
1967 Values						
Ex	193.5	186.8	218.6	220.4	183.3	1002.6
Ei	49.2	99.1	90.0	31.6	25.0	294.9
E	242.7	285.9	308.6	252.0	208.3	1297.5
Nx	219.9	229.6	247.4	143.7	178.0	1018.6
Ni	50.8	105.7	69.0	79.5	35.0	340.0
N	270.7	335.3	316.4	223.2	213.0	1358.6
1968 Values						
Ex	187.7	211.5	250.7	230.4	214.0	1094.3
Ei	63.5	111.9	111.1	41.7	33.0	361.2
E	251.2	323.4	361.8	271.1	247.0	1455.5
Nx	228.8	247.4	282.7	160.0	206.1	1125.0
Ni	59.3	111.2	92.2	95.1	48.5	406.3
N	288.1	368.6	374.9	255.1	254.6	1531.3

C. Net Trade-Creation resulting from Coordination					
	Costa Rica	El Salvador	Guatemala	Honduras	Nicaragua	Central America
1967 Values						
E	28.3	21.7	14.2	24.2	5.9	104.3
Ex	16.2	0.0	0.0	17.9	0.0	34.1
Ei	12.1	21.7	14.2	6.3	5.9	60.2
N	28.3	21.8	24.3	14.5	13.6	102.5
Nx	10.6	6.7	12.8	5.0	9.8	44.9
Ni	17.7	15.1	11.5	9.5	3.8	57.6
1968 Values						
E	22.4	29.3	30.6	30.2	9.4	132.9
Ex	0.0	5.5	−0.1	17.9	0.0	33.3
Ei	22.4	23.8	30.7	13.3	9.4	99.6
N	32.4	35.2	28.7	31.2	19.5	147.0
Nx	13.7	11.3	13.7	8.4	4.0	51.1
Ni	18.7	23.9	15.0	22.8	15.5	96.9

Finally, in section C of the table we present the differences (i.e., the solutions of section B less those in section A) which, following the traditional terminology, constitute estimates of external trade-creation, net trade-creation, trade-diversion, etc. For Central America as a whole, the increase in total imports (N) is 102.5 million C.A. pesos (at 1962 prices) in year t (1967) and 147.0 million C.A. pesos (at 1962 prices) in year $t + 1$ (1968). Thus, the net trade-creation attributable to policy coordination in the region as a whole would appear to be about 9 percent of total imports. The relative importance of net trade-creation can be seen to vary among countries from about 5 percent of total imports in Guatemala and Nicaragua to 10 percent or more in Costa Rica, El Salvador and Honduras. There is no evidence of any potential trade-suppression or even of trade-diversion.

6 conclusions, policy implications, qualifications, and suggestions for further research

Since the principal conclusions have already been stated in the individual chapters, there is no need for a detailed summary of our findings. In this concluding chapter, our presentation shall be confined to the statement or restatement of a few of the most important findings, policy implications and limitations. The present chapter is divided into two parts. Following the division of the foregoing chapters, section A deals with the evaluation of the CACM itself, and section B with the assessment of the potential benefits of policy coordination at the regional level.

A. MEASUREMENT OF THE BENEFITS OF CACM PARTICIPATION

In contrast to the findings of previous studies, and of our own application of a traditional method of measuring the benefits of CU participation in Central America, our production function method has indicated that the benefits of the formation of the customs union in Central America may have been quite substantial.

Indeed, while previous studies (mainly of the EEC) have almost invariably estimated the contribution of CU participation to the income growth rate to be less than 0.15 percent per annum, our own estimates indicate that CACM participation has raised the region's income growth rate by about 0.6 percent per annum.

Three distinctly different explanations for the discrepancy in the findings may be offered: (1) that the CACM has been more beneficial than other CUs as far as aggregate income growth is concerned; (2) that the methods employed in previous studies neither include all the effects of CU participation nor adequately account for those effects which they do include; and (3) that the methods we have used overestimate the true benefits.

We are not yet in a position to offer a definitive judgment concerning the relative importance of these explanations. Before arriving at such a judgment, among other things, it would be necessary to apply the methods developed here to other CUs (especially to the EEC),[1] a task which is clearly beyond the scope of the present study, and to duplicate the findings of the present study incorporating additional data for the years 1967 and thereafter and perhaps higher quality data for the years included in the present study.

In the meantime, it may be realistic to suppose that all of the alternative explanations mentioned above have played some role in explaining the differences between the results of this study and those of previous studies. We have already noted in the introduction, and at various other points in the subsequent discussion as well, that there have been fewer obstacles and more favorable conditions to economic integration in the Central America case than in other actual or potential cases of economic integration. At the same time, the fact that traditional methods of estimating the benefits of CU participation yield equally small estimates when applied to the CACM suggests that the difference in estimation methods may be even more important than differences in the cases studied. While there may be some suspicion that our own methods of estimation may be biased (perhaps upward) because of (1) multicollinearity and other problems and (2) the exclusion of all noneconomic variables, we have also provided even stronger reasons for believing that the estimates based on traditional methods are biased downward, in that they do not even attempt to include several important effects of CU participation and that the effects measured, typically the trade-creation effects, are accounted for only partially. Indeed, this latter suggestion is supported by the fact that when a different approach (i.e., the export performance approach) is applied, significantly larger es-

---

[1]Such an effort is, however, presently in progress and will be reported on in due course.

timates of net trade-creation and of its contribution to income growth in the CACM are obtained.

Because rather consistent results showing very small or even insignificant benefits of CU participation have been obtained by many different researchers for both the EEC and other areas using different data sources, time periods, etc., it might be contended that there is greater reason to suppose that these previous findings should be believed despite their generally admitted shortcomings. Since the shortcomings of such studies are primarily methodological, and since all such studies have utilized virtually the *same* methods, we vigorously deny this contention. The methods developed here—both for measuring the trade-creation effects and the contribution to overall income growth of CU participation are clearly more comprehensive and no less rigorous than the previously employed methods. Because each of our various estimates, i.e., the estimates of trade-creation, the estimates of tariff-homogenization, and the estimates of the overall contribution of the CACM to income growth in the region, is relatively consistent one to the other, and because of the general insensitivity of our results to alternative specifications, etc., there would seem to be reason to believe that our own estimates are not simply odd statistical artifacts.

In the process of estimating one of the effects of CU participation that is generally overlooked, i.e., the tariff-homogenizing effect, we have demonstrated that the "rules of the game" adopted for arriving at common external tariff rates out of a diversity of preunion rates among countries, tend to lead to greater homogeneity in tariff rates among commodities within countries.

Since the welfare cost of tariffs (and other sources of price distortions) increases not only with the average degree of distortion but also with the variation in the degree of distortion among the different commodities, existing estimates of the static welfare losses, which have been based on comparisons of average tariff rates alone, may seriously underestimate the social cost of the often very inhomogeneous tariff structures we find in the real world. In the absence of externalities, this conclusion supports free trade as a first-best policy for LDCs. In the presence of externalities associated with industrialization and/or various constraints on policy, it supports policy proposals for uniform effective rates of protection, such as those of Balassa (1971a), Balassa and associates (1971), Macario (1964), and the Swedish Customs Commission (1957), or for dual exchange rates such as that of Kaldor (1964). It also provides a perhaps more convincing argument than those that have previously been given as to why participation in a CU (incorporating a common external tariff) may be preferable to participation in a free-trade association.

In the specific context of Central America, this finding would recommend the abolition, or at least nonextension, of the San José Protocol in which CACM members agreed to a common surcharge on top of the existing external tariff for a five-year period due to end in 1972 or 1973, which has had the effect of increasing the average degree of distortion as well as the variation in the degree of distortion among commodities. As a substitute, one could suggest a general devaluation by the region as a whole that would perhaps be linked to a program of tariff reductions and/or reform in the direction of greater homogeneity. The same reasoning would urge some revision in the proposals currently under consideration for revising the "modus operandi," or the criteria to be used in revising the common external tariff structure of the CACM. These proposals[2] include both desirable features (those making tariffs more homogeneous within broad classes) and undesirable ones (those making tariff rates less homogeneous among these classes). The same benefits of homogeneity in distortions would presumably argue in favor of harmonization with respect to all kinds of indirect taxes and subsidies within the region. Indeed, across-the-board, comprehensive approaches to distortion harmonization and reduction would be much less likely to run aground of the theory-of-second-best qualification that when price distortions of one kind already exist reductions in distortions of another kind may not necessarily lead to welfare increases.[3]

Since the CU established in Central America has apparently rendered substantial benefits to all participating countries, and until additional evidence to the contrary is forthcoming, the most important implication of this portion of the study would seem to be that the CACM is an institution worthy of reconstitution and further strengthening, even if such achievements would require sacrifices in terms of real resources and/or national sovereignty on the part of its members. However, by virtue of the fact that the distribution of the benefits of CU participation would seem to have been somewhat skewed in favor of the more advanced members and that the benefits of the less advanced countries of the region—Honduras and Nicaragua—have been fairly small, it may be unrealistic to expect that the CACM could be reconstituted and further strengthened without some adjustment to assure somewhat greater equity in the distribution of future benefits.

Moreover, in view of our partially supported hypothesis that the findings of previous studies may have substantially underestimated the

[2]At least, this is true of those expressed in the resolutions of the meeting of the Vice Ministers of Economy of the Central American countries on October 30, 1970.

[3]The importance of the theory of second-best qualification in the Central American context would seem to be limited in view of the apparent fact that the major price distortions are those imposed by tariffs. However, this issue could only be fully resolved by a

actual or potential benefits of other actual or possible CUs, our results imply that the pessimistic conclusions (to the effect that CUs have little importance) that may have been derived from the previous empirical estimates may have been somewhat premature.

B. MEASUREMENT OF THE POTENTIAL BENEFITS OF REGIONAL COORDINATION OF MACROECONOMIC POLICIES

In chapter 4, three different versions of small-scale econometric models for each of the five Central American countries were estimated. These models have provided three alternative sets of estimates of the impact of each of the more important instruments of fiscal and monetary macroeconomic policy on each of the most important target variables, such as GNP, consumption, investment, government savings, and the balance of payments. When the five individual-country models were fitted together through intraregional trade, they have revealed the effects of the policy variables in any one country on the target variables of each and every other country. These results (the policy multipliers obtained from the reduced-form solutions to the model) have provided the basis for the simulations of the potential welfare gain to be derived from coordination of monetary and fiscal policies that were presented in chapter 5.[4]

Although the underlying econometric models are admittedly semi-hypothetical in nature, the results were sufficiently insensitive to alternative estimates of the model and to alternative sets of bounds on the allowable flexibility of the policy instruments as to command a considerable amount of confidence in the conclusion that the potential benefits of coordination of macroeconomic policies would be substantial.

The potential gains were indicated to average 3 or 4 percent of GDP for Central America as a whole, varying among countries from one percent of GDP or less in Honduras and Nicaragua to an average of 7 or 8 percent for Costa Rica and El Salvador. The small size of the potential gain for Honduras and Nicaragua might be attributed to the fact that these countries have had greater difficulty in exporting to their partner countries than have the more developed members of the CACM. Other-

---

detailed investigation of price distortions in all sectors from all sources. Such a study would be very desirable now, even though it would have been more timely before the formation of the CACM.

[4]It should be emphasized that both the models and the resulting simulations, being based almost entirely on demand considerations of the Keynesian variety, pertain only to the short run and thus are not comparable with the results of the first portion of the study, which pertain primarily to the long run.

wise, smaller countries would seem to be in a better position to benefit from policy coordination than larger countries.

The potential benefits of policy coordination among members of the CACM remained highly significant, even after allowances were made for possible errors in the model and the availability of information. The increases in terms of GNP and the other targets (including government savings and the balance of payments) generated by policy coordination among countries are attributable to the fact that with coordination the members could follow more expansionary monetary and fiscal policies than they could without coordination.

The most important conclusion of the second portion of the study is, therefore, that some of the further steps that remain to be taken on the road to more complete integration may well be even more rewarding to CACM members than the formation of the CU itself. At least this would seem to be the case in macroeconomic policy coordination at the regional level.

The difficulties that these further steps to arrive at more complete economic integration are likely to confront can hardly be underemphasized. Coordination of macroeconomic policy of the type assumed in our simulations would probably be very difficult to achieve even under ideal circumstances, let alone considering the accumulating and perhaps increasing sensitivities and fears concerning the distribution of the benefits from existing arrangements and the bitterness and frustrations that have arisen out of the soccer war of 1969, etc.

Nevertheless, the prospects for achieving some further progress toward more complete economic integration seem fairly bright in the case of Central America. For example, as early as 1962, the Central American Economic Council of Ministers declared: "that it is in the best interest of the Central American Integration Program to create the means and mechanisms necessary to assure a continuous and permanent coordination of monetary and exchange policies of the Member States." The Central American Monetary Council, established in 1964, was designed "to progressively create the basis for Central American Monetary Union" and "to foster the coordination of monetary, fiscal and exchange policies."[5]

The agreement in 1969 on the protocol on industrial incentives legislation and, more recently, the creation (subject to final approval) of the Central American Fund for Monetary Stabilization (CAFMS), the purpose of which is to provide assistance to individual members in their balance-of-payments crises, provide examples of concrete steps in the direction of policy coordination that have already been undertaken.

[5]This is stated in Article 1 of *The Agreement for Establishment of the Central American Monetary Council and Its Regulations*, July 1964.

Although it remains to be seen just how effective either of these agreements will be, or how much impact they are likely to have, both should be beneficial.

The industrial incentives legislation protocol should benefit the CACM by putting a brake on further competitive concession-making to attract industrial activities to CACM countries, thereby putting a ceiling on revenue losses associated with such concessions and reducing the disparities and distortions which may arise from varying amounts of subsidy between different kinds of activity. Although it remains to be seen what kind of conditions will be attached to CAFMS stand-by credits to the members, CAFMS should in the long run permit the Central American countries to adopt more expansionary policies and encourage (if not actually force) them to coordinate their policies to a greater extent.[6]

Thus, despite the bitterness resulting from the 1969 border war and the growing concern for equity in the distribution of the benefits of integration, a certain momentum has developed in Central American integration which makes assessments of the effects of additional forms of economic integration, such as the present one, both relevant and timely. It is to be admitted, however, that our demonstration of the potential benefits to policy coordination is based on the rather extreme comparison between no coordination and the complete coordination that might be dictated by a regional planning agency. Further research into more realistic forms and degrees of policy coordination is obviously warranted.[7] Even along the lines of the present approach, it would be interesting to determine more precisely the relationship between the degree of interdependence on the one hand and the magnitude of potential benefits of policy coordination on the other.

How much interdependence is necessary for the potential benefits of policy coordination to be important? Our study of policy coordination marks only a primitive beginning in the investigation of the potential welfare effects of forms of economic integration other than customs union. Certainly, it would be equally desirable to investigate the potential benefits of greater resource mobility in the economy of the region, of joint projects and common services, and of monetary union.

[6]The CAFMS agreement brings CACM commitment to achieve policy coordination closer to reality. According to Article 25 of the Articles of Agreement of CAFMS, "the Monetary Council shall give special attention to the possibility of developing, gradually and effectively, practical means to harmonize and coordinate financial policies of the Central America countries. In view of the fundamental importance of fiscal policy in this field, the Monetary Council shall suggest to the Ministers of Finance of Central America, through the appropriate channels the convenience of adopting procedures which will permit joint consultations." Moreover, the agreement has apparently elicited a commitment on the part of the IMF to see to it that regional interests are represented in future consultations and agreements between individual CACM countries and the IMF.

[7]An interesting approach might be to apply some version of the decomposition and decentralization procedures pioneered by Baumol and Fabian (1964).

In spite of the important influence that policies may have in shaping the direction as well as the pace of development in Central America, extraregional export growth is likely to remain the most important determinant of growth within the region. Although we have found no indication that the trade-diverting aspects of CU participation in the Central America case have yet had a deleterious effect on extraregional exports, as local industrialists become more powerful, the pressures for additional tariff protection are likely to be greater. The antiexport bias of increased protection thereby poses a very definite threat to continued growth in the long run. It should be pointed out that local industrialists can be protected as well by higher exchange rates as by higher import taxes. Devaluation by the region as a whole, coupled perhaps with tariff reduction and harmonization among commodities, should make it possible to satisfy the new industrialists without endangering future export and income growth.

The assessment of the distribution of the benefits of integration within the CACM, as was stated clearly in the introduction, is beyond the scope of this study. However, it may be appropriate to recall that our results have given some indication that the benefits of CACM participation, as of about 1966 or 1967, have been somewhat unequally distributed, and, indeed, recent developments have done little to contradict this impression. Our estimates of the additional potential benefits to be derived from policy coordination at the regional level have also indicated the strong possibility that these benefits would also be inequitably distributed. None of our results indicates that any member has suffered or would suffer an absolute loss of welfare, but the inequitable distribution of the gains, which has been apparent both in the experience to date and in our policy simulations, is likely to become a serious impediment to the realization of higher levels of integration. One additional way in which the linear programming approach to the theory of economic policy developed in chapter 5 could be related to the distribution issue deserves mention. Although not shown here, corresponding to the optimal primal solutions to the various optimization problems posed are the dual solutions consisting of a complete set of shadow prices, i.e., one shadow price for each of the constraints included in the model. Since separate constraints are set for each country, one could use the shadow prices obtained from the Central America model corresponding to these individual-country constraints as estimates of the possibility-trade-offs between equity (individual-country goals) and efficiency (regional GDP).[8]

---

[8]For an interesting theoretical analysis of the trade-off between distribution and equity, see Mera (1967).

Aside from equity in the distribution of benefits among member countries, there is also the issue of the distribution effects of CU participation on different groups and individuals. Naturally, unambiguous statements about welfare improvements cannot be made unless it is possible to show that no one person or group is worse off as a result of union after allowing for actual, or at least potential, compensation. McClelland (1972) has touched on a few such issues in the CACM, but a careful appraisal would require still more detailed and precise data on prices of regionally produced and imported goods, consumption patterns, income, etc., of different individuals and groups before and after union. The whole issue of distributional effects is certainly one that deserves a high priority in future research.

Even if the nature and magnitude of the distributional effects (actual or potential) can be determined, there is bound to be some controversy over the choice of mechanisms for controlling or compensating for the inequities. The CACM has already adopted several such mechanisms[9] and certain others are presently under consideration.[10] One such policy, which does not seem to have received attention, is that of exchange rate adjustment. We have already remarked that CACM participation has apparently preempted the use of this important instrument of economic policy, thereby imposing welfare losses on those members (probably Costa Rica, Nicaragua, and possibly Honduras) which might otherwise have been inclined to utilize this instrument. The growing trade and balance-of-payments deficits experienced in Costa Rica with respect to both extraregional and intraregional trade would seem to justify some sort of exchange rate adjustment by Costa Rica relative both to the outside world and to its CACM partners. There would seem to be little reason why periodic adjustments in the relative exchange rates among countries could not be made a part of the normal working procedures of the CACM.[11] If they were, the need for alternative mechanisms for treating the distributional effects might be alleviated considerably.

The link between the essentially microeconomic analysis of tariff distortions and welfare and the entirely macroeconomic analysis of production functions, macroeconomic models, and linear programming is

[9]Some concessions to equity considerations, especially in attracting new industrial enterprises, have been built into the Central American Bank (CABEI), the protocol on industrial incentives legislation, and the system for designating "integration industry" or monopoly status to industries requiring the entire regional market to be efficient.

[10]Among other mechanisms, recent discussions have focussed on the possibility of financial transfers to compensate for losses in tariff revenue resulting from trade-diversion.

[11]The possibility that periodic exchange rate adjustments of this sort would be destabilizing does not seem to be supported by the recent satisfactory experience of countries like Lebanon and Peru, with flexible exchange rates, and Chile and Argentina, that have followed a policy of frequent small devaluations in recent years.

admittedly still rather tenuous. The link could be strengthened by disaggregating the latter models to encompass the same three sectors specified in the former general equilibrium tariff model. Certainly, additional attention in the macroeconomic analysis could profitably be directed to more detailed analysis of the intraregional trade variables, since these variables are so important in providing the basis for the interdependencies among the policy instruments and targets between and among the individual countries and yet are admittedly rather unsatisfactorily treated in the present study.

Finally, policy-makers might wish to see a narrowing of the gap between the broad kind of policy implications derived from the present models, such as that government spending should be increased and "other" taxes reduced, and the practical policy decisions which confront them, such as exactly which type of spending should be increased, which taxes should be reduced, and which instruments of monetary policy should be exercised, etc. Further disaggregation of the policy instruments would provide the only means of meeting this criticism, but doing so would impose additional computational costs and probably would increase data requirements beyond their availabilities.

appendix a

data for estimating and forecasting with the econometric models

Note: For definitions of variables see Table 4.1 p. 83 above.

Sources: SIECA, AID/ROCAP, *International Financial Statistics*, Central Banks of each country, *United Nations Statistical Yearbook*, United Nations, *Yearbook of National Accounts Statistics* and Gabriel Siri.

Table A–1. Data for Costa Rica

	GDP	GNP	Yd	C	I_p	I_g	G	Ex	Ei	Nx	Ni	TT	NFY	K	TNET	POP
1950	227.9	246.3	216.1	190.6	31.3	4.0	19.7	55.0	.2	70.4	.3	31.3	-12.9	419.7	30.2	.82
1951	233.9	258.5	223.9	200.0	34.6	4.7	22.3	57.0	.6	85.1	.2	36.7	-12.1	507.0	34.6	.86
1952	262.3	286.2	247.0	215.4	41.7	10.1	28.1	68.9	.9	102.2	.6	40.5	-16.6	546.1	39.1	.90
1953	302.0	325.5	281.4	241.1	43.3	13.2	30.9	73.9	.5	100.6	.3	35.6	-12.1	588.9	44.1	.94
1954	304.7	342.8	296.5	256.5	40.1	13.5	34.5	68.5	1.0	109.1	.3	49.2	-11.1	627.8	46.3	.98
1955	340.0	359.8	301.1	269.1	45.8	15.1	40.0	73.7	1.1	104.1	.7	26.8	-7.0	673.0	58.7	1.02
1956	330.3	362.6	306.6	278.7	50.8	16.1	40.7	88.2	1.0	114.2	.9	35.2	-2.9	722.3	56.0	1.06
1957	358.3	389.9	328.5	295.8	61.3	14.1	43.2	70.6	1.5	127.3	.9	39.6	-8.0	779.6	61.4	1.10
1958	402.7	414.2	349.7	313.1	50.6	15.1	46.5	91.4	1.9	114.8	1.1	18.9	-7.4	825.7	64.5	1.15
1959	417.5	424.6	353.3	319.4	71.7	12.1	49.6	87.9	1.8	121.1	3.9	10.8	-3.7	888.8	71.3	1.20
1960	453.8	452.9	376.3	339.1	63.3	16.9	58.1	102.2	2.4	124.7	3.5	1.0	-1.9	946.8	76.6	1.25
1961	466.3	462.6	392.7	344.5	69.5	13.8	57.0	107.3	1.2	123.0	4.0	-1.0	-2.7	1006.5	69.9	1.30
1962	494.7	488.2	410.3	361.7	65.0	21.3	62.0	111.1	1.3	124.2	3.5	0.0	-6.5	1067.6	77.9	1.34
1963	535.9	531.9	446.7	387.0	72.1	18.8	82.0	111.3	1.3	135.4	3.8	1.8	-5.8	1131.8	85.2	1.39
1964	544.0	542.0	453.0	402.6	63.0	18.0	79.4	115.9	14.8	141.4	8.3	6.1	-8.1	1184.5	89.0	1.44
1965	576.6	570.2	476.1	432.8	84.5	26.3	91.2	110.1	18.3	172.2	14.4	4.6	-11.0	1275.7	94.1	1.49
1966	622.4	621.8	519.8	455.0	83.0	25.0	94.5	124.3	25.9	161.1	23.2	13.3	-13.9	1350.8	102.0	1.54
1967	673.4	658.0	557.0	490.7	95.1	29.0	101.9	131.0	31.0	169.0	34.0	3.0	-18.4	1441.1	101.0	1.59
1968												2.0	-18.4			

Table A–1 (Continued)

	Te	Tn	To	Te/Ex	Tn/Nx	To/GDP	MS	RM	BP	SG	Zcm	Nus	RCR	NiCM–NiCR	TIME	P
1950	1.3	14.8	14.1	.02364	.21022	.06187	38.6	23.1	−3.1	7.6	0	75	0	6.4	0	.80
1951	1.5	16.0	17.0	.02632	.18801	.07311	39.9	25.2	−9.1	0.9	0	74	0	8.6	1,000	.85
1952	2.0	17.1	20.0	.02903	.16732	.07625	48.6	30.8	−3.0	0.0	0	78	0	8.8	2,000	.82
1953	1.7	22.1	20.3	.02300	.21968	.06722	54.0	34.2	−1.8	−1.7	0	82	0	10.4	3,000	.81
1954	2.3	26.3	17.7	.03358	.24106	.05809	57.8	36.1	−10.2	3.6	0	76	0	13.0	4,000	.85
1955	3.3	32.7	22.7	.04478	.31412	.06676	57.8	35.4	−23.6	−0.8	0	85	0	12.1	5,000	.88
1956	2.6	33.1	20.3	.04467	.28959	.06146	57.6	35.3	−24.5	4.1	0	92	0	12.5	6,000	.89
1957	3.2	34.0	24.2	.04533	.26709	.06754	61.7	38.8	−11.1	2.9	0	95	0	15.7	7,000	.90
1958	3.9	37.5	23.1	.04267	.32666	.05736	64.5	40.5	−28.2	9.6	0	100	0	19.6	8,000	.93
1959	3.7	42.0	25.6	.04209	.34682	.06132	68.3	42.3	−24.5	1.6	0	119	0	26.4	9,000	.92
1960	3.5	43.7	29.4	.03425	.35044	.06479	68.8	43.8	−22.2	−0.9	0	114	1,000	29.1	10,000	.94
1961	3.4	40.0	26.5	.03169	.32520	.05938	64.8	41.0	−21.8	−5.4	0	113	1,000	32.6	11,000	.97
1962	4.2	41.6	32.1	.03780	.33494	.06623	72.0	43.0	−28.0	−15.6	0	128	1,000	46.7	12,000	1.00
1963	4.1	47.2	33.9	.03684	.34860	.06571	77.9	46.1	−21.0	−15.4	1,000	133	1,000	68.1	13,000	1.03
1964	5.4	43.8	39.8	.04659	.30976	.07453	80.5	46.6	−64.6	−23.4	1,000	141	1,000	97.9	14,000	1.06
1965	5.7	45.9	42.5	.05177	.26655	.07371	84.7	49.3	−34.7	−19.1	1,000	160	1,000	121.2	15,000	1.06
1966	5.6	45.5	50.9	.04505	.28243	.08239	88.2	50.2	−43.4	−35.0	1,000	189	1,000	149.5	16,000	1.06
1967	5.5	42.0	53.5	.04198	.24852	.07945	114.7	61.2			1,000	204	1,000	180.0	17,000	1.09
1968												250		204.8		

Note: All variables except the tax rate variables, Zcm, Nus, R^{CR}, POP, P, and TIME are in millions of C.A. pesos at 1962 prices.

Table A–2. Data for El Salvador

	GDP	GNP	Yd	C	Ip	Ig	G	Ex	Ei	Nx	Ni	TT	NFY	K	TNET	Te	Tn	POP
1950	374.0	404.1	358.7	315.9	30.2	10.1	29.6	62.6	2.5	74.2	2.7	32.1	-2.0	776.8	45.4	8.5	8.5	1.84
1951	381.3	426.0	381.0	339.4	35.7	11.9	31.1	57.8	2.2	91.4	5.4	46.7	-2.0	805.1	45.0	11.8	13.6	1.89
1952	409.9	454.6	408.2	361.7	37.8	12.6	34.0	62.1	2.0	95.5	4.8	47.4	-2.7	835.4	46.4	12.1	13.1	1.94
1953	439.2	502.4	451.4	399.0	39.5	13.2	37.7	66.2	2.9	112.8	6.5	66.3	-3.1	867.2	51.0	13.3	18.5	1.99
1954	444.3	506.6	446.2	401.5	38.8	12.9	42.4	58.1	4.5	106.0	7.9	64.6	-2.3	897.2	60.4	16.9	19.6	2.05
1955	467.2	526.1	470.5	428.7	40.0	13.3	40.7	68.8	4.1	121.5	6.9	62.3	-3.4	928.1	55.7	17.3	19.6	2.11
1956	503.8	560.9	502.7	439.1	55.9	18.7	43.0	77.8	5.2	127.8	8.1	62.0	-4.9	979.5	58.2	15.6	21.1	2.18
1957	530.7	584.3	514.9	449.8	62.0	20.6	48.1	81.5	6.4	129.0	8.7	56.9	-3.3	1037.6	69.4	20.7	24.6	2.25
1958	542.2	573.1	511.2	454.7	49.7	19.7	47.9	90.3	8.2	117.8	10.5	34.4	-3.5	1081.1	61.9	13.8	23.1	2.32
1959	542.0	557.1	499.8	447.2	39.7	21.3	48.9	101.7	10.5	114.8	12.5	18.6	-3.5	1115.1	57.3	9.6	22.7	2.39
1960	564.7	582.0	518.8	484.7	64.3	14.6	49.0	92.9	12.3	139.6	13.5	20.4	-3.1	1166.1	63.2	10.3	27.4	2.45
1961	608.3	615.3	553.4	494.2	52.5	16.4	53.4	108.2	15.0	116.8	14.6	10.2	-3.2	1205.6	61.9	9.7	24.0	2.53
1962	653.9	651.9	588.4	536.6	55.2	13.5	55.5	131.1	18.7	134.7	22.0	0.0	-2.0	1244.2	63.5	8.4	24.0	2.63
1963	680.2	678.6	612.7	570.9	63.0	16.2	54.0	131.2	30.0	157.5	27.9	0.2	-1.8	1292.3	65.9	9.0	23.7	2.72
1964	727.8	731.5	656.7	614.9	84.6	15.2	53.5	145.7	36.8	182.8	39.2	5.5	-1.8	1359.7	74.8	11.4	23.2	2.82
1965	761.8	784.7	699.7	628.4	81.7	29.1	56.0	152.7	45.3	189.0	42.4	25.0	-2.1	1436.5	85.0	14.1	24.0	2.93
1966	794.9	806.5	726.2	656.8	94.2	35.5	59.2	138.1	59.0	195.9	52.0	15.1	-3.5	1530.3	80.3	12.6	23.2	3.04
1967	830.7	831.5	744.0	686.3	92.4	26.0	65.4	136.1	77.1	197.5	55.0	5.0	-4.2	1610.4	87.5	11.9	22.3	3.15
1968												6.0	-4.2					

Table A-2 (Continued)

	To	Te/Ex	Tn/Nx	To/GDP	CR	MS	RM	BP	SG	Zcm	Nus	RES	NiCM-NiES	TIME	P
1950	28.4	.13578	.11455	.07594	44.0	66.8	52.6	7.9	2.0	0	75.	0	4.4	0	0.77
1951	19.6	.20415	.14880	.05140	42.2	65.5	50.9	8.5	-0.2	0	74.	0	3.4	1,000	0.89
1952	21.2	.19485	.13713	.05172	46.9	77.6	60.7	13.0	0.1	0	78.	0	4.6	2,000	0.87
1953	19.2	.20091	.16401	.04372	49.0	75.9	56.2	11.0	5.1	0	82.	0	4.2	3,000	0.93
1954	23.9	.29088	.18491	.05379	61.8	79.6	57.5	3.4	1.6	0	76.	0	5.4	4,000	0.92
1955	18.8	.25145	.16132	.04026	79.2	78.4	54.2	4.2	-3.5	0	85.	0	5.9	5,000	1.01
1956	21.5	.20051	.16510	.04268	98.9	88.4	60.0	3.8	0.7	0	92.	0	5.3	6,000	1.02
1957	24.0	.25399	.19147	.04522	117.3	92.0	62.3	1.1	-5.7	0	95.	0	7.9	7,000	0.98
1958	25.0	.15282	.19616	.04611	110.1	82.5	57.2	0.0	-12.9	0	100.	1,000	10.2	8,000	1.03
1959	25.0	.09440	.19774	.04613	119.6	84.8	60.2	-30.6	-0.4	0	110.	1,000	17.8	9,000	1.02
1960	25.5	.11087	.19628	.04516	138.4	79.7	57.8	-1.2	-8.1	0	114.	1,000	19.1	10,000	1.02
1961	28.2	.08965	.20548	.04636	133.7	77.9	59.3	-8.9	-5.5	1,000	113.	2,000	22.0	11,000	1.00
1962	31.1	.06407	.17817	.04756	127.8	77.8	61.9	-25.5	-4.2	1,000	128.	2,000	28.2	12,000	1.00
1963	33.2	.06860	.15048	.04881	138.4	92.5	72.1	-35.8	6.1	1,000	133.	2,000	44.0	13,000	1.01
1964	40.2	.07824	.12691	.05523	155.7	92.3	75.0	-10.5	-0.5	1,000	141.	2,000	67.0	14,000	1.03
1965	46.9	.09234	.12698	.06104	165.5	97.7	83.0	-39.2	-14.4	1,000	160.	3,000	93.2	15,000	1.03
1966	44.5	.09124	.11843	.05598	186.9	102.0	86.2	-38.5		1,000	189.	4,000	120.7	16,000	1.03
1967	53.3	.08744	.11291	.06416	189.3	104.0	101.0			1,000	204.	4,000	159.0	17,000	1.02
1968													187.8		1.03

Note: All variables except the tax rate variables, Zcm, Nus, R^{ES}, POP, P, and TIME are in millions of C.A. pesos at 1962 prices.

Table A–3. Data for Guatemala

	GDP	GNP	Yd	C	Ip	Ig	G	Ex	Ei	Nx	Ni	TT	NFY	K	TNET	Te	POP
1950	684.0	701.9	648.4	576.8	60.4	19.6	49.2	75.7	0.1	96.2	1.6	22.5	−4.6	1413.8	53.5	3.4	2.80
1951	695.1	712.6	652.7	583.2	58.1	20.2	53.6	67.7	0.3	87.2	0.8	19.7	−2.2	1456.8	59.9	8.6	2.89
1952	708.8	724.5	654.3	582.8	44.7	23.1	61.8	74.5	1.1	78.2	1.0	17.9	−2.2	1488.2	70.2	13.4	2.98
1953	734.9	749.9	675.4	616.8	41.6	24.9	62.4	76.4	1.4	87.8	0.8	23.9	−8.9	1517.5	74.5	12.1	3.08
1954	749.3	773.6	692.9	650.5	40.5	25.5	59.3	70.6	1.5	97.5	1.1	33.4	−9.1	1545.6	80.7	12.4	3.18
1955	767.6	794.9	707.5	654.6	55.1	34.0	56.6	78.9	1.7	111.8	1.5	33.6	−6.3	1596.1	87.4	20.9	3.28
1956	839.4	874.1	781.6	690.2	89.8	50.4	64.7	85.7	1.4	141.3	1.5	39.9	−5.2	1696.4	92.5	17.3	3.38
1957	887.4	912.5	812.6	729.5	92.5	59.4	69.7	89.4	2.7	154.0	1.8	31.7	−6.6	1805.9	99.9	17.9	3.48
1958	919.1	923.5	821.7	769.4	84.7	48.9	69.1	97.6	3.3	151.6	2.3	12.5	−8.1	1894.4	101.8	13.9	3.58
1959	959.1	956.2	854.8	794.0	82.7	40.3	73.9	116.7	4.3	149.7	3.1	5.2	−8.1	1970.0	101.4	12.9	3.70
1960	992.0	988.4	886.2	830.8	78.2	27.5	83.2	121.8	5.0	146.9	7.6	7.0	−10.6	2026.4	102.2	12.1	3.81
1961	1,031.9	1,016.3	911.4	847.1	78.9	32.5	87.0	121.2	8.6	134.5	8.9	−3.5	−12.1	2087.1	104.9	10.8	3.93
1962	1,066.6	1,054.7	976.2	902.1	79.3	27.3	77.2	131.4	3.4	142.9	11.2	0.0	−11.9	2141.5	78.5	8.9	4.05
1963	1,165.0	1,143.7	1,069.0	977.2	103.8	22.2	76.4	167.6	17.3	179.8	19.7	−6.6	−14.7	2214.0	74.6	6.1	4.18
1964	1,220.8	1,208.1	1,122.9	1,024.0	121.4	32.9	83.5	148.1	29.6	192.4	26.3	4.3	−17.0	2313.0	85.2	6.1	4.30
1965	1,270.3	1,248.9	1,142.6	1,050.2	124.5	30.9	95.1	169.6	35.7	204.2	31.5	−3.4	−18.0	2410.6	106.3	8.1	4.44
1966	1,323.4	1,279.7	1,172.9	1,054.6	127.8	33.1	92.4	196.2	50.9	197.8	33.8	−15.4	−28.3	2511.2	106.8	8.0	4.58
1967	1,372.4	1,321.3	1,221.3	1,067.3	183.1	36.9	99.8	173.8	60.7	207.1	42.1	−17.9	−33.2	2669.4	100.0	6.0	4.72
1968												−19.6	−33.2				

Table A–3. (Continued)

	Tn	To	Te/Ex	Tn/Nx	To/GDP	CR	MS	RM	BP	SG	Z^{cm}	Nus	R^G	$Ni^{CM}-Ni^G$	TIME
1950	19.3	30.8	.04491	.20062	.04503	26.8	58.9	51.2	−2.5	−13.9	0	75.	0	5.5	0
1951	24.0	27.3	.12703	.27523	.03928	30.9	60.4	52.3	12.1	−14.7	0	74.	0	8.0	1,000
1952	24.2	32.6	.17987	.30946	.04599	30.4	63.7	57.1	4.2	−12.8	0	78.	0	8.4	2,000
1953	25.2	37.2	.15838	.28702	.05062	40.0	76.0	68.7	−2.2	−4.1	0	82.	0	9.9	3,000
1954	24.9	43.4	.17564	.25538	.05792	41.5	77.6	69.7	−5.4	−3.2	0	76.	0	12.2	4,000
1955	23.3	43.2	.26489	.20841	.05628	41.1	86.7	75.3	−21.0	−22.6	0	85.	0	11.3	5,000
1956	29.2	46.0	.20187	.20665	.05480	51.0	103.9	91.1	−38.6	−29.2	0	92.	0	11.9	6,000
1957	32.1	49.9	.20022	.20844	.05623	68.4	119.5	96.5	−48.6	−16.2	0	95.	0	14.8	7,000
1958	35.0	52.9	.14242	.23087	.05756	84.7	108.8	85.4	−34.7	−12.8	0	100.	0	18.4	8,000
1959	38.4	50.1	.11054	.25651	.05224	85.1	111.0	90.0	−31.3	−8.5	0	119.	0	27.2	9,000
1960	35.3	54.8	.09934	.24030	.05563	91.5	110.0	88.6	−29.2	−14.6	0	114.	0	25.0	10,000
1961	36.7	57.4	.08911	.27286		100.7	116.1	94.6			0	113.	1,000	27.7	11,000
1962	26.5	43.1	.06773	.18544	.04041	109.7	112.2	92.9	−31.2	−26.0	1,000	128.	1,000	39.0	12,000
1963	25.1	43.4	.03640	.13960	.03725	122.8	125.4	104.6	−35.9	−24.0	1,000	133.	1,000	52.2	13,000
1964	26.4	52.7	.04119	.13921	.04318	138.5	137.7	112.3	−53.7	−35.5	1,000	141.		79.9	14,000
1965	29.9	68.3	.04776	.14643	.05377	152.0	143.0	121.4	−51.8	−9.7	1,000	160.	2,000	104.1	15,000
1966	25.9	72.9	.04077	.13094	.05509	167.6	156.4	132.4	−28.2	−18.7	1,000	189.	3,000	138.9	16,000
1967	26.0	68.0	.03452	.12554	.04955	197.0	156.6	132.4	−65.8	−36.7	1,000	204.	3,000	171.9	17,000
1968														212.7	

Note: All variables except the tax rate variables, Z^{cm}, Nus, R^G, POP, and TIME are in millions of C.A. pesos at 1962 prices.

Table A–4. Data for Honduras

	GDP	GNP	Yd	C	Ip	Ig	G	Ex	Ei	Nx	Ni	TT	NFY	K	TNET	Te	POP
1950	273.5	251.5	227.3	197.6	30.1	6.4	16.9	67.5	3.9	47.1	1.8	2.7	−24.7	547.0	24.2	0.6	1.39
1951	287.2	268.4	243.3	207.1	38.4	8.0	17.3	72.6	3.9	58.2	1.9	1.6	−20.4	569.8	25.1	0.6	1.43
1952	297.8	287.5	260.4	220.4	43.7	13.0	20.4	68.7	4.1	70.4	2.1	4.0	−14.3	602.0	27.1	0.8	1.47
1953	316.5	308.5	283.2	238.2	44.5	11.6	19.5	70.9	4.2	70.4	2.0	8.0	−16.0	643.7	25.3	0.6	1.51
1954	296.3	300.4	275.3	245.0	32.7	10.1	20.5	52.4	4.3	66.6	2.1	9.0	−4.9	683.7	25.1	1.0	1.56
1955	308.4	309.0	281.2	252.1	40.9	7.2	22.8	51.1	5.2	68.7	2.2	5.8	−5.2	709.4	27.8	1.1	1.61
1956	336.3	330.6	300.8	261.0	38.7	11.9	25.4	65.9	6.6	71.8	1.4	7.1	−12.8	739.8	29.8	1.3	1.66
1957	359.2	355.7	319.6	287.0	43.4	12.0	27.2	65.3	6.1	79.4	2.4	−1.9	−1.6	771.9	36.1	1.5	1.71
1958	367.6	358.1	325.1	290.3	38.7	8.2	29.9	71.7	6.7	73.8	4.1	−3.7	−5.8	808.0	33.0	1.4	1.77
1959	381.4	370.5	336.1	295.4	35.9	10.0	30.1	75.7	8.0	67.3	6.4	−8.4	−2.5	834.5	34.4	1.9	1.82
1960	387.9	374.8	339.0	302.7	39.3	11.5	30.5	70.1	8.7	69.6	5.3	−9.2	−3.9	859.5	35.8	1.8	1.88
1961	402.0	399.4	362.7	319.7	33.8	13.5	31.9	73.2	9.1	72.9	6.3	−1.9	−0.7	888.8	36.7	1.6	1.94
1962	426.2	419.6	386.0	333.2	54.5	5.6	31.7	73.2	12.9	76.1	8.8	0.0	−6.6	913.9	33.6	1.7	2.00
1963	436.2	429.3	394.4	342.6	49.3	14.3	39.8	76.1	12.6	85.3	13.2	−0.8	−6.1	951.2	34.9	2.1	2.07
1964	461.8	454.2	415.6	365.8	52.0	11.7	45.2	85.2	16.8	86.9	18.0	−1.1	−6.5	991.0	38.6	2.1	2.14
1965	499.8	486.9	440.9	377.2	54.5	12.2	48.1	113.0	21.1	99.9	26.3	−1.7	−11.3	1029.0	46.0	2.1	2.21
1966	524.9	510.5	459.1	394.1	56.4	13.1	51.4	129.1	19.8	106.6	32.4	−2.0	−12.4	1070.9	51.3	2.6	2.28
1967	561.4	538.0	485.0	424.0	60.1	16.6	53.7	134.7	22.0	109.0	40.7	−7.7	−15.7	1113.5	53.0	2.5	2.36
1968												−7.7	−15.7	1162.4		3.0	2.44

Table A-4 (Continued)

	Tn	To	Te/Ex	Tn/Nx	To/GDP	MS	RM	BP	SG	Zcm	Nus	RHO	NiCM-NiH	TIME	P
1950	9.6	14.0	.00889	.20382	.05119	28.0	22.5	-2.4	0.2	0	75	0	5.3	0	0.64
1951	11.0	13.5	.00826	.18900	.04701	26.9	21.6	-10.0	-6.3	0	74	0	6.9	1,000	0.61
1952	12.0	14.3	.01164	.17045	.04802	30.4	24.3	-5.3	-5.8	0	78	0	7.3	2,000	0.65
1953	10.5	14.2	.00846	.14915	.04487	33.7	26.2	-17.9	-5.5	0	82	0	8.7	3,000	0.74
1954	12.0	12.1	.01908	.18018	.04084	36.8	31.1	-14.0	-2.2	0	76	0	11.2	4,000	0.77
1955	10.8	15.8	.02153	.15866	.05123	30.0	24.6	-6.4	-7.5	0	85	0	10.6	5,000	0.77
1956	13.9	14.6	.01973	.19359	.04341	34.6	27.7			0	92	0	12.0	6,000	
1957	16.2	18.4	.02297	.20403	.05122	33.8	25.6	-13.9	-3.1	0	95	0	14.2	7,000	0.95
1958	15.6	16.0	.01953	.21138	.04353	32.1	24.2	-9.0	-5.1	0	100	1,000	16.6	8,000	0.98
1959	16.6	15.9	.02510	.24666	.04169	33.3	23.8	-0.9	-5.7	0	119	1,000	23.9	9,000	0.99
1960	17.8	16.2	.02568	.25575	.04176	33.2	24.1	-9.2	-6.2	0	114	1,000	27.3	10,000	0.97
1961	18.3	16.8	.02186	.25103	.04179	33.1	23.4	0.5	-8.7	0	113	2,000	30.3	11,000	0.99
1962	17.4	14.5	.02322	.22865	.03402	36.3	25.2	-5.4	-3.7	1,000	128	2,000	41.4	12,000	1.00
1963	17.9	14.9	.02760	.20985	.03416	38.4	27.1	-16.7	-19.2	1,000	133	2,000	58.7	13,000	1.025
1964	16.9	19.6	.02465	.19448	.04244	41.6	28.5	-10.5	-11.3	1,000	141	2,000	88.2	14,000	1.077
1965	19.6	23.8	.02301	.19620	.04761	46.7	30.8	-5.1	-14.3	1,000	160	2,000	109.3	15,000	1.120
1966	20.2	28.6	.01936	.18949	.05449	47.5	31.7	-4.5	-13.2	1,000	189	2,000	140.3	16,000	1.120
1967	20.0	31.0	.01485	.18349	.05522	52.0	36.1	-16.4	-17.3	1,000	204	2,000	173.3	17,000	1.160
1968													202.6		

Note: All variables except the tax rate variables, Zcm, Nus, R^{HO}, POP, P, and TIME are in millions of C.A. pesos at 1962 prices.

Table A–5. Data for Nicaragua

	GDP	GNP	Yd	C	Ip	Ig	G	Ex	Ei	Nx	Ni	TT	NFY	K	TNET	Te	POP
1950	204.7	194.9	174.7	154.4	16.0	3.8	20.1	44.3	0.9	34.5	0.3	-2.6	-7.3	418.9	20.2	1.6	1.04
1951	218.4	216.4	194.9	162.8	23.2	4.5	19.6	42.6	2.8	36.6	0.5	5.2	-7.2	436.1	21.5	2.2	1.06
1952	255.4	251.9	225.7	191.9	30.5	7.3	22.0	51.2	1.7	48.3	0.9	2.3	-5.8	462.9	26.2	2.4	1.08
1953	262.0	263.1	234.7	202.3	32.8	9.4	24.4	54.2	1.7	61.7	1.1	9.0	-7.9	503.4	28.4	2.3	1.10
1954	286.4	296.4	266.6	231.9	41.7	10.4	27.6	52.7	2.3	78.3	1.9	17.2	-7.2	542.7	29.8	2.0	1.13
1955	306.0	319.6	286.5	240.7	39.7	12.2	27.7	74.1	1.1	88.0	1.5	23.4	-9.7	581.0	33.2	4.1	1.17
1956	305.4	311.2	273.5	243.5	33.8	14.2	28.6	66.1	.7	80.0	1.5	10.6	-4.8	614.5	37.7	6.2	1.21
1957	331.3	331.5	292.4	263.9	30.9	16.9	29.9	76.1	1.2	84.8	2.8	1.9	-1.7	646.9	39.1	5.7	1.25
1958	332.4	326.0	288.3	262.7	30.3	15.8	30.2	82.3	1.4	87.6	2.7	-2.8	-3.6	676.8	37.7	3.5	1.29
1959	338.0	319.6	283.0	236.3	35.2	14.3	29.6	97.1	4.2	74.3	4.4	-15.8	-2.6	709.4	36.6	1.3	1.33
1960	342.0	330.9	291.4	265.0	35.3	10.4	30.3	79.2	2.5	78.0	2.7	-9.0	-2.1	737.4	39.5	1.2	1.37
1961	364.2	358.6	318.2	283.4	35.6	14.2	32.6	84.4	1.8	84.9	2.8	-3.4	-2.2	768.8	40.4	1.2	1.41
1962	402.5	399.5	360.9	321.0	41.5	16.7	33.6	99.2	3.5	108.3	4.7	0.0	-3.0	799.4	38.6	0.9	1.45
1963	432.9	419.4	379.4	320.5	52.4	18.8	36.8	125.4	4.7	118.4	7.3	-9.4	-4.1	850.6	40.0	0.7	1.50
1964	464.0	446.5	402.0	337.1	62.3	21.2	40.5	149.0	7.0	138.7	14.4	-9.5	-8.0	912.8	44.5	0.7	1.54
1965	506.3	483.0	428.1	376.3	64.7	26.1	44.6	159.3	12.4	156.2	21.0	-8.5	-14.8	980.7	54.9	0.9	1.60
1966	525.8	502.4	447.8	403.7	80.3	31.5	48.0	149.4	16.2	172.0	31.3	-12.5	-10.9	1068.0	54.6	1.3	1.66
1967	547.3	506.3	450.9	413.4	81.1	27.0	53.6	155.3	21.7	162.6	42.2	-28.4	-12.6	1149.4	55.4	1.4	1.72
1968												-25.0	-12.6				1.78

Table A-5 (Continued)

	Tn	To	Te/Ex	Tn/Nx	To/GDP	CR	MS	RM	BP	SG	Nus	Zcm	NiCM-NiN	R^N	P
1950	8.5	10.1	.03612	.24638	.04934	23.6	27.3	18.1			75	0	6.8	0	0.64
1951	9.6	9.7	.05164	.26230	.04441	26.5	28.2	19.7	6.3	-2.6	74	0	8.3	0	0.76
1952	12.3	11.5	.04688	.25466	.04503	31.9	33.4	22.9	0.2	-3.1	78	0	8.5	0	0.77
1953	14.4	11.7	.04244	.23339	.04466	41.8	38.0	24.7	-5.8	-5.4	82	0	9.6	0	0.87
1954	15.0	12.8	.03795	.19157	.04469	57.0	42.0	25.7	-15.2	-8.2	76	0	11.4	0	0.90
1955	17.3	11.8	.05533	.19659	.03856	53.8	36.6	21.4	-0.6	-6.7	85	0	11.3	0	1.06
1956	18.6	12.9	.09380	.23250	.04224	60.4	37.0	22.5	-8.9	-5.1	92	0	11.9	0	1.03
1957	19.0	14.4	.07490	.22406	.04347	58.8	37.5	23.6	-10.1	-7.7	95	0	13.8	0	0.99
1958	19.8	14.4	.04253	.22603	.04332	57.8	34.5	21.8	-13.0	-8.3	100	0	18.0	0	1.04
1959	21.2	14.1	.01339	.28533	.04172	51.0	35.8	23.2	4.2	-7.3	119	0	25.9	0	1.01
1960	23.0	15.3	.01515	.29487	.04474	52.2	38.1	24.1	-10.1	-1.2	114	0	29.9		0.99
1961	23.1	16.1	.01422	.27208	.04421	54.5	39.4	24.6	-7.1	-6.4	113	0	33.8	1,000	0.99
1962	21.8	15.9	.00907	.20129	.03950	59.0	50.4	32.8	-13.3	-11.7	128	1,000	45.5	2,000	1.00
1963	20.8	18.5	.00558	.17568	.04274	64.6	56.8	37.2	-9.1	-15.6	133	1,000	64.6	2,000	1.00
1964	19.1	24.7	.00470	.13771	.05323	76.7	63.1	40.0	-14.6	-17.2	141	1,000	91.8	2,000	1.04
1965	22.2	31.8	.00565	.14213	.06281	94.9	71.5	42.9	-28.8	-15.8	160	1,000	114.6	2,000	1.07
1966	21.7	31.6	.00870	.12616	.06010	110.4	70.5	44.0	-61.1	-24.9	189	1,000	141.8	2,000	1.14
1967	21.8	33.2	.00901	.13407	.05883	121.9	67.0	41.4	-68.8	-25.2	204	1,000	171.8	2,000	1.18
1968													207.7		

Note: All variables except the tax rate variables, Zcm, Nus, R^N, POP, P, are in millions of C.A. pesos at 1962 prices.

appendix b

supplementary calculations

Table B-1-A. The Effects in Millions of C.A. Pesos at 1962 Prices of a 1% Increase in the Export Tax Rate (Te/Ex) via Model 1

Country & variable affected	Country in which action is taken	Costa Rica	El Salvador	Guatemala	Honduras	Nicaragua
Central America						
GNPt		−25.28	−4.93	−5.16	−46.03	−0.97
GNPt+1		−13.31	−1.24	−2.56	−23.54	−0.32
Costa Rica						
GNPt		−17.43	−0.09	−0.19	−2.98	−0.05
SGt		−1.45	−0.01	−0.02	−0.35	−0.01
BPt		−3.40	−0.02	−0.04	−0.40	−0.01
GNPt+1		−7.18	−0.06	−0.13	−1.18	−0.04
SGt+1		−0.79	−0.01	−0.02	−0.28	−
BPt+1		2.42	0.01	0.01	0.08	−
El Salvador						
GNPt		−3.06	−4.57	−0.36	−3.06	−0.10
SGt		−0.25	0.25	−0.03	−0.22	−0.01
BPt		−0.40	−	−0.05	−0.45	−0.01
GNPt+1		−2.09	−0.99	−0.26	−3.09	−0.05
SGt+1		−0.17	−0.08	−0.02	−0.19	0.01
BPt+1		−0.02	0.26	−	−0.02	−
Guatemala						
GNPt		−3.63	−0.21	−4.48	−6.63	−0.12
SGt		−0.34	−0.02	0.35	−0.84	−0.01
BPt		−0.61	−0.04	−0.05	−0.51	−0.02
GNPt+1		−3.20	−0.15	−2.03	−4.20	−0.09
SGt+1		−0.29	−0.01	−0.19	−0.30	−0.01
BPt+1		0.18	0.01	0.55	0.08	0.01
Honduras						
GNPt		−0.45	−0.03	−0.05	−32.45	−0.02
SGt		−0.05	−	−0.01	−1.31	−
BPt		−0.11	0.01	−0.01	−4.77	−
GNPt+1		−0.36	−0.02	−0.04	−14.30	−0.01
SGt+1		−0.04	−	−0.01	−0.62	−
BPt+1		0.06	−	0.01	−1.85	−
Nicaragua						
GNPt		−0.71	−0.04	−0.08	−0.91	−0.68
SGt		−0.09	−0.01	−0.01	−0.09	0.64
BPt		−0.16	−0.01	−0.02	−0.16	0.30
GNPt+1		−0.47	−0.02	−0.06	−0.77	−0.13
SGt+1		−0.06	−	−0.17	−0.06	−0.02
BPt+1		0.01	−	−0.15	0.01	0.08

Table B-1-B. The Effects in Millions of C.A. Pesos at 1962 Prices of a 1% Increase in Import Duty Rates (Tn/Nx) via Model 1

Country & variable affected	Country in which action is taken	Costa Rica	El Salvador	Guatemala	Honduras	Nicaragua
Central America						
GNPt		2.19	7.80	0.34	1.87	1.56
GNPt+1		1.15	1.96	0.17	1.15	0.51
Costa Rica						
GNPt		1.51	0.14	0.01	1.61	0.09
SGt		0.88	0.02	–	0.89	0.01
BPt		0.96	0.03	–	0.96	0.02
GNPt+1		0.62	0.10	0.01	0.82	0.06
SGt+1		0.07	0.01	–	0.07	0.01
BPt+1		−0.21	−0.01	–	0.21	−0.01
El Salvador						
GNPt		0.26	7.22	0.02	−0.27	0.17
SGt		0.02	1.41	–	0.02	0.01
BPt		0.03	1.71	–	0.03	0.02
GNPt+1		0.18	1.57	0.02	0.18	0.08
SGt+1		0.02	0.13	–	0.02	0.01
BPt+1		–	−0.40	–	–	–
Guatemala						
GNPt		0.31	0.33	0.30	0.32	0.20
SGt		0.03	0.03	1.29	0.03	0.02
BPt		0.05	0.06	1.21	0.05	0.03
GNPt+1		0.27	0.24	0.13	0.28	0.14
SGt+1		0.03	0.02	0.01	0.03	0.01
BPt+1		−0.02	−0.03	−0.04	−0.02	−0.02
Honduras						
GNPt		0.04	−0.04	–	0.04	0.02
SGt		–	–	–	–	–
BPt		0.01	0.01	–	0.01	0.01
GNPt+1		0.03	0.03	–	0.03	0.02
SGt+1		–	–	–	–	–
BPt+1		−0.01	0.01	–	−0.01	–
Nicaragua						
GNPt		0.06	0.06	0.01	0.06	1.09
SGt		0.01	0.01	–	0.01	0.82
BPt		0.01	0.01	–	0.01	0.85
GNPt+1		0.04	0.03	–	0.04	0.21
SGt+1		0.01	–	0.01	0.01	0.03
BPt+1		–	–	0.01	–	−0.12

Table B-1-C. The Effects in Millions of C. A. Pesos at 1962 Prices of a 1% Increase
in "Other" Tax Rates (To/GDP) via Model 1

Country & variable affected	Country in which action is taken	Costa Rica	El Salvador	Guatemala	Honduras	Nicaragua
Central America						
GNPt		−10.10	−15.21	−23.14	−12.19	−7.42
GNPt+1		−5.31	−3.82	−11.46	−5.31	−2.41
Costa Rica						
GNPt		−6.96	−0.28	−0.84	−2.96	−0.41
SGt		3.71	−0.03	−0.09	−0.71	−0.05
BPt		2.41	−0.06	−0.18	−0.41	−0.09
GNPt+1		−2.87	−0.19	−0.58	−0.98	−0.27
SGt+1		−0.31	−0.02	−0.08	−0.21	−0.03
BPt+1		0.96	0.02	0.03	−0.46	0.03
El Salvador						
GNPt		−1.22	−14.08	−1.62	−1.42	−0.79
SGt		−0.10	4.69	−0.14	−0.10	−0.07
BPt		−0.16	3.72	−0.21	−0.18	−0.10
GNPt+1		−0.83	−3.06	−1.17	−1.05	−0.40
SGt+1		−0.07	−	−0.10	−0.09	0.03
BPt+1		−0.01	−	−0.02	−0.02	0.01
Guatemala						
GNPt		−1.45	0.64	−20.06	−2.42	−0.94
SGt		−0.14	0.06	7.85	−0.33	−0.09
BPt		−0.24	0.11	5.54	−0.55	−0.16
GNPt+1		−1.28	−0.46	−9.08	−1.46	−0.67
SGt+1		−0.12	−0.04	−0.85	−0.18	−0.06
BPt+1		−0.07	0.05	2.45	−0.09	−0.08
Honduras						
GNPt		−0.18	0.08	−0.24	−5.14	−0.12
SGt		−0.02	0.01	−0.03	−0.42	−0.01
BPt		−0.04	0.02	−0.06	−0.33	−0.03
GNPt+1		−0.14	−0.05	−0.20	−1.64	−0.07
SGt+1		−0.02	−0.01	−0.02	−0.22	−0.01
BPt+1		0.02	0.01	0.03	−0.19	0.02
Nicaragua						
GNPt		−0.29	−0.13	−0.38	−0.25	−5.17
SGt		−0.04	0.02	−0.05	−0.03	4.04
BPt		−0.06	0.03	−0.08	−0.06	3.07
GNPt+1		−0.19	−0.06	−0.27	−0.18	−1.01
SGt+1		−0.02	−0.01	−0.74	−0.02	−0.13
BPt+1		−	0.01	−0.66	−	0.39

Table B-1-D. The Effects in Millions of C. A. Pesos at 1962 Prices of a One Million
C. A. Peso Increase in Government Expenditure (G or Ig) via Model 1

Country & variable affected	Country in which spending is increased Costa Rica	El Salvador	Guatemala	Honduras	Nicaragua
Central America					
GNPt	2.57	2.73	2.59	2.02	1.77
GNPt+1	1.26	0.68	1.28	0.11	0.39
Costa Rica					
GNPt	1.77	0.05	0.09	0.17	0.10
SGt	−0.81	0.01	0.01	0.20	0.01
BPt	0.61	0.01	0.02	0.04	0.02
GNPt+1	0.66	0.03	0.08	0.05	0.06
SGt+1	0.07	−	0.01	0.01	0.01
BPt+1	−0.22	−	−	−0.03	0.01
El Salvador					
GNPt	0.31	2.53	0.18	0.33	0.19
SGt	0.03	0.79	0.01	0.03	0.02
BPt	0.04	0.67	0.02	0.04	0.02
GNPt+1	0.20	0.55	0.13	0.05	0.08
SGt+1	0.02	0.05	0.01	−	0.01
BPt+1	−	0.14	−	−0.02	0.01
Guatemala					
GNPt	0.37	0.12	2.25	0.40	0.22
SGt	0.03	0.01	−0.79	0.04	0.02
BPt	0.06	0.02	−0.62	0.07	0.04
GNPt+1	0.31	0.08	1.02	0.14	0.13
SGt+1	0.03	0.01	0.10	0.01	0.01
BPt+1	−0.02	−0.01	−0.27	−0.06	0.02
Honduras					
GNPt	0.05	0.01	0.03	1.04	0.03
SGt	0.01	−	−	−0.88	−
BPt	0.01	−	0.01	−0.75	0.01
GNPt+1	0.04	0.01	0.02	−0.15	0.01
SGt+1	−	−	−	−0.02	−
BPt+1	−0.01	−	−	0.11	−0.01
Nicaragua					
GNPt	0.07	0.02	0.04	0.08	1.23
SGt	0.01	−	0.01	0.01	0.84
BPt	0.02	0.01	0.01	0.02	0.73
GNPt+1	0.05	0.01	0.03	0.01	0.12
SGt+1	0.01	−	−	−	0.01
BPt+1	−	−	−	0.01	0.07

Table B-1-E. The Effects in Millions of C. A. Pesos at 1962 Prices of a 1 Million
C. A. Pesos Increase in the Stock of Reserve Money (RM) via Model 1

Country & variable affected	Country in which action is taken	Costa Rica	El Salvador	Guatemala	Honduras	Nicaragua
Central America						
GNPt		2.52	4.41	1.18	2.68	6.54
GNPt+1		1.34	1.51	0.71	0.64	1.89
Costa Rica						
GNPt		1.73	0.43	0.04	0.30	0.36
SGt		0.28	0.05	–	0.03	0.04
BPt		0.15	0.09	0.01	0.06	0.08
GNPt+1		−0.73	0.21	0.04	0.13	0.23
SGt+1		−0.08	C.02	–	0.01	0.03
BPt+1		0.24	0.05	–	--0.04	0.03
El Salvador						
GNPt		0.30	2.53	0.18	0.57	0.69
SGt		0.03	0.30	0.01	0.05	0.06
BPt		0.04	−0.04	0.02	0.07	0.09
GNPt+1		−0.21	0.66	0.07	0.16	0.32
SGt+1		−0.02	0.05	0.01	0.01	0.03
BPt+1		−0.01	0.14	–	0.03	0.02
Guatemala						
GNPt		0.36	0.98	2.35	0.68	0.83
SGt		0.03	0.09	0.22	0.06	0.08
BPt		0.06	0.16	−0.37	0.11	0.14
GNPt+1		−0.32	0.52	0.57	0.33	0.55
SGt+i		−0.03	0.05	0.05	0.03	0.05
BPt+1		0.02	0.11	−0.16	−0.08	0.07
Honduras						
GNPt		0.04	0.12	0.01	1.00	0.10
SGt		0.01	0.01	–	0.13	0.01
BPt		0.01	0.03	–	−0.47	0.02
GNPt+1		−0.04	0.05	0.01	−0.02	0.06
SGt+1		–	0.01	–	–	0.01
BPt+1		0.01	−0.02	–	0.02	0.02
Nicaragua						
GNPt		0.07	0.19	0.04	0.13	4.55
SGt		0.01	0.02	–	0.02	0.60
BPt		0.02	0.04	–	0.03	0.26
GNPt+1		−0.05	0.06	0.02	0.04	0.73
SGt+1		−0.01	0.01	–	–	0.09
BPt+1		–	0.01	–	−0.01	0.42

Table B-1-F. The Effects in Millions of C. A. Pesos at 1962 Prices of a One Million C. A. Pesos Increase in the Adjustment for Terms of Trade (TT) or Net Factor Income from Abroad (NFY) via Model 1

Country & variable affected	Country in which TT or NFY is increased	Costa Rica	El Salvador	Guatemala	Honduras	Nicaragua
Central America						
GNPt		2.73	2.87	2.71	2.10	1.84
GNPt+1		1.44	0.72	1.34	1.14	0.60
Costa Rica						
GNPt		1.88	0.05	0.10	0.18	0.10
SGt		0.14	0.01	0.01	0.02	0.01
BPt		0.35	0.01	0.02	0.04	0.02
GNPt+1		0.78	0.04	0.09	0.14	0.07
SGt+1		0.09	–	0.01	0.02	0.01
BPt+1		−0.26	–	–	−0.01	−0.01
El Salvador						
GNPt		0.33	2.66	0.19	0.35	0.20
SGt		0.03	0.17	0.01	0.03	0.02
BPt		0.04	0.30	0.02	0.05	0.03
GNPt+1		0.23	0.58	0.14	0.22	0.10
SGt+1		0.02	0.05	0.01	0.02	0.01
BPt+1		–	0.15	–	–	–
Guatemala						
GNPt		0.39	0.12	1.02	0.41	0.23
SGt		0.04	0.01	0.17	0.04	0.22
BPt		0.07	0.02	0.35	0.07	0.40
GNPt+1		0.35	0.09	1.06	0.35	0.16
SGt+1		0.03	0.01	0.10	0.03	0.02
BPt+1		−0.02	−0.01	−0.29	−0.02	−0.02
Honduras						
GNPt		0.05	0.02	0.03	1.08	0.29
SGt		0.01	–	–	0.08	–
BPt		0.01	–	0.01	0.22	0.01
GNPt+1		0.04	0.01	0.02	0.37	0.02
SGt+1		–	–	–	0.04	–
BPt+1		−0.01	–	–	−0.26	−0.01
Nicaragua						
GNPt		0.08	0.02	0.04	0.08	1.28
SGt		0.01	–	0.01	0.01	0.12
BPt		0.02	0.01	0.01	0.02	0.24
GNPt+1		0.05	0.01	0.03	0.05	0.25
SGt+1		0.01	–	–	0.01	0.03
BPt+1		–	–	–	–	−0.15

Table B-2-A. The Effects in Millions of C. A. Pesos at 1962 Prices of a 1% Increase in Export Tax Rate (Te/Ex) via Model 3

Country & variable affected	Country in which action is taken	Costa Rica	El Salvador	Guatemala	Honduras	Nicaragua
Central America						
GNPt		−20.24	−4.42	−5.50	−42.25	−1.40
GNPt+1		−7.51	−1.22	−4.59	−29.28	−0.41
Costa Rica						
GNPt		−18.94	−0.01	−0.09	−2.15	−
SGt		−2.21	−	−0.01	−0.30	−
BPt		−4.27	−	−0.02	−0.53	−
GNPt+1		−6.22	−0.01	−0.02	−1.80	−
SGt+1		−0.87	−	−	−0.25	−
BPt+1		1.79	−	0.01	−0.06	−
El Salvador						
GNPt		−0.43	−4.38	−0.15	−3.80	−
SGt		−0.04	0.12	−0.02	−0.38	−
BPt		−0.06	−0.11	−0.02	−0.56	−
GNPt+1		−0.28	−1.13	−0.03	3.22	−
SGt+1		−0.03	−0.12	−	−0.32	−
BPt+1		0.03	0.41	0.02	0.16	−
Guatemala						
GNPt		−0.64	−0.02	−5.17	−5.74	−
SGt		−0.06	−	0.31	−0.51	−
BPt		−0.11	−	−0.14	−0.95	−
GNPt+1		−0.80	−0.03	−4.50	−8.09	−
SGt+1		−0.07	−	−0.40	−0.72	−
BPt+1		0.06	−	0.71	0.34	−
Honduras						
GNPt		−0.10	−	−0.04	−29.32	−
SGt		−0.01	−	−	−2.14	−
BPt		−0.02	−	−0.01	−6.10	−
GNPt+1		−0.08	−	−0.01	−14.86	−
SGt+1		−0.01	−	−	−1.28	−
BPt+1		0.01	−	0.01	5.42	−
Nicaragua						
GNPt		−0.14	−0.01	−0.05	−1.23	−1.40
SGt		−0.02	−	−0.01	−0.14	0.56
BPt		−0.03	−	−0.01	−0.26	0.35
GNPt+1		−0.12	−	−0.02	−1.37	−0.51
SGt+1		−0.01	−	−	−0.15	−0.06
BPt+1		0.02	−	0.01	0.13	0.19

Table B-2-B. The Effects in Millions of C. A. Pesos at 1962 Prices of a 1% Increase in Import Duty Rate (Tn/Nx) via Model 3

Country & variable affected	Country in which action is taken	Costa Rica	El Salvador	Guatemala	Honduras	Nicaragua
Central America						
GNPt		0.53	5.25	1.71	3.15	3.42
GNPt+1		0.15	0.32	1.35	2.18	0.85
Costa Rica						
GNPt		0.49	0.01	0.03	0.16	−
SGt		0.91	−	−	0.02	−
BPt		0.86	−	0.01	0.03	−
GNPt+1		0.12	−	−	0.13	−
SGt+1		0.02	−	−	0.02	−
BPt+1		−0.03	−	−	−	−
El Salvador						
GNPt		0.01	−5.20	0.05	0.28	−
SGt		−	1.36	−	0.03	−
BPt		−	1.56	0.01	0.04	−
GNPt+1		0.01	0.29	0.01	0.24	−
SGt+1		−	0.03	−	0.02	−
BPt+1		−	−0.10	−0.01	−0.01	−
Guatemala						
GNPt		0.02	0.03	1.61	0.43	−
SGt		−	−	1.35	0.04	−
BPt		−	−	1.37	0.07	−
GNPt+1		0.02	0.03	1.33	0.60	−
SGt+1		−	−	0.12	0.05	−
BPt+1		−	−	−0.21	−0.03	−
Honduras						
GNPt		−	−	0.01	2.18	−
SGt		−	−	−	0.58	−
BPt		−	−	−	0.82	−
GNPt+1		−	−	−	1.11	−
SGt+1		−	−	−	0.10	−
BPt+1		−	−	−	−0.40	−
Nicaragua						
GNPt		−	0.01	0.02	0.09	3.42
SGt		−	−	−	0.01	0.87
BPt		−	−	−	0.02	1.14
GNPt+1		−	−	0.01	0.10	1.08
SGt+1		−	−	−	0.01	0.12
BPt+1		−	−	−	−0.01	−0.40

Table B–2–C. The Effects in Millions of C. A. Pesos at 1962 Prices of a 1% Increase in "Other" Tax Rate (To/GDP) via Model 3

Country & variable affected	Country in which action is taken	Costa Rica	El Salvador	Guatemala	Honduras	Nicaragua
Central America						
GNPt		−7.83	−11.37	−25.81	−8.94	−7.16
GNPt+1		−2.25	−0.71	−20.34	−6.19	−1.79
Costa Rica						
GNPt		7.32	−0.02	−0.42	−0.46	−
SGt		3.44	−	−0.06	−0.06	−
BPt		2.11	−0.01	−0.10	−0.11	−
GNPt+1		−1.79	−0.01	−0.07	−0.38	−
SGt+1		−0.25	−	−0.01	−0.05	−
BPt+1		0.52	−	0.06	−0.01	−
El Salvador						
GNPt		−0.16	−11.26	−0.74	−0.81	−
SGt		−0.02	4.74	−0.07	−0.08	−
BPt		−0.02	3.89	−0.11	−0.12	−
GNPt+1		−0.10	−0.63	−0.14	−0.68	−
SGt+1		−0.01	−0.06	−0.01	−0.01	−
BPt+1		−0.01	0.22	0.10	0.03	−
Guatemala						
GNPt		−0.25	−0.06	−24.24	−1.12	−
SGt		−0.02	−0.01	7.56	−0.11	−
BPt		−0.04	−0.01	4.93	−0.20	−
GNPt+1		−0.29	−0.06	−19.98	−1.71	−
SGt+1		−0.03	−0.01	−1.79	−0.15	−
BPt+1		0.03	0.01	3.12	−0.07	−
Honduras						
GNPt		−0.04	−0.01	−0.17	−6.20	−
SGt		−	−	−0.02	3.71	−
BPt		−0.01	−	−0.04	2.26	−
GNPt+1		−0.03	−0.01	−0.06	−3.14	−
SGt+1		−	−	−0.01	−0.27	−
BPt+1		−	−	0.04	1.15	−
Nicaragua						
GNPt		−0.05	−0.01	−0.24	−0.26	−7.16
SGt		−0.01	−	−0.03	−0.03	3.87
BPt		−0.01	−	−0.05	−0.05	2.70
GNPt+1		−0.04	−0.01	−0.10	−0.28	−2.26
SGt+1		−	−	−0.01	−0.03	−0.26
BPt+1		0.01	−	0.06	0.03	0.85

Table B-2-D. The Effects in Millions of C. A. Pesos at 1962 Prices of a One Million C. A. Peso Increase in Government Expenditure (G or Ig) via Model 3

Country & variable affected	Country in which action is taken	Costa Rica	El Salvador	Guatemala	Honduras	Nicaragua
Central America						
GNPt		2.00	2.05	2.89	2.47	1.71
GNPt+1		0.57	0.13	2.28	1.71	0.54
Costa Rica						
GNPt		1.87	–	–	0.13	–
SGt		–0.74	–	0.01	0.02	–
BPt		–0.54	–	0.01	0.03	–
GNPt+1		0.46	–	0.01	0.10	–
SGt+1		0.06	–	–	0.01	–
BPt+1		0.13	–	0.01	–	–
El Salvador						
GNPt		0.04	2.03	0.08	0.22	–
SGt		–	0.80	0.01	0.02	–
BPt		0.01	0.70	0.01	0.03	–
GNPt+1		0.03	0.11	0.02	0.19	–
SGt+1		–	0.01	–	0.02	–
BPt+1		–	0.04	–0.01	–0.01	–
Guatemala						
GNPt		0.06	0.01	2.72	0.34	–
SGt		–	–	–0.76	0.03	–
BPt		0.01	–	–0.55	0.06	–
GNPt+1		0.07	0.01	2.24	0.47	–
SGt+1		0.01	–	0.20	0.04	–
BPt+1		–0.01	–	–0.35	–0.02	–
Honduras						
GNPt		0.01	–	0.02	1.71	–
SGt		–	–	–	–0.85	–
BPt		–	–	–	–0.62	–
GNPt+1		0.01	–	0.01	0.87	–
SGt+1		–	–	–	0.07	–
BPt+1		–	–	–	–0.32	–
Nicaragua						
GNPt		0.01	–	0.03	0.07	1.71
SGt		–	–	–	0.01	–0.81
BPt		–	–	0.01	0.01	–0.65
GNPt+1		0.01	–	0.01	0.08	0.54
SGt+1		–	–	–	0.01	0.06
BPt+1		–	–	–0.01	–0.01	–0.20

Table B–2–E. The Effects in Millions of C. A. Pesos at 1962 Prices of a One Million
C. A. Peso Increase in the Flow of Reserve Money (DRM) via Model 3

Country & variable affected	Country in which action is taken	Costa Rica	El Salvador	Guatemala	Honduras	Nicaragua
Central America						
GNPt		7.98	4.22	0.18	−0.47	2.56
GNPt+1		8.29	6.09	0.04	−0.33	2.79
Costa Rica						
GNPt		7.47	0.38	−	−0.02	−
SGt		1.37	0.05	−	−	−
BPt		−0.30	0.09	−	−0.01	−
GNPt+1		7.44	0.48	−	−0.02	−
SGt+1		1.16	0.07	−	−	−
BPt+1		0.61	0.05	−	−	−
El Salvador						
GNPt		0.17	2.46	0.01	−0.04	−
SGt		0.02	0.36	−	−	−
BPt		0.02	−0.29	−	−0.01	−
GNPt+1		0.23	3.21	−	−0.04	−
SGt+1		0.02	0.42	−	−	−
BPt+1		0.01	−0.59	−	−	−
Guatemala						
GNPt		0.25	1.01	0.17	−0.06	−
SGt		0.02	0.09	0.22	−0.01	−
BPt		0.04	1.17	−0.71	−0.01	−
GNPt+1		0.48	1.86	0.04	−0.09	−
SGt+1		0.04	0.17	0.18	−0.01	−
BPt+1		0.01	0.01	−0.59	−	−
Honduras						
GNPt		0.04	0.16	−	−0.32	−
SGt		−	0.01	−	−	−
BPt		0.01	0.03	−	−0.04	−
GNPt+1		0.06	0.23	−	−0.17	−
SGt+1		0.01	0.02	−	−0.01	−
BPt+1		−	−	−	0.06	−
Nicaragua						
GNPt		0.05	0.22	−	−0.01	2.56
SGt		0.01	0.02	−	−	0.30
BPt		0.01	0.04	−	−	−0.30
GNPt+1		0.08	0.32	−	−0.01	2.79
SGt+1		0.01	0.04	−	−	0.32
BPt+1		−	−	−	−	0.58

Table B-2-F. The Effects in Millions of C. A. Pesos at 1962 Prices of a One Million C. A. Peso Increase in Terms of Trade Adjustment (TT) or Net Factor Income from Abroad (NFY) via Model 3

Country & variable affected	Country in which TT or NFY is increased	Costa Rica	El Salvador	Guatemala	Honduras	Nicaragua
Central America						
GNPt		2.75	2.94	3.65	3.11	2.53
GNPt+1		0.76	0.18	2.85	2.19	0.78
Costa Rica						
GNPt		2.64	–	–	0.11	–
SGt		0.23	–	–	0.02	–
BPt		0.53	–	0.01	0.03	–
GNPt+1		0.65	–	0.02	0.13	–
SGt+1		0.09	–	–	0.02	–
BPt+1		−0.19	–	–	0.01	–
El Salvador						
GNPt		0.04	2.94	0.08	0.19	–
SGt		--	0.19	0.01	0.02	–
BPt		0.01	0.33	0.01	0.03	–
GNPt+1		0.03	0.16	0.04	0.23	–
SGt+1		–	0.02	–	0.02	–
BPt+1		–	0.06	−0.01	–	–
Guatemala						
GNPt		0.06	0.01	3.49	0.29	–
SGt		0.01	–	0.22	0.03	–
BPt		0.01	–	0.49	0.05	–
GNPt+1		0.07	0.01	2.77	0.50	–
SGt+1		0.01	–	0.25	0.05	–
BPt+1		–	–	−0.47	–	–
Honduras						
GNPt		0.01	–	0.02	2.46	–
SGt		–	–	–	0.13	–
BPt		–	–	–	0.47	–
GNPt+1		0.01	–	0.01	1.25	–
SGt+1		–	–	–	0.11	–
BPt+1		–	–	–	−0.46	–
Nicaragua						
GNPt		0.01	–	0.02	0.06	2.53
SGt		–	–	–	0.01	0.17
BPt		–	–	0.01	0.01	0.42
GNPt+1		0.01	–	0.02	0.09	0.78
SGt+1		–	–	–	0.01	0.09
BPt+1		–	–	–	–	−0.30

Table B–3. Historical Forecasts Using Model 1 1951–66

Variable	1951	1952	1953	1954	1955	1956	1957
1 GNPG	723.9122	738.4053	773.7871	769.4272	759.9852	923.3722	974.4108
2 GDPG	706.4122	722.7053	758.7871	745.1272	732.6852	888.6722	949.3108
3 YDG	665.4843	662.7040	692.9547	685.0351	676.0743	828.6172	871.9748
4 CG	608.8911	606.3411	634.0867	626.8229	618.6042	758.5150	798.2822
5 IPG	43.2204	44.8382	50.8528	54.2543	60.5332	75.1565	94.3553
6 EXG	71.8442	69.7511	79.1151	72.8314	70.1327	88.3195	92.6265
7 EIG	-8.4864	-0.2659	6.8347	7.6413	-2.3839	8.6551	6.8885
8 NXG	80.6824	81.7843	97.4378	101.6536	109.1110	148.3046	160.7920
9 NIG	2.1748	1.0749	1.9643	-0.9309	-4.3100	8.7693	11.1497
10 TEG	9.8416	14.1644	12.8703	13.9771	21.3241	17.0237	17.1198
11 TNG	23.7353	29.3518	29.4861	25.5144	19.8978	28.7559	31.9462
12 TOG	24.8510	32.1851	38.4761	44.9006	42.6891	48.9754	53.3699
13 KG	1441.3879	1488.3182	1526.7478	1558.8168	1601.4932	1681.7540	1807.7453
14 MSG	60.0173	66.0812	79.2905	81.3613	88.2657	105.8884	112.5827
15 CRG	12.9842	22.2905	42.5631	45.7412	56.3376	83.3834	93.6573
16 SGG	-15.3721	-9.1987	-6.4676	0.0921	-6.6891	-20.3451	-26.6640
17 TOE	-1.9993	2.3260	1.5476	4.0499	-9.7522	-25.3994	-47.3268
18 GNPE	410.6046	450.1914	542.8713	524.0809	505.6784	581.5845	590.1980
19 GDPE	365.9046	405.4914	479.6713	461.7809	446.7784	524.4845	536.5980
20 YDE	336.5085	402.5235	490.0306	458.5022	453.1513	522.7991	522.4509
21 CE	322.9801	357.1306	440.1074	410.2113	405.1374	471.1795	470.8493
22 IPE	31.5395	41.4523	40.1569	45.2538	42.8909	49.3084	54.1335
23 EXE	53.4815	65.5034	65.4287	59.3793	65.6554	79.8387	78.9014
24 EIE	-2.2459	3.8370	7.1547	7.6992	-0.3056	10.1812	9.8669
25 NXE	84.7380	101.4338	116.1324	107.8800	115.8262	135.1105	131.0520
26 NIE	-1.8874	7.5980	7.9439	8.1826	4.7734	12.6128	14.8102
27 TEE	12.2128	12.7612	13.2115	19.3828	17.0555	14.6812	18.6272
28 TNE	12.8078	13.5546	19.0556	20.6591	18.6633	21.7758	24.6622
29 TOE	19.0754	21.3521	20.5737	25.5368	16.8083	22.3284	24.4577
30 KE	800.9170	839.0248	867.8719	903.6738	930.9609	972.9059	1029.7460
31 MSE	73.8233	81.8271	78.1519	79.2136	76.5185	81.2554	83.1338
32 CRE	67.7702	101.4148	85.9658	90.4288	79.0995	99.0116	106.9077
33 SGE	1.0960	1.0679	1.9408	10.2787	-1.4729	-2.9145	-0.9530
34 BPE	13.0850	5.0085	11.7071	13.3159	3.6502	-0.6034	-3.4849
35 GNPN	221.1558	252.5669	284.6027	304.9782	301.9995	314.1189	320.2917
36 GDPN	223.1558	256.0669	283.5027	294.9782	288.2995	308.3189	320.0917
37 YDN	195.7695	223.5698	253.6211	274.9561	273.8652	276.0596	283.5153
38 CN	168.5588	193.4145	220.2828	239.3579	238.3826	240.3445	247.0105
39 IPN	20.6540	28.2838	35.3274	36.1660	33.7723	36.8492	35.4535
40 EXN	40.3651	52.4444	61.1050	66.1643	60.9564	68.8288	75.4694
41 EIN	0.5769	2.3392	3.7353	3.1508	-0.7707	3.9521	3.4027

42 NXN	35.8460	50.5478	67.5609	82.6197	80.5820	80.4338	84.3622
43 NIN	-4.7471	-0.8328	3.1869	5.2412	3.3591	4.0218	3.6823
44 TEN	3.0026	2.8185	2.6119	2.3536	3.5458	6.4439	5.1605
45 TNN	12.4570	14.4453	15.5470	14.3035	14.4101	17.8476	17.7615
46 TON	9.9268	11.7332	12.8226	13.3650	10.1784	13.7679	13.8543
47 KN	433.5815	460.7813	496.0549	537.3810	575.1048	617.5242	651.4910
48 MSN	30.6471	35.8850	38.8313	40.4682	33.4298	35.2303	37.0308
49 CRN	34.8059	40.6860	44.8116	47.9347	44.4163	47.6647	50.9132
50 SGN	1.2863	-0.3030	-2.8184	-7.9979	-11.7557	-4.7406	-10.0236
51 BPN	7.8431	1.5685	-4.8075	-8.5457	-10.0553	-5.8748	-8.9724
52 GNPC	256.8110	281.5184	326.4091	365.1239	345.9285	398.4127	397.9130
53 GDPC	232.2110	257.6184	302.9091	327.0239	326.1285	366.1127	366.3130
54 YDC	223.2865	242.1444	280.6082	316.8363	288.7294	340.0890	336.4036
55 CC	198.6277	215.1906	248.9734	280.7925	256.1062	301.2154	297.9785
56 IPC	31.7972	37.8869	39.9224	45.0936	52.5962	54.9445	57.7145
57 EXC	57.8072	63.2806	75.6173	71.3632	64.9012	69.4732	75.5673
58 EIC	-2.6886	2.0229	4.5423	3.1951	-2.6084	3.1867	3.6748
59 NXC	84.7966	101.8668	107.4410	114.1754	100.1884	112.4579	122.4956
60 NIC	-4.4641	-2.9042	2.8053	7.2451	-0.2215	7.0492	3.4265
61 TEC	1.2489	1.6895	1.6738	2.3857	3.0625	3.2330	3.5277
62 TNC	14.5828	16.8110	24.1216	28.2905	32.7127	33.2386	33.3981
63 TOC	17.6928	20.8736	20.0055	17.6114	21.4241	21.8520	24.5836
64 KC	504.2047	542.3119	585.5699	632.7711	679.8012	727.2195	776.0570
65 MSC	39.2501	47.8112	53.3077	56.7145	56.4993	57.1200	62.7557
66 SGC	6.5246	1.1741	1.7009	0.2876	2.0991	1.5237	4.2094
67 BPC	-0.6139	-9.7591	-6.5866	-8.7622	-17.8740	-14.5472	-15.0800
68 GNPH	266.1160	290.6126	316.7467	314.9833	299.7749	332.6487	339.4500
69 GDPH	284.9160	300.9126	324.7467	310.8833	299.1749	338.3487	342.9500
70 YDH	240.9464	263.7246	289.5840	289.0400	272.5433	303.1118	305.7365
71 CH	211.4067	231.0135	253.2725	252.8042	238.6044	264.9168	267.1761
72 IPH	37.8999	41.4613	40.5304	43.2167	35.1235	37.1348	38.8181
73 EXH	64.7971	62.1907	81.2328	55.4162	51.1706	66.1932	61.5705
74 EIH	2.9048	4.3531	5.4989	5.8999	4.2135	7.2287	7.2930
75 NXH	59.6834	68.2188	77.6636	71.0152	65.1142	70.9164	69.7034
76 NIH	-2.2909	3.2872	9.2243	6.0386	-5.1770	3.5085	1.4043
77 TEH	0.4472	0.6397	0.7993	1.0422	1.1334	1.3109	1.4518
78 TNH	11.2857	11.6214	11.9383	12.8462	10.1920	13.7729	14.2755
79 TOH	13.4368	14.6269	14.4250	12.0550	15.9063	14.4531	17.9862
80 KH	601.4549	641.4113	679.7379	719.9242	733.9885	770.3398	803.4206
81 MSH	25.4353	29.2392	32.0997	38.4980	31.4530	35.7286	33.8722
82 SGH	-0.1304	-6.5120	-3.9373	-4.6566	-2.7684	-7.7631	-5.4865
83 BPH	-8.4906	-15.2622	-8.1562	-11.6376	-3.9530	-6.7030	-5.7442
84 CCM	1510.4644	1603.0903	1796.7227	1809.9889	1756.8347	2036.1712	2081.2967
85 ITCM	214.4110	260.0226	279.0898	295.8844	306.7161	364.6935	403.4750
86 GNPCM	1878.5997	2013.2947	2244.4169	2278.5936	2213.3665	2550.1370	2622.2635
87 GDPCM	1812.5997	1942.7947	2149.6169	2139.7936	2093.0665	2425.9370	2515.2635

Table B-3. (Continued)

Variable	1958	1959	1960	1961	1962	1963	1964	1965	1966
1 GNPG	918.5135	932.9425	924.1990	1005.4096	1055.5331	1090.3206	1193.1839	1271.0727	1311.4857
2 GDPG	914.1135	935.8425	927.7990	1021.0096	1067.4331	1111.6206	1205.8839	1292.4727	1355.1857
3 YDG	821.6848	837.2793	829.5776	905.0867	977.6746	1018.1954	1104.5823	1162.8329	1198.9639
4 CG	752.1567	766.4598	759.3959	828.6520	895.2290	932.3942	1011.6275	1065.0543	1098.1933
5 IPG	87.0285	81.5935	81.7698	81.8336	82.1941	92.3506	112.2767	127.3745	134.4211
6 EXG	101.0626	121.3432	118.8154	121.3141	135.4027	146.8288	154.8016	171.4051	197.9807
7 EIG	1.6549	-0.9698	0.8267	9.7444	12.8477	23.6331	24.2091	35.3240	44.4907
8 NXG	142.4425	144.5456	144.7808	129.0328	149.4454	168.0583	191.9876	201.2044	207.4508
9 NIG	3.3466	2.2407	-1.0719	11.0018	13.2950	14.1278	21.4435	31.4808	37.9494
10 TEG	12.7263	11.1548	10.0765	9.3537	8.3263	6.3183	7.1550	8.6116	9.4730
11 TNG	31.1821	35.6869	33.2035	34.6318	25.7007	22.8607	28.0630	31.6545	30.6848
12 TOG	52.9203	48.8215	51.3414	56.3375	43.8316	42.9463	53.3835	67.9737	72.3639
13 KG	1896.6810	1968.9335	2000.7698	2090.0736	2144.4166	2202.5131	2303.8267	2412.4745	2517.8561
14 MSG	101.9388	107.7925	107.3414	114.6662	113.8998	127.2142	136.3253	146.9076	159.4864
15 CRG	77.3219	86.3057	85.6134	96.8549	95.6787	116.1125	130.0956	146.3365	165.6414
16 SGG	-21.1713	-18.5368	-16.0786	-19.1770	-26.6415	-26.4747	-27.7985	-17.7602	-12.9783
17 BPG	-38.6717	-29.3109	-27.6667	-24.5760	-26.3900	-33.0242	-47.1203	-47.3561	-46.6288
18 GNPE	586.3339	576.3094	552.2245	641.7881	626.4885	651.0189	647.2866	799.9378	858.3752
19 GDPE	555.4339	561.2094	534.9245	634.7881	628.4885	652.6189	643.5866	777.0378	846.7752
20 YDE	523.6511	516.0560	493.0377	576.5721	564.1182	586.2065	579.5023	715.6208	772.1635
21 CE	471.9873	464.7855	442.9588	522.1686	510.3595	531.3043	524.9472	654.0188	707.6343
22 IPE	51.9061	53.4324	50.1087	53.4412	58.3868	69.8673	74.5040	85.5463	92.6623
23 EXE	91.3500	104.4308	104.6037	112.1196	120.9497	131.5886	136.3821	144.2900	150.5948
24 EIE	8.1088	6.5410	7.5523	18.3399	22.2883	30.4246	33.2156	45.8915	56.7134
25 NXE	124.9346	125.6320	124.2839	121.9128	131.9053	151.0098	162.2543	193.0543	205.7476
26 NIE	10.5837	12.5484	9.6151	19.1684	20.5906	29.7562	31.9080	44.7546	49.7820
27 TEE	12.2744	9.2199	10.4829	9.6612	8.6466	10.0965	11.3241	13.2131	13.7862
28 TNE	24.4347	24.7432	24.3698	25.2470	23.0442	22.0298	20.4847	24.6780	25.2878
29 TOE	25.9737	26.2902	24.3342	30.3079	30.6794	32.6860	35.9754	46.4258	47.1376
30 KE	1083.2661	1128.8049	1151.9312	1206.7887	1247.3468	1299.1623	1349.6965	1440.3538	1528.7498
31 MSE	78.9686	81.4187	79.4586	80.6837	82.8071	91.1376	93.5060	100.0397	102.6532
32 CRE	89.3989	99.6982	91.4587	96.6084	105.5345	140.5523	150.5083	177.9732	188.9592
33 SGE	-4.9172	-9.9466	-4.4132	-4.5840	-6.6297	-5.3877	-0.9157	-0.7830	-8.4883
34 BPE	-5.1595	-12.1085	-4.4430	-3.6217	-11.2579	-20.3527	-20.8645	-24.7273	-36.6214
35 GNPN	311.7687	315.3890	326.3662	354.9077	407.8613	433.4731	447.3345	474.4857	505.6921
36 GDPN	318.1687	333.7890	337.4662	360.5077	410.8613	446.9731	464.8345	497.7857	529.0921
37 YDN	277.9573	279.2282	286.8886	316.1510	369.6509	391.8393	401.3578	419.7617	449.0297
38 CN	242.0413	243.1776	250.0266	276.1895	324.0227	343.8609	352.3712	368.8258	394.9937
39 IPN	34.9397	34.7618	33.5283	35.0082	48.5809	59.4174	62.8376	66.3937	68.5283
40 EXN	75.2164	85.1206	90.1626	83.5781	109.6843	124.4738	136.6724	150.5437	161.6820
41 EIN	1.2255	-0.0069	-0.0080	3.8384	4.0846	6.8597	7.5188	11.7408	14.6474
42 NXN	80.3885	73.0682	76.3771	80.8097	114.2690	129.1596	140.8300	151.8866	167.7479

43 NIN	0.8657	0.0959	0.5661	3.9968	11.5421	14.4790	15.4353	18.6317	22.5115
44 TEN	2.8072	0.8241	1.0192	0.8637	0.8388	0.7886	0.8824	1.1368	1.5072
45 TNN	17.2149	21.5798	23.1137	21.7364	21.1089	21.3983	19.8981	22.3744	23.7739
46 TON	13.7893	13.7569	15.3447	16.1566	16.2627	19.4470	25.1962	31.2127	31.3813
47 KN	681.4672	708.9418	735.5933	768.0732	814.8609	857.6324	913.3726	982.5737	1056.2108
48 MSN	34.0845	36.3761	37.8492	38.6677	52.0898	59.2918	63.8750	68.6218	70.4224
49 CRN	50.5275	54.1519	57.1497	59.6463	71.7920	79.1758	84.5545	90.0586	93.3071
50 SGN		-7.7392	-1.2224	-7.9433	-12.0896	-13.9662	-15.7233	-16.0761	-22.8376
51 BPN	-11.2123	-6.4504	2.1114	-2.9900	-15.0422	-25.4051	-29.5742	-31.5338	-37.3299
52 GNPC	389.0911	395.4824	445.8599	466.1731	487.6209	546.3892	536.5243	580.4359	618.5109
53 GDPC	377.5911	388.3824	446.7599	469.8731	494.1209	550.3892	538.5243	586.8359	619.1109
54 YDC	326.3133	327.2361	371.2563	394.3872	407.8811	458.7875	447.8938	488.2249	516.9682
55 CC	289.1162	289.9266	328.5896	348.9055	360.7572	405.4683	395.9003	431.3231	456.5684
56 IPC	56.6204	61.5594	65.1259	64.9385	69.6350	71.0759	74.7199	83.3209	82.4888
57 EXC	83.6664	89.8677	102.7238	107.9188	107.9399	115.3110	110.9650	112.2997	123.7256
58 EIC	0.7678	-0.8039	-2.2216	3.4480	5.5528	9.1918	11.4832	18.2870	22.8119
59 NXC	116.0869	117.9807	119.7335	122.7568	128.7935	137.9345	143.9691	162.4116	168.1924
60 NIC	-1.9073	-4.1132	2.7244	3.3808	4.2705	13.5232	7.9750	13.4832	17.7914
61 TEC	3.6253	3.8211	3.6754	3.6671	4.1757	4.3860	5.0253	5.5083	5.3994
62 TNC	38.3302	41.0780	41.9465	39.9385	42.6258	46.5739	43.8510	43.9357	47.2388
63 TOC	20.8223	23.3472	28.9817	28.1803	32.9383	36.6418	39.7542	42.7670	48.9044
64 KC	831.8304	878.7169	948.6059	1001.8685	1072.2725	1130.7859	1196.2249	1264.5084	1351.2963
65 MSC	65.8839	69.1514	72.0010	68.8605	72.4066	77.4851	78.9416	83.4629	85.4766
66 SGC	1.1778	6.5463	-0.3964	0.9859	-3.5602	-13.1983	-8.7696	-25.2889	-17.9573
67 BPC	-18.2454	-17.7036	-22.8556	-18.4709	-26.0712	-30.9549	-31.4959	-51.7081	-40.0463
68 GNPH	361.4141	359.5270	376.5090	405.5446	418.1003	437.6309	457.7544	490.5902	513.2098
69 GDPH	370.9141	370.4270	389.6090	411.1446	424.7003	444.5309	465.3544	493.5902	527.6098
70 YDH	328.0732	325.7132	340.4309	371.0908	384.0463	402.4179	417.7015	435.6102	462.0406
71 CH	286.4029	284.3714	297.0400	323.4312	334.5829	350.3965	363.5522	378.9675	401.7180
72 IPH	40.1028	39.5586	43.4269	41.8238	50.7200	52.2953	48.8538	51.4764	54.6170
73 EXH	79.7772	68.1989	73.7661	75.7235	79.4446	73.0603	91.0698	105.1398	125.2445
74 EIH	6.8742	6.6529	6.7639	11.1410	12.4108	14.7294	15.2389	18.5399	20.5969
75 NXH	74.4653	67.3062	70.0257	74.7416	78.1412	84.8577	91.4196	97.1212	107.3819
76 NIH	5.8777	1.1487	3.3622	11.6333	11.6166	15.1935	18.8408	23.7122	31.6847
77 TEH	1.5754	1.7431	1.8996	1.6617	1.8372	2.0249	2.1801	2.3497	2.4969
78 TNH	15.7110	16.8202	17.9851	18.5605	17.6369	17.6047	17.7845	19.0040	20.5070
79 TOH	16.0545	15.2505	16.1935	17.2315	14.5799	15.5834	20.0883	23.6263	28.1654
80 KH	836.1028	863.1961	892.9394	921.9038	947.3725	994.0158	1026.7788	1067.8289	1111.8445
81 MSH	32.8413	32.9896	33.9633	33.7579	36.5005	39.3610	41.6320	44.9642	46.6455
82 SGH	-4.7592	-6.2862	-5.9218	-7.9463	-3.2460	-18.8870	-16.8471	-15.3200	-13.3308
83 BPH	-3.1916	-4.5030	-5.9578	-2.1104	-4.5025	-19.1614	-11.5517	-10.1537	-7.6251
84 CCM	2041.7044	2048.7209	2078.0109	2299.3468	2424.9512	2563.4242	2648.3984	2898.1894	3059.1077
85 ITCM	378.2975	368.9057	354.8597	367.3452	393.9168	435.3070	472.1919	538.8119	570.9175
86 GNPCM	2567.1213	2579.6502	2625.1587	2876.8231	2995.6042	3158.8328	3282.0836	3606.5222	3807.2737
87 GDPCM	2536.2213	2589.6502	2636.5587	2897.3231	3025.6042	3206.1328	3318.1836	3647.7222	3877.7737

Table B–4. Historical Forecasts Using Model 2 1951–66

Variable	1951	1952	1953	1954	1955	1956	1957
1 GNPG	746.4872	755.0591	771.8544	759.7662	755.8400	927.4136	965.7084
2 GDPG	728.9872	739.3591	756.8544	735.4662	728.5400	892.7136	940.6084
3 YDG	686.1964	678.1947	691.1000	677.1443	672.6565	831.8699	863.8072
4 CG	628.0419	620.7097	632.5352	619.7471	615.6349	761.5268	790.7920
5 IPG	42.0740	43.0069	52.6930	53.5440	61.9799	80.3020	92.8715
6 EXG	73.9631	71.9805	79.7860	71.6300	70.3497	87.2142	90.5554
7 EIG	-5.4647	1.3342	2.2000	2.8713	-2.5873	3.6259	3.1233
8 NXG	83.9375	82.7959	97.3998	96.9577	107.9598	151.0403	160.4950
9 NIG	-0.5104	-0.2237	0.2599	-0.3313	-0.5228	4.0150	5.3388
10 TEG	9.9784	14.2937	12.9162	13.9208	21.3211	16.9566	16.9988
11 TNG	24.3578	29.5731	29.4681	24.2893	19.3897	29.4115	31.9599
12 TOG	25.9546	32.9975	38.3701	44.4118	42.4726	49.1756	52.9426
13 KG	1440.2415	1486.4869	1528.5880	1558.1065	1602.9399	1686.8995	1806.2615
14 MSG	60.7486	66.2296	76.8454	77.7256	84.2751	104.3452	110.3362
15 CRG	26.5345	32.0170	35.1167	43.7694	47.2566	53.5916	64.2076
16 SGG	-13.5092	-8.0356	-6.5456	-1.6781	-7.4165	-19.5562	-27.1988
17 BPG	2.5713	6.4425	-0.6737	2.1750	-12.3747	-29.5152	-47.0551
18 GNPE	423.6925	460.1634	541.5695	519.7201	512.9652	581.0695	584.4278
19 GDPE	378.9925	415.4634	478.3695	457.4201	454.0652	523.9695	530.8278
20 YDE	377.2170	410.1329	487.9038	455.0888	460.9813	522.4161	518.0786
21 CE	333.2833	364.4635	438.1335	407.0488	412.6307	470.8260	466.7173
22 IPE	34.4273	41.3533	39.0276	45.0923	40.4529	48.4531	52.8835
23 EXE	60.6339	75.9616	69.2103	58.2504	62.5767	80.3101	74.8943
24 EIE	-1.6815	2.8100	4.8635	4.8726	1.1255	7.2955	7.3566
25 NXE	90.9623	107.3393	119.7831	105.6033	112.3883	134.9877	128.4644
26 NIE	-0.2918	8.3856	3.9823	7.5408	4.3324	9.6275	11.2595
27 TEE	13.1790	13.9238	13.7351	19.1127	16.7122	14.7238	18.0210
28 TNE	13.6552	14.3584	19.5521	20.3504	18.1971	21.7593	24.3105
29 TOE	19.6413	21.7483	20.3785	25.1682	17.0745	22.1703	24.0176
30 KE	803.8048	838.9258	866.7426	903.5123	928.5229	972.0506	1028.4960
31 MSE	66.4504	80.2110	73.1533	78.7611	75.9754	86.5870	91.9547
32 CRE	43.4261	55.5438	52.5851	55.6555	68.2353	93.7792	116.0968
33 SGE	3.4755	3.4306	2.7657	9.3313	-2.0162	-3.0466	-2.3509
34 BPE	12.9819	7.7467	13.5084	12.2789	5.8816	0.0904	-3.8730
35 GNPN	243.8279	258.1642	282.5153	286.5199	308.5919	321.0299	310.0868
36 GDPN	245.8279	261.6642	281.4153	276.5199	294.8919	315.2299	309.8868
37 YDN	215.1448	228.0432	251.5912	258.4910	279.7855	282.7474	274.5872
38 CN	185.6847	197.2433	218.3451	224.5281	243.6106	246.2648	238.9523
39 IPN	24.9869	28.8119	35.6228	34.8235	31.7426	40.1597	32.5896
40 EXN	52.8034	57.7022	62.0969	55.8235	59.4797	67.4251	69.4880
41 EIN	0.8205	2.3584	1.9110	1.8011	0.3176	2.1178	2.3250
42 NXN	45.9222	53.8843	66.6537	74.8754	80.7554	79.9253	79.9031

43 NIN	-3.3546	-0.1328	3.7068	3.5809	-0.5967	3.6122	0.3651
44 TEN	3.1776	2.8973	2.6336	2.2285	3.5302	6.4096	5.0721
45 TNN	14.6137	15.3034	15.6159	13.3414	14.7893	17.8082	17.0615
46 TON	10.8918	11.9203	12.6746	12.4591	10.4869	14.0647	13.3661
47 KN	437.9144	461.3094	496.3503	536.0385	573.0751	620.8347	648.6271
48 MSN	29.6843	32.9030	36.1933	39.7344	36.1926	38.4503	38.8583
49 CRN	28.3508	32.5455	38.5105	47.7455	55.7939	55.1320	59.9553
50 SGN	4.5831	0.8210	-2.8759	-9.9710	-11.0937	-4.5175	-11.3004
51 BPN	9.0562	2.8091	-5.2526	-10.8317	-6.6613	-8.1946	-8.2551
52 GNPC	237.7933	292.3769	339.2090	382.3848	322.4885	380.7601	401.2018
53 GDPC	213.1933	268.4769	315.7090	344.2848	302.6885	348.4601	369.6018
54 YDC	205.4697	251.2901	291.4378	332.5800	268.4650	324.5138	339.9820
55 CC	183.1881	223.3708	258.5787	294.6588	238.4324	287.5851	301.1500
56 IPC	31.2276	43.4265	41.2953	42.1549	40.8370	45.0073	54.5579
57 EXC	56.1425	65.8914	81.1382	74.2905	64.8279	68.1838	77.4971
58 EIC	1.1127	1.7619	1.6109	1.2349	-1.8299	1.7516	1.2353
59 NXC	85.8554	105.2130	110.7173	114.9490	94.7504	109.6442	120.3170
60 NIC	-2.6033	-1.0393	0.2969	1.1053	-0.0714	1.2234	1.8215
61 TEC	1.1687	1.7824	1.8959	2.4938	3.0380	3.1633	3.5906
62 TNC	14.8289	17.7007	24.9890	28.4950	31.2175	32.4703	32.8212
63 TOC	16.3260	21.6036	20.8862	18.8161	19.7680	20.6126	24.8080
64 KC	503.6351	547.8515	586.9428	629.8324	668.0420	717.2823	772.9004
65 MSC	41.0270	48.3494	53.7426	56.8612	56.4271	57.4483	63.3655
66 SGC	5.3236	2.8868	3.6712	1.8049	-1.0765	-0.5538	3.9198
67 BPC	-3.6224	-12.6204	-4.7650	-2.4288	-11.8810	-8.6323	-11.8061
68 GNPH	275.8076	304.5731	319.8922	321.4602	298.0928	319.8140	326.5349
69 GDPH	294.6076	314.8731	327.8922	317.3602	297.4928	325.5140	330.0349
70 YDH	249.5154	276.5316	292.9890	295.5399	270.4439	291.3505	293.9416
71 CH	219.3672	242.4447	256.5028	258.6818	237.2445	255.1031	257.3165
72 IPH	38.9500	40.1846	40.9580	42.4935	37.0830	36.0695	38.7082
73 EXH	69.2680	66.6817	75.1222	52.6279	55.4738	63.9161	60.7912
74 EIH	3.1309	4.5677	4.6990	5.0804	4.1656	5.7683	5.8003
75 NXH	62.7134	70.3338	76.2487	69.6371	67.2981	68.7981	67.1833
76 NIH	-1.3049	2.0718	4.2410	2.4862	-0.8241	3.8447	4.5980
77 TEH	0.5396	0.7330	0.6736	0.9884	1.2249	1.2660	1.4383
78 TNH	11.8738	12.0308	11.6659	12.5830	10.6157	13.3674	13.7931
79 TOH	13.8788	15.2776	14.5637	12.3489	15.8082	13.8301	17.3618
80 KH	602.5050	640.1346	680.1655	719.2010	735.9480	769.2745	803.3107
81 MSH	27.5543	30.2228	32.9440	39.4603	30.6193	33.7995	33.0104
82 SGH	0.9922	-5.3585	-4.1968	-4.6797	-2.3511	-8.8365	-6.6068
83 BPH	-7.8096	-11.4562	-8.6685	-10.3150	-6.2347	-8.6585	-8.6898
84 CCM	1549.5651	1648.2319	1804.0953	1084.6646	1747.5531	2021.3057	2054.9280
85 ITCM	220.9659	262.8831	281.8967	290.0082	293.8954	361.2916	394.6107
86 GNPCM	1927.6085	2070.3368	2255.0405	2269.8512	2197.9784	2530.0871	2587.9597
87 GDPCM	1861.6085	1999.8368	2160.2405	2131.0512	2077.6784	2405.8871	2480.9597

Table B-4. (Continued)

Variable	1958	1959	1960	1961	1962	1963	1964	1965	1966
1 GNPG	897.2554	933.9575	917.9947	989.3540	1048.9381	1067.2980	1207.4604	1278.5917	1311.3861
2 GDPG	892.8554	936.8575	921.5947	1004.9540	1060.8381	1088.5980	1220.1604	1299.9917	1355.0861
3 YDG	801.4357	837.8221	824.2164	889.8859	971.6695	966.9995	1118.3041	1169.8090	1198.7577
4 CG	733.6391	766.9810	754.5137	814.6886	889.6294	912.8401	1023.9951	1071.1906	1097.7171
5 IPG	84.3527	78.0439	79.4065	85.6515	81.8043	92.5893	115.3736	128.0594	132.1846
6 EXG	101.0926	122.9461	118.9169	119.7913	135.8838	145.3183	152.8763	171.2257	199.9883
7 EIG	2.1633	5.1693	4.9195	7.6397	12.8466	21.3637	22.9249	33.4978	43.3879
8 NXG	142.3733	145.2477	142.0486	128.5198	148.4839	166.0042	191.6640	201.4696	207.0968
9 NIG	4.0189	5.2351	4.8133	13.7973	15.3420	16.1092	19.7456	28.5122	36.5950
10 TEG	12.7298	11.2405	10.0858	9.2768	8.3556	6.2424	7.0510	8.5906	9.5570
11 TNG	31.2219	36.0205	32.6562	34.6410	25.3993	22.2399	27.9940	31.8176	30.6799
12 TOG	51.8680	48.8744	51.0362	55.5503	43.5138	41.8161	54.1113	68.3745	72.3915
13 KG	1894.0052	1965.3839	1998.4065	2093.8915	2144.0268	2202.7518	2306.9236	2413.1594	2515.6196
14 MSG	108.1632	114.3708	110.1110	117.0765	114.8835	125.4094	134.2924	148.0881	155.4283
15 CRG	77.7651	94.8970	94.0881	101.7195	109.0006	120.3429	134.7084	152.9739	167.1740
16 SGG	-22.1803	-18.0646	-16.9217	-20.0318	-27.2314	-28.3015	-27.2437	-17.2173	-12.8715
17 BPG	-38.7363	-25.2674	-26.6255	-30.4861	-26.9955	-36.7314	-48.3084	-46.6582	-44.0156
18 GNPE	554.9500	565.5235	547.0975	626.7495	625.4040	662.8798	667.6639	805.3123	840.9817
19 GDPE	524.0500	550.4235	529.7975	619.7495	627.4040	664.4798	663.6639	782.4123	829.3817
20 YDE	495.6217	506.0706	490.1416	562.4542	563.0054	597.0504	599.1725	721.0260	756.1836
21 CE	445.4444	455.3424	440.2533	508.7529	509.2750	541.5248	543.5351	658.9632	692.2669
22 IPE	50.3589	54.1563	53.8995	50.8433	56.7454	71.8874	74.4113	86.7817	91.1855
23 EXE	84.4626	100.9035	90.7361	115.2740	123.6821	135.1595	138.0899	144.8948	151.2994
24 EIE	7.9009	11.0089	11.7988	16.7379	22.0645	28.4388	31.1365	43.3817	55.6811
25 NXE	117.5035	125.9579	119.4056	119.1086	130.9036	152.8728	160.6205	193.9536	205.7766
26 NIE	14.2134	15.2297	11.0847	22.5501	22.4594	29.8579	31.2884	42.7556	49.9746
27 TEE	11.7214	9.0840	9.3206	10.0638	9.0198	10.3928	11.3451	12.9688	13.4776
28 TNE	23.4252	24.7873	23.7070	24.8659	22.9082	22.2828	20.2629	24.7994	25.2907
29 TOE	24.1816	25.5816	23.9283	29.3655	30.4707	33.1538	36.8833	46.5181	46.0298
30 KE	1081.7189	1129.5288	1155.7220	1204.1908	1245.7054	1301.1824	1349.6038	1441.5892	1527.2730
31 MSE	85.2662	85.7453	80.3944	79.8304	78.9588	90.0555	93.8837	100.1283	98.8690
32 CRE	35.3169	119.5850	122.4603	138.1094	133.1050	139.1277	152.0699	173.1894	180.3880
33 SGE	-8.2717	-10.7471	-6.6440	-5.5048	-6.6014	-4.3706	-0.2087	-0.8137	-9.9019
34 BPE	-8.4534	-14.1751	-10.6553	-2.6468	-9.6164	-20.7324	-18.9825	-25.5326	-37.1707
35 GNPN	309.5031	327.1277	333.1577	398.2779	423.4416	425.0762	429.8670	466.4742	524.2520
36 GDPN	315.9031	345.5277	344.2577	403.8779	426.4416	438.5762	447.3670	489.7742	547.6520
37 YDN	275.4925	289.5885	293.8356	356.6652	384.8723	384.9978	385.6729	412.5362	465.2088
38 CN	239.7636	252.3952	256.2011	312.5041	337.7810	337.8935	338.4984	362.5711	409.7722
39 IPN	34.7239	34.1737	36.9223	32.9497	43.3666	54.8707	62.0694	69.8146	73.2932
40 EXN	73.5976	93.7102	90.4957	90.0998	110.2275	117.0639	125.5881	145.2115	172.1015
41 EIN	1.8550	2.2189	1.3528	4.4924	4.5914	6.7204	7.3204	10.8279	14.1361
42 NXN									177.4909

43 NIN	-1.7128	2.0207	5.3616	-3.8258	7.3020	10.2439	11.8332	18.1693	23.6600
44 TEN	2.7887	0.9452	1.0307	0.9585	0.8468	0.6832	0.7298	1.0519	1.6195
45 TNN	17.5508	22.2745	22.6557	22.4502	20.6381	20.2440	19.0541	22.0618	25.1402
46 TON	13.6711	14.3196	15.6557	18.2040	17.0844	19.1503	24.4101	30.8242	32.2834
47 KN	681.2514	708.3537	738.9873	766.0147	809.6466	853.0857	912.6044	985.9946	1060.9757
48 MSN	35.1980	36.7399	37.3468	39.1174	51.5159	57.5580	61.4969	69.0860	74.0448
49 CRN	56.3543	56.7185	52.4504	54.4857	64.5351	71.7594	78.3051	91.8189	107.7374
50 SGN	-11.9894	-6.3608	-1.3779	-5.0873	-11.7307	-15.5216	-17.5060	-16.8620	-20.4569
51 BPN	-10.9843	-3.3412	-0.6658	6.1242	-8.0060	-23.2880	-32.4009	-36.7115	-38.3134
52 GNPC	373.3871	391.0501	452.7873	425.0392	466.9677	527.8470	511.0955	583.6875	635.4538
53 GDPC	361.8871	383.9501	453.6873	428.7392	473.4671	531.8470	513.0955	590.0875	636.0538
54 YDC	313.1193	323.8424	378.2392	359.9889	390.1223	441.3164	426.4372	490.9708	531.3915
55 CC	277.5925	286.9962	334.7000	318.6953	345.1211	390.0162	376.9678	433.5612	469.0085
56 IPC	51.9874	57.8396	60.2416	52.5325	67.8887	72.6696	70.3861	82.9458	80.0091
57 EXC	83.2106	93.1237	105.0193	96.6593	100.4517	110.4122	105.5730	115.1335	130.6321
58 EIC	0.0681	1.3673	0.2833	3.4752	5.8618	8.6192	9.9612	16.5871	22.8974
59 NXC	110.9682	114.8493	117.3567	109.9285	124.3957	139.3187	136.3716	162.6410	171.6939
60 NIC	1.6033	2.2274	4.2003	3.4945	4.7599	11.3515	10.8210	12.9991	14.2995
61 TEC	3.6002	3.9493	3.7794	3.2336	3.8891	4.2088	4.8187	5.6284	5.6951
62 TNC	36.9430	40.2197	41.2917	36.5030	41.4497	46.9538	41.8509	44.0667	48.2494
63 TOC	19.7247	23.0387	29.4770	25.3137	31.5065	35.3681	37.9888	43.0216	50.1178
64 KC	827.1974	874.9971	943.7216	989.4625	1070.5262	1132.3796	1191.8911	1264.1333	1348.8166
65 MSC	64.6081	67.7191	71.1997	64.4062	68.3746	77.8090	79.5806	86.0557	87.4034
66 SGC	-1.3322	5.5077	-0.4519	-5.7497	-6.4546	-14.2694	-12.7417	-24.7833	-15.4377
67 BPC	-17.7928	-15.4857	-17.1543	-16.9886	-29.3421	-35.6388	-33.6854	-50.3194	-33.0638
68 GNPH	353.4656	367.5565	360.3131	411.1645	412.0140	435.3167	447.1082	475.9104	534.9514
69 GDPH	362.9656	378.4565	373.4131	413.7645	418.6140	442.2167	454.7082	488.9104	549.3514
70 YDH	321.0384	332.6357	325.4725	374.1677	378.4139	400.1114	407.9199	431.2432	482.1400
71 CH	280.4629	290.3693	284.2505	325.8464	329.4735	348.0078	354.6779	374.6009	418.0774
72 IPH	41.8263	39.5217	40.2666	44.5180	48.8656	50.4803	48.6915	51.5112	56.3958
73 EXH	70.4426	75.7820	70.9381	69.4054	78.7264	75.2329	86.3820	103.8410	132.4166
74 EIH	7.4211	8.1098	8.1879	10.9810	12.4280	14.2776	14.9177	17.9219	20.2306
75 NXH	72.6824	70.2403	67.8842	72.3273	77.3124	85.0821	89.9799	96.6847	109.6185
76 NIH	2.6049	5.1860	4.3457	10.0590	10.8671	14.7997	16.8811	22.5798	32.6505
77 TEH	1.3846	1.8993	1.8428	1.5332	1.8224	2.0703	2.0828	2.3195	2.6365
78 TNH	15.3687	17.3871	17.5752	18.0966	17.4768	17.6448	17.5025	18.9129	20.9264
79 TOH	15.6739	15.6344	15.4227	17.3670	14.3309	15.4902	19.6029	23.4348	29.2485
80 KH	837.8263	863.1592	889.7791	924.5980	945.5181	992.2003	1026.6165	1067.8637	1113.6233
81 MSH	32.9326	32.2543	34.2125	33.0584	35.5873	38.9502	40.5618	44.7665	48.4851
82 SGH	-5.6728	-5.1792	-7.1594	-8.4032	-3.6999	-18.8947	-17.7118	-15.6329	-11.6886
83 BPH	-6.9235	-2.4345	-6.2040	-4.5999	-3.6251	-17.2714	-13.1612	-10.5017	-4.0218
84 CCM	1976.9024	2052.0842	2069.9186	2280.4873	2411.2800	2530.2823	2637.6742	2900.8869	3086.8421
85 ITCM	370.9491	361.7352	351.6365	356.7951	383.0706	432.7974	469.9320	543.8127	571.2683
86 GNPCM	2488.5613	2585.2153	2611.3503	2850.5851	2976.7654	3118.4176	3263.1949	3609.9761	3847.0250
87 GDPCM	2457.6613	2595.2153	2622.7503	2871.0851	3006.7654	3165.7176	3299.2949	3651.1761	3917.5250

Table B-5. Historical Forecasts Using Model 3 1951–66

Variable	1951	1952	1953	1954	1955	1956	1957
1 GNPG	745.4693	751.2839	763.9140	755.3968	758.4186	922.1953	971.2718
2 GDPG	727.9693	735.5839	748.9140	731.0968	731.1186	887.4953	946.1718
3 YDG	685.3847	674.8241	683.8545	673.1764	674.9714	827.0448	868.8257
4 CG	627.0978	617.4090	625.6940	615.8973	617.5441	757.0638	795.3958
5 IPG	42.0740	43.0069	52.6930	53.5440	61.9799	80.3020	92.8715
6 EXG	73.9631	71.9805	79.7860	71.6300	70.3497	87.2142	90.5554
7 EIG	-4.3266	1.1496	0.5394	1.3686	-1.7358	2.3682	3.2793
8 NXG	83.5549	81.9160	96.1669	96.4515	108.9973	150.4605	161.4577
9 NIG	1.0843	0.9462	0.9315	-0.8085	-1.3781	4.0925	3.5725
10 TEG	9.9784	14.2937	12.9162	13.9208	21.3211	16.9566	16.9988
11 TNG	24.1982	29.3526	29.1646	24.1022	19.5231	29.2792	32.2328
12 TOG	25.9080	32.8134	37.9786	44.1974	42.6030	48.9147	53.2145
13 KG	1440.2415	1486.4869	1528.5880	1558.1065	1602.9399	1686.8995	1806.2615
14 MSG	60.7486	66.2296	76.8454	77.7256	84.2751	104.3452	110.3362
15 CRG	26.5345	32.0170	35.1167	43.7694	47.2566	53.5916	64.2076
16 SGG	-13.7154	-8.4403	-7.2406	-2.0795	-7.1528	-19.9494	-26.6539
17 BPG	2.4974	5.9680	-1.7729	1.6555	-11.7053	-30.2705	-46.0955
18 GNPE	426.8197	460.7047	539.2075	516.7861	513.8013	578.9640	583.3995
19 GDPE	382.1197	416.0047	476.0075	454.4861	454.9013	521.8640	529.7995
20 YDE	380.0345	410.6205	485.7757	452.4454	461.7346	520.5191	517.1522
21 CE	335.9522	364.9254	436.1176	404.5448	413.3443	469.0290	465.8397
22 IPE	34.4273	41.3533	39.0276	45.0923	40.4529	48.4531	52.8835
23 EXE	60.6339	75.9616	69.2103	58.2504	62.5767	80.3101	74.8943
24 EIE	-0.1414	3.0765	3.7003	3.4277	1.5373	6.2586	6.8502
25 NXE	92.0301	107.5241	118.9766	104.6014	112.6738	134.2688	128.1133
26 NIE	-0.2778	8.3881	3.9717	7.5276	4.3361	9.6180	11.2549
27 TEE	13.1790	13.9238	13.7351	19.1127	16.7122	14.7238	18.0210
28 TNE	13.8002	14.3835	19.4426	20.2143	18.2359	21.6617	24.2628
29 TOE	19.8059	21.7768	20.2542	25.0138	17.1185	22.0595	23.9635
30 KE	803.8048	838.9258	866.7426	903.5123	928.5229	972.0506	1028.4960
31 MSE	66.4504	80.2110	73.1533	78.7611	75.9754	86.5870	91.9547
32 CRE	43.4261	55.5438	52.5851	55.6555	68.2353	93.7792	116.0968
33 SGE	3.7851	3.4842	2.5318	9.0408	-1.9334	-3.2551	-2.4527
34 BPE	13.4402	7.8260	13.1623	11.8491	6.0041	-0.2181	-4.0237
35 GNPN	239.4893	258.9129	288.9450	291.8942	305.1290	326.1301	309.1683
36 GDPN	241.4893	262.4129	287.8450	281.8942	291.4290	320.3301	308.9683
37 YDN	211.2794	228.6968	257.3217	263.3676	276.8465	287.2950	273.8203
38 CN	182.4241	197.9970	223.5906	228.9962	241.0477	250.3896	238.3419
39 IPN	24.9869	28.8119	35.6228	34.8235	31.7426	40.1597	32.5896
40 EXN	52.8034	57.7022	62.0969	55.8235	59.4797	67.4251	69.4880
41 EIN	1.0675	2.5251	1.9845	1.7107	0.2060	2.1111	2.0716
42 NXN	44.7681	54.5209	69.2916	77.2235	79.5990	81.7635	79.5310

43 NIN	-0.8755	-0.5976	-0.0418	0.2361	1.3478	0.7920	0.7920
44 TEN	3.1776	2.8973	2.6336	2.2285	3.5302	6.4096	5.0721
45 TNN	14.2812	15.3104	15.9789	13.5484	14.4305	18.1099	16.9393
46 TON	10.7511	12.0084	13.0107	12.7497	10.3218	14.3156	13.3365
47 KN	437.9144	461.3094	496.3503	536.0385	573.0751	620.8347	648.6271
48 MSN	29.6843	32.9030	36.1933	39.7344	36.1926	38.4503	38.8583
49 CRN	28.3508	32.5455	38.5105	47.7455	55.7939	55.1820	59.9553
50 SGN	4.1100	0.9160	-2.1768	-9.4734	-11.6175	-3.9649	-11.4521
51 BPN	7.9783	2.8040	-4.0684	-9.9255	-7.5612	-7.2193	-8.5633
52 GNPC	239.5607	292.6828	337.8740	380.7267	322.9610	379.5701	400.6207
53 GDPC	214.9607	268.7828	314.3740	342.6267	303.1610	347.2701	369.0207
54 YDC	206.9899	251.5533	290.2896	331.1537	268.8714	323.4903	339.4822
55 CC	184.5213	223.6015	257.5717	293.4079	238.7889	286.6874	300.7117
56 IPC	31.2276	43.4265	41.2953	42.1549	40.8370	45.0073	54.5579
57 EXC	56.1425	65.8914	81.1382	74.2905	64.8279	68.1838	77.4971
58 EIC	0.1672	1.9255	0.8968	0.3479	1.5771	1.1150	0.9244
59 NXC	86.3167	105.2928	110.3689	114.5162	94.8737	109.3336	120.1653
60 NIC	-2.5533	-1.0306	0.2591	1.0584	-0.0581	1.1898	1.8051
61 TEC	1.1687	1.7824	1.8959	2.4959	3.0383	3.1633	3.5906
62 TNC	14.9521	17.7221	24.8959	28.3794	31.2504	32.3873	32.7807
63 TOC	16.4499	21.6250	20.7926	18.6998	19.8011	20.5292	24.7672
64 KC	503.6351	547.8515	586.9428	629.8324	668.0420	717.2823	772.9004
65 MSC	41.0270	48.3494	53.7426	56.8612	56.4271	57.4483	63.3655
66 SGC	5.5708	2.9296	3.4845	1.5730	-1.0104	-0.7202	3.8385
67 BPC	-3.1882	-12.5453	-5.0930	-2.8362	-11.7649	-8.9246	-11.9489
68 GNPH	276.5459	304.7009	319.3346	320.7676	298.2902	319.3170	326.2922
69 GDPH	295.3459	315.0009	327.3346	316.6676	297.6902	325.0170	329.7922
70 YDH	250.1900	276.6484	292.4795	294.9070	270.6243	290.8963	293.7198
71 CH	219.9434	242.5444	256.0675	258.1411	237.3986	254.7151	257.1270
72 IPH	38.9500	40.1846	40.9580	42.4935	37.0830	36.0695	38.7082
73 EXH	69.2680	66.6817	75.1222	52.6279	55.4738	63.9161	60.7912
74 EIH	3.5633	4.6426	4.3724	4.6747	4.2812	5.4771	5.6582
75 NXH	62.8607	70.3593	76.1374	69.4989	67.3375	68.6989	67.1348
76 NIH	-1.1819	2.0930	4.1481	2.3708	-0.7913	3.7619	4.5576
77 TEH	0.5396	0.7330	0.6736	0.9884	1.2249	1.2660	1.4383
78 TNH	11.9022	12.0357	11.6445	12.5564	10.6233	13.3483	13.7838
79 TOH	13.9141	15.2838	14.5370	12.3157	15.8177	13.8064	17.3502
80 KH	602.5050	640.1346	680.1655	719.2010	735.9480	769.2745	803.3107
81 MSH	27.5543	30.2228	32.9440	39.4603	30.6198	33.7995	33.0104
82 SGH	1.0559	-5.3475	-4.2449	-4.7394	-2.3341	-8.8793	-6.6277
83 BPH	-7.6476	-11.4281	-8.7909	-10.4670	-6.1913	-8.7676	-8.7430
84 CCM	1549.9388	1646.4774	1799.0414	1800.9873	1748.1235	2017.8850	2057.4161
85 ITCM	220.9659	262.8831	281.8967	290.0082	293.8954	361.2916	394.6107
86 GNPCM	1927.8848	2068.2851	2249.2751	2265.5714	2198.6002	2526.1765	2590.7525
87 GDPCM	1861.8848	1997.7851	2154.4751	2126.7714	2078.3002	2401.9765	2483.7525

Table B-5. (Continued)

Variable	1958	1959	1960	1961	1962	1963	1964	1965	1966
1 GNPG	914.1714	949.3417	936.9798	1026.1061	1076.1818	1096.3981	1247.6873	1343.8170	1401.8468
2 GDPG	909.7714	952.2417	940.5798	1041.7061	1088.0818	1117.6981	1260.3873	1365.2170	1445.5468
3 YDG	816.8186	851.8466	841.5606	923.1829	996.4750	1023.4759	1155.0108	1229.2244	1281.1436
4 CG	747.6819	779.8183	770.3814	845.2658	912.5076	937.2796	1057.9563	1126.0435	1173.6768
5 IPG	84.3527	78.0439	79.4065	85.6515	81.8043	92.5893	115.3736	128.0594	132.1846
6 EXG	101.0926	122.9461	118.9169	119.7913	135.8838	145.3183	152.8763	171.2257	199.9883
7 EIG	4.0140	5.2755	4.5569	10.2486	10.5237	18.8872	21.3151	33.3303	44.7293
8 NXG	145.1411	147.3867	144.7734	135.0295	153.1595	171.1996	198.0026	211.9679	221.8368
9 NIG	0.2286	0.6553	-1.3916	3.7216	3.9781	3.7767	5.5314	7.4760	8.6955
10 TEG	12.7298	11.2405	10.0858	9.2768	8.3556	6.2424	7.0510	8.5906	9.5570
11 TNG	31.9189	36.6210	33.3592	36.2799	26.4931	23.4278	29.5313	34.4087	34.2867
12 TOG	52.7041	49.6336	51.9742	57.3664	44.8581	43.2519	56.0942	71.5933	76.8595
13 KG	1894.0052	1965.3839	1998.4065	2093.8915	2144.0268	2202.7518	2306.9236	2413.1594	2515.6196
14 MSG	108.1632	114.3708	110.1110	117.0765	114.8835	125.4094	134.2924	148.0881	155.4283
15 CRG	77.7651	94.8970	94.0881	101.7195	109.0006	120.3429	134.7084	152.9739	167.1740
16 SGG	-20.6472	-16.7049	-15.2808	-16.5768	-24.7933	-25.6779	-23.7235	-11.4073	-4.7968
17 BPG	-35.8631	-22.7204	-23.5081	-24.3112	-22.6301	-32.0709	-42.0426	-36.2858	-29.5146
18 GNPE	555.3498	562.3447	541.9200	623.8397	613.0699	649.5703	654.4635	789.5832	822.8109
19 GDPE	524.4498	547.2447	524.6200	616.8397	615.0699	651.1703	650.7635	766.6832	811.2109
20 YDE	495.9819	503.2065	485.4767	559.8326	551.8925	585.0588	587.2792	706.8544	739.8121
21 CE	445.7857	452.6293	435.8344	506.2669	498.7481	530.1656	532.2689	645.5389	676.7587
22 IPE	50.3589	54.1563	53.8995	50.8433	56.7454	71.8874	74.4113	86.7817	91.1855
23 EXE	84.4626	100.9035	90.7361	115.2740	123.6821	135.1595	138.0899	144.8948	151.2994
24 EIE	8.0979	9.4434	9.2490	15.3049	15.9902	21.8842	24.6356	35.6356	46.7324
25 NXE	117.6400	124.8724	117.6376	118.1149	126.6918	148.3280	156.1130	188.5826	199.5718
26 NIE	14.2152	15.2154	11.0615	22.5371	22.4041	29.7983	31.2293	42.6851	49.8932
27 TEE	11.7214	9.0840	9.3206	10.0638	9.0198	10.3928	11.3451	12.9688	13.4776
28 TNE	23.3438	24.6398	23.4669	24.7309	22.3361	21.6656	19.6057	24.0699	24.4480
29 TOE	24.2027	25.4143	23.6558	29.2124	29.8214	32.4532	36.1884	45.6902	45.0732
30 KE	1081.7189	1129.5288	1155.7220	1204.1908	1245.7054	1301.1824	1349.6038	1441.5892	1527.2730
31 MSE	85.2662	85.7453	80.3944	79.8304	78.9588	90.0555	93.8837	100.1283	98.8690
32 CRE	125.3169	119.5850	122.4603	138.1094	133.1050	139.1277	152.0699	173.1894	180.3880
33 SGE	-8.2321	-11.0618	-7.1567	-5.7929	-7.8227	-5.6885	-1.5157	-2.3712	-11.7011
34 BPE	-8.3948	-14.6409	-11.4140	-3.0732	-11.4237	-22.6826	-20.9167	-27.8373	-39.8333
35 GNPN	301.5617	325.9609	333.1885	384.0143	427.8447	429.9102	430.8390	460.1981	510.7178
36 GDPN	307.9617	344.3609	344.2885	389.6143	430.8447	443.4102	448.3390	483.4981	534.1178
37 YDN	268.4919	288.4832	293.7566	343.8248	388.7456	389.2813	386.5420	406.9029	453.1716
38 CN	233.5778	251.4520	256.1670	300.9329	341.0967	341.5756	339.1264	357.3311	398.6999
39 IPN	34.7239	34.1737	36.9223	32.9497	43.3666	54.8707	62.0694	69.8146	73.2932
40 EXN	73.5976	93.7102	90.4957	90.0998	110.2275	117.0639	125.5881	145.2115	172.1015
41 EIN	1.3328	1.5576	0.4495	3.0712	2.9136	4.9725	5.2401	7.7805	10.1172

42 NXN	78.6719	77.9731	75.6242	81.6798	114.4612	125.4339	136.5334	148.7219	171.7050
43 NIN	2.5985	2.4595	4.8218	2.4595	2.5985	5.2387	8.8516	18.7177	27.8890
44 TEN	2.7887	0.9452	1.0307	0.9585	0.8468	0.6832	0.7298	1.0519	1.6195
45 TNN	16.9677	22.2855	22.7442	21.7272	21.0468	20.6433	19.1280	21.6960	24.3079
46 TON	13.3134	14.2471	15.6570	17.5039	17.2055	19.3024	24.4391	30.5473	31.6187
47 KN	681.2514	708.3537	738.9873	766.0147	809.6466	853.0857	912.6044	985.9946	1060.9757
48 MSN	35.1980	36.7399	37.3468	39.1174	51.5159	57.5580	61.4969	69.0860	74.0448
49 CRN	56.3543	56.7185	52.4504	54.4857	64.5351	71.7594	78.3051	91.8189	107.7374
50 SGN	-12.9302	-6.4222	-1.2681	-6.5104	-11.2010	-14.9711	-17.4030	-17.5048	-21.9538
51 BPN	-12.7400	-3.5648	-0.6008	3.4318	-6.9186	-22.1361	-32.0568	-37.7476	-40.7754
52 GNPC	373.6131	389.2534	449.8611	423.3947	459.9968	520.3249	503.6350	574.7979	625.1842
53 GDPC	362.1131	382.1534	450.7611	427.0947	466.4968	524.3249	505.6350	581.1979	625.7842
54 YDC	313.3137	322.2970	375.7222	358.5743	384.1262	434.8461	420.0200	483.3243	522.5580
55 CC	277.7630	285.6410	332.4927	317.4548	339.8627	384.3421	371.3401	426.8555	461.2619
56 IPC	51.9874	57.8396	60.2416	52.5325	67.8887	72.6696	70.3861	82.9458	80.0091
57 EXC	83.2106	93.1237	105.0193	96.6593	100.4517	110.4122	105.5730	115.1335	130.6321
58 EIC	0.1890	0.4062	1.2821	2.5954	2.1326	4.5950	5.0700	11.8314	17.4034
59 NXC	111.0272	114.3804	116.5929	109.4992	122.5762	137.3554	134.4243	160.3207	169.0134
60 NIC	1.6097	2.1766	4.1175	3.4480	4.5627	11.1387	10.6099	12.7476	14.0089
61 TEC	3.6002	3.9493	3.7794	3.2336	3.8891	4.2088	4.8187	5.6284	5.6951
62 TNC	36.9587	40.0945	41.0877	36.3883	40.9637	46.4293	41.3307	43.4469	47.5334
63 TOC	19.7405	22.9127	29.2718	25.1983	31.0177	34.8406	37.4656	42.3982	49.3977
64 KC	827.1974	674.9971	943.7216	989.4625	1070.5262	1132.3796	1191.8911	1264.1333	1348.8166
65 MSC	64.6081	67.1191	71.1997	64.4062	68.3746	77.8090	79.5806	86.0557	87.4034
66 SGC	-1.3006	5.2565	-0.8611	-5.9797	-7.4294	-15.3213	-13.7850	-26.0264	-16.8738
67 BPC	-17.7373	-15.9271	-17.8732	-17.3926	-31.0547	-37.4868	-35.4912	-52.5034	-35.5868
68 GNPH	353.5600	366.8061	359.0908	410.4775	409.1022	432.1746	443.9919	472.1971	530.6617
69 GDPH	363.0600	377.7061	372.1908	413.0775	415.7022	439.0746	451.5919	485.1971	545.0617
70 YDH	321.1247	331.9499	324.3556	373.5400	375.7532	397.2404	405.0724	427.8502	478.2203
71 CH	280.5365	289.7836	283.2964	325.3102	327.2007	345.5553	352.2455	371.7026	414.7292
72 IPH	41.8263	39.5217	40.26666	44.5180	48.8656	50.4803	48.6915	51.5112	56.3958
73 EXH	70.4426	75.7820	70.9381	69.4054	78.7264	75.2329	86.3820	103.8410	132.4166
74 EIH	7.4764	7.6703	7.4720	10.5787	10.7226	12.4373	13.0925	15.7471	17.7181
75 NXH	72.7012	70.0905	67.6402	72.1902	76.7312	84.4549	89.3578	95.9435	108.7622
76 NIH	2.6207	5.0610	4.1420	9.9446	10.3819	14.2762	16.3618	21.9611	31.9358
77 TEH	1.3846	1.8993	1.8428	1.5332	1.8224	2.0702	2.0828	2.3195	2.6365
78 TNH	15.3723	17.3583	17.5283	18.0702	17.3650	17.5242	17.3829	18.7704	20.7617
79 TOH	15.6784	15.5985	15.3642	17.3341	14.1615	15.3398	19.4537	23.2570	29.0432
80 KH	837.8263	863.1592	889.7791	924.5980	945.5181	992.2003	1026.6165	1067.8637	1113.6233
81 MSH	32.9326	32.2543	34.2125	33.0584	35.5873	38.9502	40.5618	44.7665	48.4851
82 SGH	-5.6647	-5.2439	-7.2648	-8.4625	-3.9510	-19.1657	-17.9805	-15.9531	-12.0586
83 BPH	-6.9028	-2.5992	-6.4722	-4.2641	-4.2641	-17.9610	-13.8451	-11.3166	-4.9632
84 CCM	1985.3449	2059.3241	2078.1719	2295.2332	2419.4159	2538.9181	2652.9371	2927.4715	3125.1265
85 ITCM	370.9491	361.7352	351.6365	356.7951	383.0706	432.7974	469.9320	543.8127	571.2683
86 GNPCM	2498.2561	2593.7068	2621.0402	2867.8324	2986.1952	3128.3781	3280.6166	3640.5934	3891.2214
87 GDPCM	2467.3561	2603.7068	2632.4402	2888.3324	3016.1952	3175.6781	3316.7166	3681.7934	3961.7214

references

Adelman, Irma, and Je, Kim Mahn. 1969. An econometric model of the Korean economy (1956-66). In *Practical approaches to development planning: Korea's second five year plan,* I. Adelman, ed., Baltimore: The Johns Hopkins University Press.

Agarwala, R. 1970. *An econometric model of India.* London: Frank Cass.

Allen, Robert L. 1961. Integration in less developed areas. *Kyklos* 14: 314-36.

Alonso, William. 1971. The Economics of Urban Size. *Regional Science Association Papers* 26: 67-83.

Anderson, James E. 1970. General equilibrium and the effective rate of protection. *Journal of Political Economy* 78, no. 4, Part I (July/August): 717-24.

Arndt, Sven W. 1968. On discriminating vs. non-preferential tariff policies. *Economic Journal* 78, no. 312 (December): 941-48.

————. 1969. Customs union and the theory of tariffs. *American Economic Review* 59, no. 1 (March): 108-18.

Ayala, Antonio V. 1964. "The use of a policy model for analyzing some Philippine growth alternatives: 1963-66." Ph.D. dissertation, Georgetown University, June 1964.

Bain, Joseph S. 1954. Economies of scale, concentration and conditions of entry in 20 manufacturing industries. *American Economic Review* 44, no. 1 (March): 15-39.

————. 1966. *International differences in industrial structure: eight nations in the 1950's.* New Haven: Yale University Press.

Balassa, Bela. 1961. *The theory of economic integration.* Homewood, Ill.: Richard D. Irwin.

————. 1965a. Tariff protection in industrial countries: an evaluation. *Journal of Political Economy* 73, no. 6 (December): 573-94.

_____. 1965*b*. *Economic development and integration.* Mexico City: Centro de Estudios Monetarios Latinoamericanos.

_____. 1967. Trade creation and trade diversion in the European market. *Economic Journal* 77, no. 305 (March): 1–21.

_____. 1971*a*. Trade policies in developing countries. *American Economic Review, Papers and Proceedings* 61, no. 2 (May): 178–87.

_____. 1971*b*. Regional integration and trade liberalization in Latin America. *Journal of Common Market Studies* 10, no. 1 (September): 58–77.

_____ and Associates. 1971. *The structure of protection in developing countries.* Baltimore: The Johns Hopkins University Press.

Ball, R. J. 1973. *The international linkage of national economic models.* Amsterdam: North-Holland Pub. Co.

Basmann, Robert L. 1971. The Brookings quarterly econometric model: science or number mysticism? *The current state of econometrics.* Chicago: Rand McNally.

Baumol, William J., and Fabian, Tibor. 1964. Decomposition, pricing for decentralization and external economies. *Management Science* 11, no. 1 (September): 1–32.

Belson, David. 1970. "An engineering approach to economic models." Ph.D. dissertation. Los Angeles: University of Southern California.

Bentick, B. L. 1963. Estimating trade creation and trade diversion. *Economic Journal* 73, no. 290 (June): 219–25.

Bertrand, Trent J. 1972. Decision rules for effective protection in less developed economies. *American Economic Review* 62, no. 4 (September): 743–46.

_____ and Vanek, Jaroslav. 1971. The theory of tariffs, taxes and subsidies: some aspects of the second best. *American Economic Review* 61, no. 5 (December): 925–31.

Bhambri, R. S. 1962. Customs unions and underdeveloped countries. *Economia Internazionale* 15: 235–55.

Brown, A. J. 1961. Economic separatism versus a common market in developing countries. *Yorkshire Bulletin of Economic and Social Research* 13 (May and November): 235–58.

Brown, Murray. 1966. *On the theory and measurement of technological change.* Cambridge: Cambridge University Press.

Bruton, Henry J. 1967. Productivity growth in Latin America. *American Economic Review* 57, no. 5 (December): 1099–1116.

Cabezon, P. 1969. "An evaluation of commercial policy in the Chilean economy." Ph.D. dissertation, University of Wisconsin.

Cable, V. 1969. The football war and the Central American common market. *International Affairs* (October): 669–70.

Carnoy, Martin. 1970. A welfare analysis of Latin American economic union: six industry studies. *Journal of Political Economy* 78, no. 4, Part 2 (July–August): 626–54.

Carter, Nicholas G. 1970. "A macro-econometric model of Jamaica, 1959–66." Mimeographed. Washington, D.C.: International Bank for Reconstruction and Development.

Castillo, Carlos M. 1966. *Growth and integration in Central America.* New York: Frederick A. Praeger.

Caves, Richard E. 1965. Vent-for-surplus models of trade and growth. In *Trade and growth and the balance of payments,* Baldwin et al. Chicago and Amsterdam: Rand McNally and North-Holland Publishing Company.

Chenery, Hollis B. 1959. The interdependence of investment decisions. In *The allocation of economic resources,* M. Abramovitz et al. Stanford: Stanford University Press.

──────. 1960. Patterns of industrial growth. *American Economic Review* 51, no. 4 (September): 624–54.

Christensen, Laurits R., Jorgenson, Dale W., and Lau, Lawrence J. 1973. Transcendental logarithmic production frontiers. *Review of Economics and Statistics* 55, no. 1 (February): 28–45.

Clague, Christopher. 1971. Tariff preferences and separable utility. *American Economic Review, Papers and Proceedings* 61, no. 2 (May): 184–94.

Cochrane, D., and Orcutt, G. H. 1949. Application of least squares regression to relationships containing autocorrelated error terms. *Journal of the American Statistical Association* 44, no. 245 (March): 32–61.

Cohen, Benjamin. 1969. "Optimal international development of India and Pakistan." Paper presented to the International Economic Association Conference on Economic Development in South Asia, Kandy, Ceylon (June).

Conrad, Alfred H. 1968. Econometric models in development planning—Pakistan, Argentina, Liberia. In *Development policy—theory and practice,* Gustav F. Papanek, ed. Cambridge, Mass.: Harvard University Press.

Cooper, C. A., and Massell, B. F. 1965. Toward a general theory of customs union for developing countries. *Journal of Political Economy* 73, no. 3 (October): 461–76.

Cooper, Richard N. 1968. "On the theory of policy in an integrated economy." Mimeographed.

──────. 1969. Macroeconomic policy adjustment in interdependent economies. *Quarterly Journal of Economics* 83, no. 1 (February): 1–24.

Corden, W. Max. 1970. The efficiency effects of trade and protection. In *Studies in international economics,* McDougall, I. A., and Snape, R. H., eds. Amsterdam: North-Holland Publishing Company.

──────. 1972a. Economies of scale and customs union theory. *Journal of Political Economy* 80, no. 3, Part 1 (May, June): 465–75.

──────. 1972b. Monetary integration. *Essays in international finance,* no. 93. Princeton: Princeton University International Finance Section (April).

D'Arge, Ralph. 1969. Note on customs unions and direct foreign investment. *Economic Journal* 79, no. 314 (June): 324–27.

DePrano, Michael, and Nugent, Jeffrey B. 1966. "A global financial model of Ecuador." Mimeographed. Quito: Junta Nacional de Planificacion.

De Vries, Barend A. 1967. *The export experience of developing countries.* Washington, D.C.: IBRD, Occasional Paper, no. 3.

Dhrymes, Phoebus J., and Kurz, Mordecai. 1964. Technology and scale in electricity generation. *Econometrica* 32: 287–315.

Dudley, Leonard. 1972. Learning and productivity change in metal products. *American Economic Review* 62, no. 4 (September): 662–69.

Duquesne de la Vinelle, L. 1965–66. La creation du commerce attributable au Marché commun et son incidence sur le volume du produit national de la communauté. *Information Statistiques* 4 (1965): 61–70, and 3 (1966): 5–31.

Durbin, J., and Watson, G. S. 1950–51. Testing for serial correlation in least-squares regression. *Biometrika* 37, 38 (December 1950 and Jan. 1951): 409–28 and 159–78, respectively.

Dutta, M., and Su, V. 1969. An econometric model of Puerto Rico. *Review of Economic Studies* 36, no. 3 (July): 319–29.

El Daly, El Sayed Abdel. 1967. "An econometric model of growth with reference to the UAR." Ph.D. dissertation, Rutgers University.

Erlenkotter, Donald 1970. Economic integration and dynamic location planning. *The Swedish Journal of Economics* 74: 8–18.

Escuela Nacional de Economia. 1970. *Un modelo de política económico para Mexico*. Mexico: Universidad Nacional Autonoma de Mexico.

Evans, H. David. 1970. A programming model of trade and protection. In *Studies in international economics*, McDougall, J. A., and Snape, R. H., eds. Amsterdam: North-Holland Publishing Company.

———. 1971. Effects of protection in a general equilibrium framework. *Review of Economics and Statistics* 53 (May): 147–56.

———. 1972. *A general equilibrium analysis of protection*. Amsterdam: North-Holland Publishing Company.

Evans, Michael K. 1968. "An econometric model of part of the Israeli economy." Philadelphia: University of Pennsylvania. Discussion paper, no. 86.

Fei, J. H., and Ranis, Gustav. 1961. A theory of economic development. *American Economic Review* 51, no. 4 (September): 533–64.

Foster, E., and Sonnenschein, H. 1970. Price distortion and economic welfare. *Econometrica* 48 (March): 281–97.

Fox, K. A., Sengupta, J. K., and Thorbecke, E. 1966. *The theory of quantitative economic policy and stabilization*. Amsterdam: North-Holland Publishing Company.

Frank, Charles, Meeraus, Alex, and Stoutjesdijk, Ardy. 1973. Planning the chemical industries: the case of fertilizers in East Africa. In *Industrial planning with economies of scale*, Stoutjesdijk and Westphal, eds. Amsterdam: North-Holland Publishing Company.

Gehrels, Franz. 1956–57. Customs union from a single-country view-point. *Review of Economic Studies* 24: 61–64.

Ghai, Dharam. 1965. Territorial distribution of the benefits and costs of the East Africa common market. In *Federation in East Africa*, Lays, C., and Robson, P. eds. Nairobi.

Green, Reginald H., and Krishna, K. G. V. 1967. *Economic cooperation in Africa, retrospect and prospect*. Nairobi: Oxford University Press.

Grubel, Herbert G. 1970. The theory of intra-industry trade. *Studies in international economics*, McDougall, I. A., and Snape, R. H., eds. Amsterdam: North-Holland Publishing Company.

Halabuk, L., Kenessey, Z., and Theiss, E. 1965. An econometric model of Hungary. *Economics of Planning* 5, no. 3 (September): 30–40.

Haldi, John, and Whitcomb, David. 1967. Economies of scale in industrial plants. *Journal of Political Economy* 75, no. 3, Part 1 (August): 373–85.

Hansen, Bent. 1958. *The economic theory of fiscal policy.* Cambridge, Mass.: Harvard University Press.

Hansen, Roger. 1967. *Central America: regional integration and economic development.* Washington, D.C.: National Planning Association.

Harberger, Arnold C. 1959. Using the resources at hand more effectively. *American Economic Review, Papers and Proceedings* 59, no. 2 (May): 134–47.

Hazlewood, Arthur. 1966. The shiftability of industry and the measurement of gains and losses in the East African common market. *Bulletin of the Oxford University Institute of Economics and Statistics* 28, no. 2 (May): 63–72.

Heller, H. Robert. 1968. *International trade: theory and empirical evidence.* Englewood Cliffs, N.J.: Prentice-Hall.

Henley, Donald S. 1967. "Regional trade and market performance: a study of the Central American common market." DBA Thesis. Cambridge, Mass.: Harvard University.

Hirsch, Werner Z. 1956. Firm progress ratios. *Econometrica* 24, no. 2 (April): 136–43.

Hirschman, Albert O. 1958. *The strategy of economic development.* New Haven: Yale University Press.

Islam, Nurul. 1965. *A short-term model for Pakistan economy: an econometric analysis.* Lahore, Karachi, Dacca: Oxford University Press.

Janssen, L. H. 1961. *Free trade, protection and customs union.* Leiden: Kroese.

Joel, C. 1971. The incentives in Central American development. *Economic Development and Cultural Change* 19, no. 1 (January): 229–52.

Johnson, Harry G. 1958a. The gains from freer trade with Europe: an estimate. *Manchester School of Economic and Social Studies* 26, no. 3 (September): 171–81.

———. 1958b. Marshallian analysis of discriminating tariff reduction: an extension. *Indian Journal of Economics* 39, Part 2 (October): 171–81.

———. 1965a. The costs of protection and self sufficiency. *Quarterly Journal of Economics* 79, no. 3 (August): 356–72.

———. 1965b. An economic theory of protectionism, tariff bargaining and the formation of customs unions. *Journal of Political Economy* 73, no. 2 (June): 256–83.

———. 1966. Factor market distortions and the shape of the transformation curve. *Econometrica* 34, no. 3 (July): 686–98.

Kahnert, F., Richards, P., Stoutjesdijk, E., and Thomopoulos, P. 1969. *Economic integration among developing countries.* Paris: OECD.

Kaldor, Nicholas. 1964. Dual exchange rates and economic development. *Economic Bulletin for Latin America* 9, no. 2 (November): 215–33.

———. 1971. The truth about the dynamic effects. *New Statesman* 12 (March): 1–9.

Karnes, Thomas L. 1961. *The failure of union: Central America, 1824–60.* Chapel Hill: University of North Carolina Press.

Keesing, Donald B. 1965. Thailand and Malaysia: a case for a common market. *Malayan Economic Review* 10, no. 2 (October): 102–13.

Kemp, Murray. 1969. *A contribution to the general equilibrium theory of preferential trading.* Amsterdam: North-Holland Pub. Co.

Klein, Lawrence R. 1965. What kind of macroeconometric model for developing economies? *Econometric Annual of the Indian Economic Journal* 13 no. 3: 313–24.

Krause, Lawrence B. 1968. *European economic integration and the United States.* Washington, D.C.: Brookings Institution.

Krauss, Melvyn B. 1972. Recent development in customs union theory: an interpretive survey. *Journal of Economic Literature* 10, no. 2 (June): 413–36.

Kravis, Irving B. 1970. Trade as a handmaiden of growth: similarities between the nineteenth and twentieth centuries. *Economic Journal* 80, no. 320 (December): 850–72.

Kreinin, Mordechai E. 1964. On the dynamic effects of a customs union. *Journal of Political Economy* 72, no. 2 (April): 193–99.

———. 1968. Israel and the European economic community. *Quarterly Journal of Economics* 82, no. 2 (May): 325–42.

———. 1969. Trade creation and diversion by the EEC and EFTA. *Economia Internazionale* 22 (May): 273–80.

Lage, G. M. 1966. "The welfare cost of trade restrictions: a linear programming analysis." Ph.D. dissertation, University of Minnesota.

———. 1970. A linear programming analysis of tariff protection. *Western Economic Journal* 8, no. 2 (June): 167–85.

Lamfalussy, Alexander. 1961. Europe's progress due to common market? *Lloyds Bank Review* (October), reprinted in L. B. Krause, *The common market: progress and controversy.* Englewood Cliffs, N.J.: Prentice-Hall, 1964.

———. 1963. "Intra-European trade and the competitive position of the EEC." Paper read to the Manchester Statistical Society (March 1963).

Lawrence, Roger. 1968*a*. Primary products preferences and economic welfare: The EEC and Africa. In *The open economy*, Kenen, Peter, and Lawrence, Roger, eds. New York: Columbia University Press.

———. 1968*b*. "Protection in the Central American common market in 1966." Mimeographed.

Leibenstein, Harvey. 1966. Allocative efficiency vs. X-efficiency. *American Economic Review* 56, no. 3 (June): 392–415.

Lewis, Arthur W. 1954. Economic development with unlimited supplies of labour. *The Manchester School* 22 (May): 139–91.

Liesner, H. H. 1958. The European common market and British economy. *Economic Journal* 68, no. 270 (June): 302–16.

Lipsey, R. G. 1957. The theory of customs union: trade diversion and welfare. *Economica* 24 (February): 40–46.

———. 1960. The theory of customs union: a general survey. *Economic Journal* 70, no. 270 (September): 496–513.

Little, Ian M. D., Scitovsky, Tibor, and Scott, Maurice. 1970. *Industry and trade in some developing countries: a comparative study.* London: Oxford University Press.

Lovell, Michael C., and Prescott, Edward. 1968. "Multiple regressions with inequality constraints: pretesting bias, hypothesis testing and efficiency." Philadelphia: University of Pennsylvania. Discussion Paper No. 109.

Macario, Santiago. 1964. Protectionism and industrialization in Latin America. *Economic Bulletin for Latin America* 9, no. 1 (March): 61–101.

Major, R. L., and Hays, S. 1970. Another look at the common market. *National Institute Economic Review* 54 (November): 29–43.

Makower, H., and Morton, G. 1953. A contribution towards a theory of customs unions. *Economic Journal* 62, no. 249 (March): 33–49.

Marwah, K. 1969. "An econometric model of India: estimating prices, their role and source of change." Mimeographed.

———. 1969. "An econometric model of Colombia: a prototype devaluation view. *Econometrica* 37, no. 2 (April): 228–51.

McClelland, Donald H. 1968. "The common market's contribution to Central American growth—a first approximation." Paper presented to the California Institute of International Studies Conference on Economic Integration in Latin America (May).

———. 1972. *The Central American common market, economic policies, economic growth, and choices for the future.* New York: Praeger.

McKinnon, Ronald I. 1966. Intermediate products and differential tariffs: a generalization of Lerner's symmetry theorem. *Quarterly Journal of Economics* 80 (November): 584–615.

Mead, Donald C. 1968. The distribution of gains in customs unions between developing countries. *Kyklos* 21, Fasc. 4: 713–36.

Meade, James. 1955. *The theory of customs unions.* Amsterdam: North-Holland Publishing Company.

Mennes, L. B. M., Tinbergen, Jan, and Waardenburg, J. George. 1969. *The element of space in development planning.* Amsterdam: North-Holland Publishing Company.

Mera, Koichi. 1967. Tradeoff between aggregate efficiency and interregional equity: a static analysis. *Quarterly Journal of Economics* 81, no. 4 (November): 658–74.

Michaely, Michael. 1965. On customs unions and the gains from trade. *Economic Journal* 75, no. 299 (September): 577–83.

Mikesell, Raymond F. 1965. The theory of common markets as applied to regional arrangements among developing countries. In *International trade theory in a developing world*, Harrod and Hague, eds. New York: St. Martin's Press, pp. 205–29.

Mishan, Edward J. 1966. The welfare gains of a trade-diverting customs union reinterpreted. *Economic Journal* 76, no. 303 (September): 669–72.

———. 1968. What is producer's surplus. *American Economic Review* 58, no. 5, Part 1 (December): 1269–82.

Moore, Frederick T. 1959. Economies of scale: some statistical evidence. *Quarterly Journal of Economics* 73, no. 2 (May): 232–45.

Moscarella, Joseph. 1964. La integración económica Centroamericana. In *Integracion de America Latina*, Wiónczek, M. S., ed. Mexico, Buenos Aires: Funda de Cultura Economica.

Naranjo Villalobos, F. E. 1970. "Un Modelo Macroeconométrico de Política Fiscal para Costa Rica." (July). Mimeographed.

Narasimham, N. V. A. 1956. *A short-term planning model for India.* Amsterdam: North-Holland Publishing Co.

Naya, Seiji. 1968. Variations in export growth among developing Asian countries. *Economic Record* (December): 480–87.

Negishi, Tokashi. 1969. The customs union and the theory of second best. *International Economic Review* 10, no. 2: 391–98.

Nerlove, Marc. 1965. *Estimation and identification of Cobb-Douglas production functions.* Chicago: Rand McNally.

Newlyn, W. F. 1965. Gains and losses in the East African common market. *Yorkshire Bulletin of Economic and Social Research* 17, no. 2 (November): 117–29.

Nugent, Jeffrey B. 1966. "Country study—Argentina." Washington, D.C.: Agency for International Development.

———. 1968. La estructura arancelaria y el costo de protección en America Central. *El Trimestre Economico* (October–December).

———. 1973a. Exchange rate movements and economic development in the late nineteenth century. *Journal of Political Economy* 81, no. 4.

———. 1973b. "Customs unions and tariff dispersion." Mimeographed.

———. 1973c. "Comparative export performance of less developed countries 1949–67." Mimeographed.

———, and DePrano, Michael E. 1966. "The effects of long-run and short-run planning goals on economic policy instruments." Paper presented to the Econometric Society, Washington, D.C.

———, and Akbar, Mohammed Ali. 1971. "The Welfare Cost of Tariffs when Tariff Rates Vary among Commodities." Mimeographed.

Nurkse, Ragnar. 1965. Patterns of trade and development. In *Equilibrium and growth in world economy,* Haberler, G., and Stern, R., eds., Cambridge: Harvard University Press.

Ooms, Van Doorn. 1966. "Regionalization and export performance: a study of primary commodities." Ph.D. dissertation, Yale University.

Pavlopoulos, Pavlos. 1966. *A statistical model of the Greek economy 1949–1959.* Amsterdam: North-Holland Publishing Co.

PEP (Political and Economic Planning). 1959. *Tariffs and trade in Western Europe.* London: Allen and Unwin.

———. 1962. *Atlantic tariffs and trade.* London: Allen and Unwin.

Pincus, Joseph. 1962. *The Central American common market.* Mexico City: U.S. Agency for International Development.

Rapping, Leonard. 1965. Learning and World War II production functions. *Review of Economics and Statistics* 47, no. 1 (February): 81–86.

Resnick, Stephen A. 1968. An empirical study of economic policy in the common market. In *Studies in economic stabilization.* Ando, Albert, Brown, E. Cary, and Friedlander, Ann F., eds. Washington, D.C.: Brookings Institution.

———, and Truman, Edwin M. 1972. "An empirical examination of bilateral trade in Western Europe." Discussion Paper No. 16. New Haven: Yale University, Department of Economics.

Robson, Peter. 1964. *Economic integration in Africa.* London: Allen and Unwin.

―――――, ed. 1972. *International economic integration.* Middlesex, England: Penguin Books.

Scaperlanda, Anthony. 1967. The EEC and U.S. foreign investment: some empirical evidence. *Economic Journal* 77, no. 305 (March): 23–26.

―――――, and Mauer, L. J. 1969. The determinants of U.S. direct investment in the EEC. *American Economic Review* 59, no. 4, Part 1 (September): 558–68.

Schiavo-Campo, Salvatore. 1971. "Import structure and import substitution in Central America." Mimeographed.

Schmitter, Philippe C. 1970. Central American integration: spillover, spill-around or encapsulation? *Journal of Common Market Studies* 9, no. 1 (September): 1–48.

Schmitz, Andrew. 1970. The impact of trade blocs on foreign direct investment. *Economic Journal* 80, no. 319 (September): 724–30.

Scitovsky, Tibor. 1958. *Economic theory and Western European integration.* Stanford, Calif.: Stanford University Press.

―――――. 1963. International trade and economic integration as a means of overcoming the disadvantages of a small nation. In *Economic consequences to the size of nations,* Robinson, E. A. G., ed. London: Macmillan.

Segal, Aron. 1967. The integration of developing countries: some thoughts on East Africa and Central America. *Journal of Common Market Studies* 5, no. 3 (March): 252–82.

Sheshinski, Eytan. 1967. Tests of the learning-by-doing hypothesis. *Review of Economics and Statistics* 49, no. 4 (November): 568–78.

SIECA. 1965. "Statistical and descriptive data of Central America and Panama," and *Series Estadísticas Históricas Seleccionadas.* Guatemala City: SIECA.

Soonthornsima, Chinnawoot. 1964. *A macroeconomic model for economic development of Thailand.* Thailand: Thammosat University Press.

Stigler, George S. 1958. The economies of scale. *Journal of Law and Economics* 1, no. 1: 54–71.

Suits, Daniel B. 1964. *An econometric model of the Greek economy.* Athens: Center of Planning and Economic Research.

Swedish Customs Tariff Commission. 1957. *Revision of the Swedish customs tariff.* Stockholm.

Taylor, Lester D. 1968. "A small econometric model of Colombia." Mimeographed.

Theil, Henri. 1964. *Optimal decision rules for government and industry.* Amsterdam: North-Holland Publishing Company.

―――――. 1965. Linear decision rules for macrodynamic problems. In *Quantitative planning of economic policy,* Hickman, Bert G., ed. Washington, D.C.: The Brookings Institution.

Thorbecke, E. 1969. "The structure and performance of the Guatemalan economy, 1950–1966. Mimeographed.

―――――, and Condos, A. 1967. Macroeconomic growth and development models of the Peruvian economy. In *Theory and design of economic development.* Adelman, I. and Thorbecke, E., eds. Baltimore: The Johns Hopkins University Press.

Tinbergen, Jan. 1952. *On the theory of economic policy.* Amsterdam: North-Holland Publishing Company.

――――. 1963. *The trend towards integration.* Athens: Center of Economic Research, Lecture Series No. 6.

――――. 1964. *Economic policy: principles and design.* Amsterdam: North-Holland Publishing Company.

Truman, Edwin M. 1967. "The European economic community: trade creation and trade diversion." Ph.D. dissertation, Yale University.

Tullock, Gordon. 1967. The welfare costs of tariffs, monopolies and theft. *Western Economic Journal* 5, no. 2 (June): 224–32.

United Nations. 1963. *A study of industrial growth.* New York: United Nations.

――――, ECAFE. 1964. *Review of long-term economic projections for selected countries in the ECAFE region.* Development Programming Techniques Series no. 5. Bangkok, 1964 (contains a macromodel for Indonesia), sales no. 65, 11.F.6 E/CN. 11/674.

――――. 1967. *Sectoral aspects of long-term economic projections with special reference to Asia and the Far East.* Development Programming Techniques Series, no. 6. Bangkok, 1967 (contains macromodels of Thailand and Ceylon), sales no. 67, 11.F.4, E/CN. 11/674.

――――. 1970. *International development strategy for the second United Nations development decade.* New York: United Nations.

Van Eijk, C. J., and Sandee, Jan. 1959. Quantitative determination of an optimum economic policy. *Econometrica* 27, no. 1 (January): 1–13.

Van Rijckeghem, Willy. 1965. "A model of inflation in the Argentine economy, 1950–1963." Mimeographed. Buenos Aires: CONADE.

Vanek, J. 1965. *General equilibrium of international discrimination.* Cambridge: Harvard University Press.

Verdoorn, P. J. 1954. A customs union for Western Europe—advantages and feasibility. *World Politics* (July): 482–500.

――――, and Meyer zu Schlochtern, F. J. M. 1964. Trade creation and trade diversion in the common market. In *Intégration Européenne et réalité économique.* Bruges: College of Europe, pp. 95–137.

Villagrán-Kramer, Francisco. 1967. *Integración económica Centroamericana: aspectos sociales y políticos.* Guatemala: University of San Carlos.

Viner, Jacob. 1950. *The customs union issue.* New York: Carnegie Endowment for International Peace.

Waelbroeck, J. 1964. Le commerce de la communauté Européenne avec les pays tiers. In *Intégration Européenne et réalité economique.* Bruges: College of Europe, pp. 139–64.

Walter, Ingo. 1967. *The European common market: growth and patterns of trade and production.* New York: Praeger.

Walters, A. A. 1963. A note on economies of scale. *Review of Economics and Statistics* 45, no. 4 (November): 425–27.

Waters, W. G. I. 1970. International transport costs and regional industrialization among less developed countries. *Journal of Common Market Studies* 9, no. 2 (December): 151–69.

Wemelsfelder, J. 1960. The short-term effect of lowering import duties in Germany. *Economic Journal* 60, no. 277 (March): 94–104.

Westphal, Larry E. 1971. *Planning investments with economies of scale.* Amsterdam: North-Holland Publishing Company.

Wilford, W. T. 1970. Trade creation in the Central American common market. *Western Economic Journal* 8, no. 1 (March): 61–69.

Williamson, John. 1971. Trade and economic growth. In *The economics of Europe: what the common market means for Britain*, Pinder, John, ed. London: Charles Knight and Company.

_____, and Bottrill, Anthony. 1971. The impact of customs unions on trade in manufactures. *Oxford Economic Papers* 13 (November).

Willmore, Larry N. 1972a. "Trade creation and trade diversion in the Central American common market." Paper presented to the Canadian Association of Latin American Studies, McGill University (June).

_____. 1972b. Free trade in manufactures among developing countries: the Central American experience. *Economic Development and Cultural Change* 20, no. 4 (July).

_____. 1972c. Direct foreign investment and industrial entrepreneurship in Central America. In *Latin American revolution: prospects for the 70's*, Polock, D., and Ritter, A., eds. New York: Praeger.

Wiónczek, Miguel S. 1968. Experience of the Central American integration program as applied to East Africa. *Industrialization and Productivity* 11 (1968).

_____. 1970. The rise and decline of Latin American economic integration. *Journal of Common Market Studies* 9, no. 1 (September): 49–66.

_____. 1972. The Central American common market. In *International economic integration*, Robson, Peter, ed. Middlesex, England: Penguin Books.

Wonnacott, R. J., and Wonnacott, P. 1967. *Free trade between the United States and Canada.* Cambridge, Mass.: Harvard University Press.

Zarembka, Paul. 1972. *Toward a theory of economic development.* San Francisco: Holden-Day, Inc.

index

208 / index

THE JOHNS HOPKINS UNIVERSITY PRESS

This book was composed in Times Roman text and
Times Roman and Vanguard display type by
Jones Composition Company, from a design by
Victoria Dudley Hirsch. It was printed on 60-lb.
Warren 1854 paper and bound in Johanna Arrestox
cloth by Universal Lithographers, Inc.

Library of Congress Cataloging in Publication Data
Nugent, Jeffrey B
    Economic integration in Central America.

    Bibliography: p.
    1. Central America—Economic integration.
2. Mercado Común Centroamericano. 3. Central
America—Economic conditions—Mathematical models.
4. Central America—Economic policy. I. Title.
HC141.N83   338.91′728   74-6832
ISBN 0-8018-1451-0